T0317002

.

JUSTICE IN A TIME OF AUSTERITY

JUSTICE IN A TIME OF AUSTERITY

Stories From a System in Crisis

Jon Robins and Daniel Newman

BRISTOL
UNIVERSITY
PRESS

First published in Great Britain in 2021 by

Bristol University Press
University of Bristol
1-9 Old Park Hill
Bristol
BS2 8BB
UK
t: +44 (0)117 954 5940
e: bup-info@bristol.ac.uk

Details of international sales and distribution partners are available at
bristoluniversitypress.co.uk

British Library Cataloguing in Publication Data
A catalogue record for this book is available from the British Library

ISBN 978-1-5292-1312-6 hardcover
ISBN 978-1-5292-1314-0 ePub
ISBN 978-1-5292-1315-7 ePdf

Cover design: blu inc
Front cover image: Neil Warburton stocksy.com 1714056

Bristol University Press uses environmentally responsible
print partners.

Printed in Great Britain by TJ Books Limited, Padstow

Jon:
Thanks to my parents, Chris and Margaret,
for their love and support.

The book is dedicated to Juliet, Bea and Eve.

Daniel:
Thanks always to Rhian for her support and encouragement.

This book is dedicated to Betsi and Iolo.

Contents

List of Abbreviations

CAB	Citizens Advice Bureau
CLAC	community legal advice centre
CLAN	community legal advice network
CLAS	Community Legal Advice Service
CPS	Crown Prosecution Service
DWP	Department for Work and Pensions
ESA	Employment and Support Allowance
HASL	Housing Action Southwark and Lambeth
IHAG	Ipswich Housing Action Group
JSA	Jobseeker's Allowance
LAA	Legal Aid Agency
LASPO	Legal Aid, Sentencing and Punishment of Offenders Act 2012
LiP	litigant-in-person
LSC	Legal Services Commission
PIP	Personal Independence Payment
PSU	Personal Support Unit
SIFA	Supporting Independence From Alcohol
UN	United Nations
UNHCR	United Nations High Commissioner

About the Authors

Jon Robins is an award-winning journalist and academic. He has written about law and justice for 20 years and runs The Justice Gap (www.thejusticegap.com). His work has regularly appeared in *The Times*, *The Observer*, *The Guardian* and *The Independent on Sunday*. His books include *Guilty Until Proven Innocent: The Crisis in Our Justice System* (Biteback Publishing, 2018), *The First Miscarriage of Justice* (Waterside Publishing, 2014), *The Justice Gap* (Legal Action Group, 2009) and *People Power* (Daily Telegraph/Lawpack, 2008).

Jon is a lecturer at Sheffield Hallam University in the Department of Law and Criminology. He is a patron of Hackney Community Law Centre and on the advisory committee for the Centre for Criminal Appeals.

Jon has won the Bar Council's legal journalist of the year award twice, and the Halsbury Legal Journalism award.

★ ★ ★

Daniel Newman is Senior Lecturer in Law at Cardiff University. His research focuses on access to justice and legal aid, with an interest in the role that social justice can play in the legal system.

He is author of *Legal Aid Lawyers and the Quest for Justice* (Hart Publishing, 2013) and has edited *Leading Works in Law and Social Justice* with Faith Gordon (Routledge, 2021). He is currently writing *Experiences of Criminal Justice* with Roxanna Dehaghani for Bristol University Press.

He has published over 30 articles in law journals, as well as writing on the justice system for specialist and generalist publications for non-academic audiences.

Acknowledgements

Projects like this don't happen without the support of enlightened funders. We would like to thank the barristers' chambers Garden Court for their generous support and we are also grateful to Ashurst LLP and the firm's pro bono manager, Rebecca Greenhalgh. We would also like to thank Cardiff University and their Research Leave Fellowship scheme for supporting the project from the outset.

We want to thank Edward Johnston, Jess Mant, Angus Nurse, Sharon Thompson and Lucy Welsh for reading through our earlier drafts of the manuscript. Errors are, of course, our own, but we are grateful for their input and encouragement.

Foreword

Baroness Shami Chakrabarti CBE PC

It was a morning in the High Court. I was a pupil barrister sitting with a treasury solicitor behind a junior member of chambers responding to an 'immigration list' of applications for permission for judicial review.

The room was grand and forbidding with its old wood-panelling and strict protocol, worthy of any cinematic depiction of British justice. It was a day like so many others during my training. Still, someone stood out. A young woman (I think originally from Uganda) had an application in the list and her solicitor was late. I read her papers which, amongst other things, asserted multiple incidents of torture and rape before her escape to the UK.

Her case was called early on, but as no representative emerged, the court obliged by putting her to the end of the list. When the other matters had all been heard, the woman referred to as 'Ms T' was asked to come forward to the innermost bar, in front even of where the QCs sit, to "make your application for permission for judicial review".

She promptly burst into tears, and the government lawyer, just as uncomfortable as I was, handed me the phone number of a leading legal aid firm, indicating that I should phone for help for our opponent.

That memory has haunted me for over 25 years. There are now so many more like it that it is hard adequately even to do justice to the telling of the denials of rights that mark out our legal system nearly a quarter of the way into the twenty-first century. So, I am grateful to Jon Robins and Dan Newman for the fine work of reportage, scholarship and advocacy that follows.

Human rights are not, as some would have us believe, a devalued currency of lawyers' tricks for clogging up a sausage machine of administrative convenience. They are about the protection of everything that a person needs to live with a modicum of dignity. That covers social and economic rights to food, shelter and the basic means of existence, and civil and political rights to fair trials and family life, and against discrimination. The bridge between the two is 'access to justice' or the advice and representation without which all other protections remain beyond reach.

Justice in a Time of Austerity was researched in one pivotal year, but the full span of its story is much longer. From the much cited, yet tarnished ideals of Magna Carta to post-war aspirations that were never bold enough on universal legal provision. From the denigration of 'fat cats' and 'gravy trains' to the Grenfell, Windrush and 'Real Daniel Blake' scandals that are testament to years of austerity. This book should be a call to arms. If you are a tribune of the people who has ever poured scorn on 'activist lawyers', I dare you to read this. If you are a lawyer or even a concerned citizen who has never felt comfortable with the 'activist' tag, it may just tempt you to reconsider.

Introduction

'I genuinely believe "access to justice" is the hallmark of a civilised society.' It was with those uplifting words that the then Lord Chancellor, Kenneth Clarke, introduced the Legal Aid, Sentencing and Punishment of Offenders Bill in the House of Commons in 2011.[1]

This book is about 'access to justice', what it means and what its absence means for our justice system and for those caught in it. The phrase has been used and abused by politicians of all colours, but never quite so strikingly as when invoked by Kenneth Clarke, perhaps the most enlightened minister to hold the ancient title of Lord Chancellor in the last decade (2010–12). There have been seven Lord Chancellors since 2010.

The Legal Aid, Sentencing and Punishment of Offenders Act 2012, or LASPO, was to represent the most radical package of reforms to the legal aid scheme since our system of publicly funded legal advice was established as a fundamental building block in the architecture of the post-Second World War welfare state. The reforms came into force in April 2013.

As our book demonstrates, the LASPO reforms were 'radical' in a wholly negative and destructive sense. The Coalition government's flagship legislation was predicated on one idea above all others: to cut £350 million a year from a total £2.1 billion budget. Such swingeing cuts took place as the Coalition government imposed its 'austerity' policies in the United Kingdom (UK).

★ ★ ★

Over a 12-month period, starting in October 2018, we interviewed people across England and Wales about their experiences of the justice system. One idea behind our book is to reframe the debate about access to justice. There is a tendency to conflate 'access to justice' with 'legal aid'.

The labels 'legal aid' and 'access to justice' are tricky. Our book is not just about legal aid because (i) post-LASPO, there is not much left; (ii) often the people we spoke to were the ones who had fallen through the gap and had no lawyers and no publicly funded legal help; and (iii) the phrase doesn't resonate with the public, who suspect that 'legal aid' is all about lawyers' fees and professional self-interest. The phrase 'access to justice' isn't quite right either, because the people that we spoke to, more often than not, were being denied justice.

We spoke to people in law centres, Citizens Advice Bureaux and community advice agencies. As a result of the 2013 legal aid cuts, increasingly people were forced to navigate the justice system without help, and so we met people in venues such as court waiting rooms or in MPs' surgeries. We did not approach law firms or advice agencies for 'case studies'.

Instead, we conducted interviews in a range of settings: for example, a foodbank in a church hall in a wealthy part of London or a community centre in a former mining town in the Welsh valleys; a homeless shelter for rough sleepers in central Birmingham; and a destitution service for asylum seekers in a city on the South coast. We didn't restrict our research to the obvious major conurbations; but we spent time in locations across the country from older industrial towns in the North blighted by the decline of manufacturing through to more disparate rural communities poorly served by public transport, let alone by the local advice sector and the courts.

It was a year defined by 'austerity'. We met people caught up in the growing housing crisis, from Grenfell survivors to the homeless or the about-to-be-homeless; and others who had fallen victim to the so-called 'hostile environment', including a number of the Windrush generation who had been denied access to benefits, lost jobs and even faced deportation. Some of our interviewees found themselves dependent on welfare benefits and foodbanks, often both. These were difficult lives made even more difficult by the chaotic roll-out of Universal Credit with its five-week wait for the first payment and punitive sanctions.

Our approach was to talk to people about what 'access to justice' meant to them, what was at stake for them and where they went for help; and then to interview those professionals who were there for them on the front line – if, indeed, anybody was there.

★ ★ ★

One theme of our book is the resourcefulness and commitment of those that remain working in social welfare law who have managed to serve their communities in the face of the advice sector's own hostile environment. Many of the professionals we spoke to (legal aid lawyers, welfare rights advisers and volunteers) worked in law centres, Citizens Advice Bureaux, advice agencies and law firms that have struggled to stay afloat in a sector that has been besieged by threats and challenges going back decades.

Politicians, aided by the media, have depicted legal aid lawyers as 'fat cats' for years. Insofar as there is any truth in that caricature, it does not apply to professionals working in the area of social welfare law. As we make clear, those that we interviewed could not fairly be accused of doing it for the money.[2]

As we make clear, the problems faced by the legal advice sector predate LASPO and austerity, although these are our starting point. The problems that beset the sector also predate the New Labour government, whose policies had such as a ruinous impact on the sector in certain parts of the country that we visited.

★ ★ ★

We write this book in the 50th anniversary year of the law centre movement. The first law centre opened in 1970 a short distance away from where Grenfell Tower was later to be built. North Kensington Law Centre marked the beginning of a social justice movement.

The remains of the 24-storey tower block are now a symbol of the disparity between the living conditions of rich and poor in our capital city. It was ever thus. North Kensington Law Centre is now based on the Lancaster West housing estate in West London, right next door to the remains of the tower. It was set up to provide advice to the tenants of the slum landlords of West London, such as the notorious Peter Rachman; and it was there almost half a century later to help the survivors of the terrible blaze that started one June day in 2017.

Since 2010 the legal not-for-profit sector has been dealt a double body blow. Before LASPO, legal aid would typically account for 40% of a law centre's income, with another 40% coming from local authorities. As a result of the 2013 cuts, the income of law centres halved and 11 were forced to close, leaving Wales without a single law centre, and only 43 in England offering specialist advice for those who cannot afford to pay a lawyer. Happily, more law centres have opened since then (and the Speakeasy in Cardiff has joined the fold over the course of our research); but the new additions to the network are largely volunteer organisations supported by little funding.

It is testimony to the tenacity of those that work in the sector that the movement has survived and new law centres have managed to open post-LASPO.

A two-nation justice system

The LASPO cuts were the deepest and most reckless since the legal aid scheme was introduced 70 years ago under the Legal Aid and Advice Act 1949. They were achieved by removing public funding for what is known as 'social welfare law' advice, or what used to be called 'poverty law': welfare benefits, housing (except where there is a risk of homelessness), employment, family law (unless there is evidence of domestic violence), and immigration and asylum.

The legal aid scheme has been cut to the bone. All that remains is what couldn't be removed because of the residual protections afforded by the European Convention on Human Rights. By the time of the 2013 cuts, the coverage provided by the legal advice sector was already threadbare and fraying. New Labour's plans to overhaul a rather patchy and chaotic sector might have been understandable; but their execution was at best chaotic and, at worst, seemingly calculated to drive advice agencies out of business.

When we started our research the Ministry of Justice's data reported that the number of not-for-profit agencies and legal aid firms offering social welfare law advice had collapsed by a third over the five years since LASPO. The withering on the vine of the civil legal aid scheme continued for the fifth consecutive year running and the number of providers was down 5% on the previous year. The scheme was in free-fall: workloads in immigration were down by 9% in the last quarter, as compared to the previous year; mental health dropped by 8%, and housing by 4%. Legal help (advice and assistance under the legal aid scheme other than representation in a court or tribunal) had collapsed to less than one-third of pre-LASPO levels.

That there is a 'crisis' in our justice system is uncontested. In 2015 the Lord Chancellor spoke of our 'two nation' justice system: there is 'the wealthy, international class' who opt to settle their cases in London with its 'gold standard of British justice'; and then there is everyone else. The rest of us have to put up with 'a creaking, outdated system'.[3]

Most commentators seem to understand the 'legal aid crisis' as being exclusively about our 'broken' criminal justice system. When lawyers talk about the campaign to save legal aid, often they mean the campaign to preserve legal aid for defence lawyers. Defence lawyers have not had a pay rise for over two decades and had an 8.75% fee cut foisted on them in 2014.

The topic of our book is the other crisis in our justice system – the one that is rarely talked about: the evisceration of our system of 'access to justice' in the civil and family courts.

As noted previously, our book is about 'access to justice', not legal aid. Many of the people we spoke to had never seen a lawyer, let alone received legal aid. Some would not be eligible. It is quite possible to be poor and not qualify for legal aid under the narrow terms of the means test. Even if they were eligible, they might not be able to find a lawyer or (most likely) their case would not have been covered by the post-LASPO scheme.

The shrinking legal aid scheme means that it has increasingly become an irrelevance. The proportion of the population eligible for legal aid has collapsed from 80% in 1980 to 29% in 2007, and could possibly be as low as 20%.[4]

Research published in 2018 demonstrated that the legal aid means test, frozen since 2010, was disqualifying people below the poverty line, which was defined as 10% to 30% below a minimum living standard.[5] Working people are called on to pay their legal costs either in full or in part by making a contribution that many would find hard or impossible to afford. Those who are out of work may be excluded if they are homeowners because they would be expected to sell their homes to cover costs.

The death of an idea

During the year of our research there was a two-week fact-finding mission to the UK by Philip Alston, the United Nations (UN) rapporteur on extreme poverty and human rights. According to his final report published in 2019, one in five people in the UK lived in poverty and close to four in ten children would do so within the next two years.[6]

The Australian human rights lawyer invoked the 17th-century English philosopher Thomas Hobbes to say that their lives were likely to be 'solitary, poor, nasty, brutish, and short'. He reckoned that 'austerity' politics, including the roll-out of Universal Credit, had contributed to the 'systematic immiseration of millions'.

In a striking but barely noted observation, Philip Alston identified the 'dramatic rolling back' of legal aid post LASPO as one of the causes of our country's 'systematic' impoverishment. He was specifically talking about the impact of the 2013 legal aid cuts.

We agree.

★ ★ ★

'Access to justice' is not an easy cause to champion. There are suspicions of lawyers' special pleading and professional self-interest. The *Guardian* columnist Jonathan Freedland memorably described legal aid as the 'most friendless wing of the welfare state' in 2006.[7] Unlike schools or hospitals, he pointed out, legal aid seemed 'technical and remote' to all but those who had to rely upon it. Certainly, the campaign against the LASPO cuts never fired the public imagination. It failed to achieve any significant change beyond a few small but important concessions.

Our book is about how poverty and social inequality are entrenched through a failing justice system. We illustrate this through our interviews, which offer illustrations as to how the denial of 'access to justice' often represents a catastrophic step in the life of the person interviewed and their family.

We argue that the LASPO regime represents the death of an idea: the end of the post-war political consensus around 'access to justice' and, in particular, the notion that legal redress should not be the preserve of the wealthy. The 2013 cuts mark the final severing of the link between our system of publicly funded law and the welfare state.

It's time to revive the campaign to save access to justice.

Structure and approach

The book is structured thematically, reflecting the concerns of our interviewees.

- *Housing crisis*: We begin with the housing crisis and the experience of those facing eviction in the housing courts; problems relating to social housing and the legacy of the Grenfell fire of June 2017; and homelessness (Chapters 1, 2 and 3, respectively).
- *Food poverty and welfare benefits*: Then, we look at issues to do with food poverty and welfare benefits and, in particular, the roll-out of Universal Credit (Chapters 3, 4 and 5).
- *Immigration and asylum*: In Chapters 6 and 7 we look at immigration, the policies that might be described as the 'hostile environment' and the treatment of asylum seekers.
- *Family*: In Chapter 8 we focus on issues to do with family break-up.

Each of these chapters features reports from different parts of the country highlighting the experience of people as they go through the justice system and speaking to the professionals to whom they typically go for help. The purpose is to map the provision of advice in a given area; and also to provide a history of the legal advice sector.

Our book is focused on the impact of austerity and, in particular, the 2013 legal aid cuts; however, we recognise that it would be misleading to suggest that the challenges faced by the sector started in 2010. In particular, austerity and the LASPO cuts have had such a calamitous effect upon the not-for-profit legal advice sector in some parts of the country because of policies introduced in the New Labour years which weakened existing provision. Chapter 9 explains why.

In Chapter 10 we call for a new understanding of 'access to justice' in a post-austerity environment and we end with our proposals as to how this might be achieved as well as remedying the worst excess of the LASPO regime.

Our interviews took place within a 12-month period; however, we have both been researching and writing about the sector for many years. Occasionally we refer to articles written outside of the year of our research, which we make clear in the text and in the notes.

During the year of our research we wrote a number of articles about our research in a number of publications including the *Guardian*, *The Justice Gap* and *Byline Times*. These are also identified in the notes.

When we use just an interviewee's forename, we have changed the name to protect their identity because of the sensitivity of the issues discussed.

1

Conveyor Belt Justice

The date is 29 October 2018. It is, relatively speaking, a quiet Monday morning at Stratford Housing Centre, which is housed in the shabby magistrates' court in the London borough of Newham. There are 12 rent possession cases on the housing list for the morning session. On a busy day, the duty adviser Simon Mullings can see as many as 20 people. "It can be manic," he tells us as we sit in the duty solicitor's office next door to the court. "You're literally running between the duty room and the court, constantly talking to housing officers and ushers."

Mullings, a senior case worker at Edwards Duthie solicitors based in the East End, has been covering the duty scheme for 15 years. His job as court duty adviser it is to provide last-minute emergency advice to those who might otherwise be evicted. He greets each tenant in the same cheery and reassuring manner: "Good afternoon, I'm Simon Mullings. I'm here to advise you about the case. I can represent you in court."

Confusion is unavoidable

It is a bewildering experience for tenants fearful of losing their homes. They don't know what to expect and don't know whether the amiable Mullings is friend or foe. "Half of them think you're the judge," he explains between clients. "I have people ask me if they are going to go to prison today."

Each tenant has roughly five minutes of Mullings' time. He shuffles through their paperwork, should they have had the foresight to bring any, and quickly tries to work out what on earth is going on. These snatched meetings are occasionally interrupted by the clerk directing him to Courtroom 12, where a deputy district judge presides over cases in about the same amount of time as Mullings has to make sense of them.

It is conveyor belt justice. The judge has to get through his list and the clerk is there to make sure he does. "The more people there are in court on any given day, the less time I have to explain what's going on and the more confusing it is for clients," says Mullings. "The confusion is unavoidable."

It is hard to think of a court process where stakes are higher and, yet, where 'access to justice' is more imperilled. This is the reason why we decide to start our 12-month journey through the justice system here: a court duty scheme in one of the poorest boroughs of London in the midst of a housing crisis marked by a collapse in homeownership, increasingly unaffordable private rented homes and a dearth of social housing.

At the time when we are in Newham, the average home costs a full-time worker eight times their salary and rents are taking up an increasing chunk of our salaries (up to 49% on average in London).[1] Meanwhile, homeownership among young adults has collapsed. Among 25- to 34-year-olds earning between £22,200 and £30,600 per year, homeownership has fallen to less than a third (27%) compared to almost two-thirds (65%) two decades before.[2]

Housing advice was removed from the legal aid scheme in 2013, under what are known as the LASPO cuts, except where there is a risk of homelessness. Such a risk is present in all cases on today's list, but hardly any of clients have seen a housing lawyer at any point, and none about their attendance in court today. Despite the government's preserving public funding for homelessness cases, applications for legal aid in such cases have fallen by a third (34%) since the cuts. This has happened at a time when the number of rough sleepers has shot up by 165% between 2010 and 2018.

Meanwhile, the legal advice sector has been decimated. Almost a third of legal aid areas in England and Wales now have one or no local legal aid housing advice providers.[3] This includes the entire county of Suffolk, which doesn't have a single housing lawyer (as we report in Chapter 3).

"If I'm not here, then the judge is presented with an experienced housing officer who has all the paperwork and a tenant who's often scared witless," Mullings tells us. "Housing officers can steamroller judges into making an order that otherwise they wouldn't." The consequence could be an eviction, or else the tenant agreeing to repay arrears which they can't afford, which will mean they will be back in court facing eviction at a later date.

One of the first people Simon Mullings sees is a distressed single mum who's £2,486 in arrears. She has been off work because her son had dislocated his leg. "I get very emotional," she apologises at one point. She and her two kids were "decanted" (her word) from their new-build flat, which was rendered uninhabitable as a result of a damp problem. Her daughter is a self-employed musician and helps out "as and when". Mullings sympathises. "I was a self-employed musician myself once," he says.

The good news is that there is a technicality – the paperwork (the amended particulars) has not been dated or signed by the housing association. Today she gets to stay in her temporary home. "Does that mean I have to come back again?" she wants to know. "I can't bear it."

Mullings goes into the waiting room, speaks to her housing officer, and a deal is struck to pay rent plus some of the arrears. It's affordable. Her relief is palpable. "Thanks for being so understanding," she says.

★ ★ ★

The housing market is not working. The 2017 general election cost the Conservatives their majority, with statisticians noting a swing among private renters to Labour in a phenomenon statisticians call 'rentquake' (as opposed to 'youthquake').[4] The issue of housing, especially the need for a new approach to be taken to social housing, is back on the political agenda after years of neglect. The shadow of Grenfell looms large (see Chapter 2).

Just before our time in Newham, the then prime minister, Theresa May, promised 'a new generation of social rented homes'. 'Many people in society – including too many politicians – continue to look down on social housing and, by extension, the people who call it their home,' she said.[5]

Housing law specialists such as Simon Mullings work under the Ministry of Justice's housing possession court duty scheme. The duty scheme means that people defending proceedings for possession can (theoretically) obtain help on the day at court.

The duty solicitor provides immediate, face-to-face help for those at risk of losing their home. The court will make an order against the defendant, give directions for trial or adjourn the matter for further investigation. The duty solicitor typically seeks an adjournment for a short period to try to resolve the matter in a way that prevents the defendant from losing their home.

In 2018 the Ministry of Justice attempted to consolidate the 113 housing duty schemes across England and Wales into just 47 schemes through the crude mechanism of a price-competitive tender. Some schemes are run by private practice law firms and some by charities; some are not run by the Ministry of Justice but instead are funded by the local authority or a charity. Some courts simply do not have cover. The Ministry of Justice wanted to contract fewer, larger, duty solicitor schemes, some covering multiple English counties and one covering an entire country (Wales). The argument was that this would make the schemes more economically viable.

Critics say the government's plans represented 'a race to the bottom' in terms of the quality of help as firms and advice agencies undercut each other.[6] Less than a third of current schemes would have remained, and so people at risk of eviction would have needed to travel much farther for help to keep their homes.

Weeks before our visit to East London, the Law Centres Network won a High Court challenge against the Ministry of Justice proposals.[7] In a scathing judgment, Mrs Justice Andrews criticised the government for its 'facile assumption', treating duty schemes in isolation. She said that it was 'beyond argument' that the schemes' users disproportionately had 'protected characteristics' under the Equality Act. For example, more than eight out of ten clients were low-income, insofar as they would have qualified for legal aid (85%); almost a third were disabled (31%); and many had mental health difficulties. The court noted that, on the ministry's own account, any savings were likely to have been 'negligible', as the cost of running the scheme was just £3.6 million or only 0.2% of the entire legal aid budget.

Until very recently courts in Cornwall had no such schemes. We spoke to Eddie Coppinger, director of the Legal Advice Centre at University House in East London. It is one of the oldest legal advice agencies in London and dates back to 1941. The centre is based in Bethnal Green and runs a webcam advice project providing an online housing duty scheme service to two of Cornwall's main courts, Bodmin and Truro.

The project is supported by a community centre in Falmouth called the Dracaena Centre. "We beam in and talk to clients before they go into the hearing," he explains. "We can talk to the clients after they come out." The Legal Advice Centre had just won the legal aid contract to cover the duty scheme.

Prior to that, neither court had coverage. The contract had been put out for tender by the Legal Aid Agency; but the Legal Advice Centre did not bid in the hope that a local firm of solicitors would step up. No one was interested. It was only after the tender closed that the Legal Advice Centre in East London approached the Legal Aid Agency and were offered the contract.

Manchester's Palais de Justice

It's Monday morning (15 October 2018) on level five of the 16-storey, glass-fronted Manchester Civil Justice Centre. District Judge Hassall has 19 cases on a busy housing list in court seven. First up is an application by a landlord concerning a tenant with mental health problems. The tenant spends a disconcerting amount of his time perched on the window ledge of his fifth floor flat, which is, the judge is informed, 'a 60 foot drop onto the concrete car park beneath'. The judge accepts that the man is a danger to himself and others as well as a disturbing presence on the estate.

Two solicitors are on today's duty scheme, which is run by the housing charity Shelter. They cover two lists: one in the morning for antisocial behaviour; and rent arrears possession cases in the afternoon on level seven. Tenants can be evicted on account of their antisocial behaviour for breach of a court order or injunction.

Next up is a case concerning the occupants of a one-bedroom flat in a block of 16. The court hears of 'overwhelming evidence of the supply, sale and production' of crack-cocaine as evidenced by 'a constant smell of ammonia' and the frequent sighting of 'people wearing respirators'. Neighbouring tenants complain of addicts blocking the stairwell using 'heroin with foil and needles'. Four residents have received death threats.

Some 19 cases are listed and four tenants turn up for the morning session. At one point, Judge Hassall expresses concern about his own potential to 'over-react' when a hearing concerns a tenant who is neither present nor represented in court. How can he properly test the evidence without the risk of adding to 'a chain of fallacies'?, he asks.

The morning's duty solicitor, Ben Taylor assists on three cases. "It's a poor turnout," he says, "but most of the cases were gas injunctions and tenants tend not to come." Landlords have to provide an annual gas safety certificate and they are allowed access to properties on 24 hours' notice to ensure that properties are compliant and safe for their occupants and neighbours. Issues often arise when tenants refuse access, and an injunction can be granted to allow entry. Non-attendance at court does not lessen the seriousness of the potential consequences of an unforgiving legal process. After the morning session ends, Taylor explains how it works. "If they don't provide access once an injunction order is given as made by the court they could end up in prison for contempt for two years plus a £5,000 fine," he says.

The Ministry of Justice only funds possession proceedings. However, the court expects the duty scheme to deal with all cases. Taylor does do this on an unpaid basis. "We might pick up paid work through the scheme but we also want the courts to have a smooth-running system," he says. "The courts don't care if it's possession because of rent arrears or whatever. They just hope that there is a duty solicitor there to help."

★ ★ ★

Two connected themes of our 12-month journey are the increasingly ragged state of disrepair of our courts (the shabby Stratford Hearing Centre is a typical example of a neglected court) and the government's court closure programme.

Over the last decade, the government has embarked on a massive programme of court sell-offs. Almost half of all courts in England and Wales were closed between 2010 and 2018: 162 out of 323 magistrates' courts and 90 county courts.[8] Underutilised, neglected courts sit on prime real estate. In answer to a parliamentary question in March 2018, it was revealed that the sale of 126 court premises in England and Wales since 2010 had raised £34 million – 'each going for little more than the average house price', as the *Guardian* put it.[9]

Manchester Civil Justice Centre is a rare thing: not only a new addition to our court estate but an architectural triumph. The £160 million building was commissioned by the New Labour government and opened for business in 2007. It is the first major court complex built in Britain since the Royal Courts of Justice in 1882 and was listed by *Design* magazine in its top ten buildings of the first decade of the 21st century. The magazine breathlessly described it as 'a spectacle of justice – a place where justice can be seen to be done', and one that tapped 'into the commercial and moral heart of Manchester'. Locals call it 'the filing cabinet' on account of its cantilevered floors.

The reality is that people living in the outskirts of Manchester, previously well served by local county courts, struggle to make the journey into town; hence the poor turnout. Just ahead of our visit to Manchester, the government had confirmed a further cull of 86 courts across the country, including 10 in the capital.

Ben Taylor calls the civil justice centre the "last dedicated property investment before the property crash". "All the courts that have been closing are being shoehorned into this building, our Palais de Justice. A huge white elephant which for a long time was half empty," he says. Courts in Tameside, Altrincham, Oldham and Bolton have been shut down and relocated to the justice centre's 47 courts.

Later we speak to the other solicitor working on the duty scheme that day, Helen Jackson, a solicitor with Shelter. The housing charity used to cover the busy Tameside duty scheme. "People may be losing their homes because they have struggled to get to court for a possession hearing," she says. "If it is a single mum with childcare responsibilities she might not have anyone to drop the kids off at school; if she hasn't got a car, which is going to be true of most people in that situation, then you have to get in for a 10 o'clock hearing – that is a struggle from outlying areas of Manchester, and it's an expense."

There is a bitter irony that the then Department of Constitutional Affairs (now Ministry of Justice), which commissioned Manchester's extravagant 'spectacle of justice', also introduced massive reorganisation of the local legal aid sector, effectively dismantling the delicate network of local legal advice provision (see Chapter 9).

Both Taylor and Jackson point out that the advice sector has withered in the intervening years. "There has been a desertification of the North West. I'm not sure that's a word but that's what I'd call it," says Taylor, who has specialised in housing law since 1992. "Over the last few years key players have pulled out. LASPO was the last nail in the coffin."

"When I first started there were a lot of providers," says Jackson. "Now, there are more demands in the city than the ability to meet them. People are sometimes waiting for appointments until it reaches desperation stage."

LASPO removed most housing from the legal aid scheme, with some exceptions. "Homelessness, disrepair where there's risk to health and possession proceedings are still in scope," says Taylor. Jackson says Shelter 'props up' a massively limited legal aid scheme through income from its charitable donations.

Fat-cat lawyers

"Do you know how much a legal aid lawyer gets paid an hour?" Ben Taylor asks me. They used to get paid £66 an hour, but he points out that now the rate is £58. "It is an absolute disgrace," he says. "The £66 rate was decided in 1997. It was that rate for 18 years, then LASPO came and it dropped to £58."

In 2015 the fact-checking charity Full Fact looked at the myth of 'fat cat' legal aid lawyers' fees following an inflammatory remark in Parliament by the then justice minister, Lord Faulks. 'The question that arises out of social welfare law is whether it is always necessary for everybody who has quite real problems to have a lawyer at £200-odd an hour, or whether there are better and more effective ways of giving advice,' Faulks had said.[10]

'There are lawyers, and there are lawyers,' began Full Fact. Some were very talented 'and their skills earn them hundreds of pounds per hour', the group said; others were equally talented but did not work in sectors that commanded 'the big bucks'. 'Squarely into this latter camp fall social welfare solicitors paid by the government to help people who can't afford a lawyer,' it said.

The fact checkers explained that when social welfare lawyers were not paid on a fixed fee, they tended to be paid £50–£70 an hour. For a relatively simple housing case a fixed fee is about £160.

If the case is more complicated, more than a day's work, an hourly rate might kick in. The rate for legal help and advice is just under £50 per hour for some social welfare cases, just over for others.

The Law Society has described the rates of pay as 'catastrophically' low and as having led to law firms leaving publicly funded work in droves.[11] The solicitors' group pointed out that fees paid for civil legal aid provision had not increased since 1994, equating to a 49% real-terms reduction. On top of this, fees were cut by a further 10% in 2011. As a result, the solicitors' group argued, more than half of local authorities in England and Wales had no publicly funded legal advice for housing.

"You don't do this job for the money," says Taylor. "You do it because you have won the lottery or maybe you're some kind of champagne socialist or else because money isn't important. I love this job. I can't imagine doing anything else. Would I advise anyone to come into this area of law who is interested in being a lawyer? No way. There is no future in legal aid."

A brutal process

We spoke to a housing judge who works on the South East circuit, on condition of anonymity. How did they manage the frenetic pace of such crowded lists? "You develop techniques," the judge told us. "The number of issues you need to be able to check on a possession case is huge and you have to take a realistic view about what information you're able to glean from a file; and what key issues you can check within the time frame. You cannot check everything."

They continued: "You never know what the defendant's going to say; whether or not they're going to turn up; and whether they are going to want representation. You are dealing with the whole myriad of key decisions very, very quickly."

Duty advisers told us that judges lean heavily on their expertise. What was the view from the judge's bench? "It is a fair point," the judge told us. "If a judge knows there is a good, reliable duty adviser they will expect the duty adviser to raise the points that are going to be relevant rather than necessarily looking in greater detail, which you might do if there was a litigant-in-person."

In the judge's experience ("so not empirical"), "about one third of people don't turn up; about one third are represented by the duty solicitor; and about a third have had to deal with the landlord, housing association or local authority beforehand". They report that the duty schemes are "well run; well attended and the quality of the advocate is usually high".

How did they feel, presiding over a court where the stakes were so high and yet so few tenants even turned up? "One of the most fundamental things you can do is to say to someone they have to leave the home they're living in," the judge replied. "In some way making an order that a mother and her three children leave the property is easier than a young single man because the woman and three kids are going to be rehoused by the local authority – not quickly, but they will be." They point out that "they might be in hotel accommodation for a few days – but they will be rehoused".

Other tenants might not be regarded as urgent cases. "If you're throwing them out, they're on the streets," the judge says. "You see so many people who were just down on their luck. Things haven't gone right for them. They've lost their job, their relationship has broken down, they have had a period of bad health and they could be two months in arrears on their rents; and the landlord can get them out. There is no defence. It is a brutal process."

Austerity: 'an ideological project'

According to the London Borough of Newham's website, the 2012 Olympics left 'a stunning legacy of state-of-the-art sports venues, a beautiful new park and a range of shopping and visitor attractions'. Six years after the Games, the borough has the dubious distinction of being the homelessness capital of the UK.

Weeks after our visit, the UN special rapporteur on extreme poverty arrived, on the eighth day of his tour of the UK, for an evidence-gathering session at Community Links, a 40-year-old charity in Canning Town. 'The room is packed, people spilling out of the doors,' the *Guardian* columnist Aditya Chakrabortty reported.[12] 'The atmosphere crackles. So it should, for this is what it feels like when an entire society is held to account.' The journalist reckoned the UN inquiry could prove to be 'one of the most significant events in British civil society this decade'.

In 2018 it was estimated that at least one in 24 people in the borough was homeless and some 14,535 households were in temporary accommodation.[13] Amanda Durbery, chief executive at a homeless shelter in Canning Town, called the Caritas Anchor House, was at the event. She tells us: "When you sit in Anchor House, from one window you can see Canary Wharf, from another the Olympic Village, and from another window the O2. You can see massive wealth. I was on the phone looking out of my window, straight ahead of me there's a Rolls Royce opposite my window, and to the side a guy sitting in a sleeping bag begging on the street." For Durbery, such disparity sums up Newham. "Massive injections of wealth side by side with people who are living in absolute poverty," she says.

In the 12 months of our project, it was reported that 612 people were seen sleeping rough in the borough.[14] As part of the government's £50 million 'rough sleeping strategy', which promises to eradicate the phenomenon by 2027, Caritas Anchor House launched a project in 2018 allowing for 20 bed spaces.

Durbery points out that the Stratford shopping centre has "probably the highest concentration of rough sleepers in a single location" in the country. "Some of those people are working. They're going to work all day and they're sleeping in the shopping centre because they can't afford any of the over-priced accommodation in the borough. They literally can't afford a roof over their head because flats are £2,000 to £3,000 a month." Regeneration, particularly post-Olympics, has "priced people on low incomes out of their own borough". "They're having to move further and further afield," she says.

★ ★ ★

In the shadow of Canary Wharf, the homelessness crisis is out of control; and within walking distance of the global centre of legal expertise there is a dearth of the most basic legal help. Labour's East Ham MP, Stephen Timms, tells us about the decline of the local advice sector; and his constituency neighbour Lyn Brown, Labour MP for West Ham, complains that "decent advice [is] severely constrained" and "small things, such as maintaining an open phone line, have become a rarity".

Both MPs' offices have taken up some of the slack. "By far the most common subject for case-work relates to housing because of an acute shortage of affordable homes and a very significant increase in private sector rented property," Brown says. "It's always been housing," agrees Timms. Nearly one quarter of his constituency case-work last month (23%) related to housing, which, together with immigration, takes up "nearly half of our time".

The local Citizens Advice in Newham was recently forced to scrap its drop-in advice sessions because its restricted service had been overwhelmed. Now people make an appointment over the phone between 10 am and 2 pm on the two days a week that it remains open. Previously there would be up to 70 people standing outside an agency with capacity to see between 15 and 20 a day. Occasionally there were fights.

"Normally we don't like to do it by phone because we know people want to see us face to face. It's easier to help and go through their documents," Benno Allerman, service manager at Citizens Advice East End says. "But it's just the sheer demand, and so we stopped having a drop-in last October. We had queues literally around the corner, around two corners. People started queuing up at two o'clock in the morning."

Allerman explains that the bureau isn't funded by Newham – by contrast, neighbouring local authorities Hackney and Tower Hamlets do support Citizens Advice. "In Newham the local authority isn't really giving any money out to the third sector," she says. "There isn't really the normal support that many other local authorities have. So we rely on trusts and other charities."

Sir Robin Wales, the former Labour mayor of Newham, was "very much against not just the Citizens Advice, but the third sector and any support that people needed". "He felt it was creating some kind of dependency, that people couldn't be bothered and should be able to [get] work," Allerman says. Wales was deselected by his party in 2018, after serving as a councillor for 23 years.

Allerman reports that the council and job centre refer people to them with little understanding of how limited their service is. She says: "Everyone seems to think that we can help, but we don't have any money to help. We're trying to run something on almost no money."

"It's a miracle that any of the charities in the borough have survived," comments Amanda Durbery. "It's only really because of the ingenuity and business sense of those charities that any of them are left standing."

★ ★ ★

In May 2019 the UN special rapporteur on extreme poverty, Philip Alston, delivered his report.[15] He didn't pull his punches.

As we recalled in the Introduction, the Australian human rights lawyer invoked the 17th-century English philosopher Thomas Hobbes, saying that life under the Coalition government's welfare reforms risked becoming 'solitary, poor, nasty, brutish, and short'. 'It might seem to some observers that the Department of Work and Pensions has been tasked with designing a digital and sanitized version of the nineteenth century workhouse, made infamous by Charles Dickens,' he continued.

The UN rapporteur called the imposition of austerity 'an ideological project' and Brexit 'a tragic distraction'. So damning was his verdict that the Work and Pensions Secretary, Amber Rudd, threatened to lodge a formal complaint about his 'barely believable' report.

Alston identified 'the decimation' of legal aid as a contributing factor to the 'immiseration of millions'. He recorded that as a result of the LASPO cuts the number of civil legal aid cases had declined by 'a staggering' 82% between 2010 and 2018. 'As a result, many poor people are unable to effectively claim and enforce their rights, have lost access to critical support, and some have even reportedly lost custody of their children,' he wrote. 'Lack of access to legal aid also exacerbates extreme poverty, since justiciable problems that could have been resolved with legal representation go unaddressed.'

★ ★ ★

The last person we see on our day in Newham at the Stratford Housing Centre is a 30-year-old Spanish man. "I just want to stop the eviction. I don't have anywhere else to go," he tells Simon Mullings as he enters the duty solicitor's room at Stratford Hearing Centre.

In court, the judge wearily points out that he is more than £9,660 in arrears – "£9,815.73 including this week's rent," the housing officer corrects. She has his rent book, which reveals that only three payments have been made. "We don't believe he has any intention of paying," she says.

Simon Mullings tells the judge that a friend has promised to pay half of his client's arrears; however, the friend is abroad. "Is there any evidence of this friend?" the judge asks. "I'm afraid not," Mullings replies. "My feeling is that your client is using the housing association as a credit agency," the judge says.

To quote our anonymous judge, it is a brutal process. The man is told he will be evicted tomorrow at 9.40 am. It's not clear if the young man has anywhere to go.

2

In the Shadow of Grenfell

The charred remains of Grenfell Tower are now a feature of the West London skyline and a symbol of the disparity between the living conditions of rich and poor in England's capital. When we visit North Kensington Law Centre (13 September 2018), literally in the shadow of the 24-storey high rise, a massive banner has recently been unfurled, obscuring the top floors. Emblazoned with a huge green heart, one side reads 'Forever in our hearts'. It is in tribute to the 72 people who died in the fire 15 months earlier.

This time last year the railings outside St Clement's Church, were covered in flowers, candles, teddy bears, as well as the posters for the still missing. Over the road from the church is Baseline Business Studios, home to the law centre where a small team of five to ten regular staff plus volunteers have been helping survivors and the bereaved in the aftermath of the tragedy. The office is so close to the tower that in the first 24 hours of the fire it was behind the police cordon. Staff had to decamp to the church's community centre, and a drop-in clinic was up and running by lunchtime the day after the fire started.

"We're part of the community," the law centre's director, Annie Campbell Viswanathan, tells us. "People know that they can come to us." We are discussing press reports about 'ambulance-chasing' lawyers 'touting for business' in the wake of the tragedy.

A solicitors' firm had been criticised for fly-posting on the Lancaster West estate offering to help victims 'kick-start any potential insurance claims and review any complex documents'. A disclaimer stated that two lawyers from the firm named on the poster, both trainee solicitors, would not be paid, but a third party 'may charge for their services'. The firm in the flyers is a leading human rights practice, Leigh Day, and its controversial work representing Iraqi citizens pursuing claims of torture and murder against British troops has piqued press interest.

"People know that with us the first port of call isn't going to be their credit card," says Viswanathan. "It has been critical since the 1940s and the beginning of the welfare state that the poor and marginalised have 'access to justice'. What we mean by that is a really good-quality legal service. We provide that and we provide it to local people."

North Kensington Law Centre occupies a small but significant place in legal history. It was the first law centre, and its creation spawned an idealistic movement with a mission to take legal rights to the poor and vulnerable who would otherwise be excluded. At their peak, there were over 60 law centres nation-wide. On the day we visit, there are just 43.

The 2013 LASPO cuts have taken their toll.

★ ★ ★

At the time of our visit the small law centre is still dealing with some 80 Grenfell clients, and the local authority, the Royal Borough of Kensington and Chelsea, is under fire over its failure to satisfactorily rehouse displaced and traumatised tenants in one of the wealthiest parts of the capital. On the first anniversary of the blaze, just 83 of the 203 surviving Grenfell households are living in a permanent home and 52 are in temporary accommodation.

"The council haven't conducted themselves well," says Viswanathan. "In public they're playing lip-service to their commitment to rehouse the survivors. We have clients who in private say they're being put under enormous pressure. They are saying that they're being told: 'We can't afford to keep you there'. It's outrageous considering all the money the council has."

By that time nearly £21 million had been spent keeping survivors in hotel rooms. According to Kensington MP Emma Dent Coad, architects working on the Lancaster West estate during the 1970s estimated it would have cost about £500,000 to build the 24-storey block. The MP is in despair at the council's response: "It's really, really shockingly bad. The number of households who are still homeless from Grenfell is shocking," she says.

The council has spent £235 million on securing 307 properties. The MP is frustrated that the council did not consider the specific needs of survivors – for example, those that are disabled.

Spike Western started as a volunteer with North Kensington Law Centre and is now a Grenfell support paralegal working with survivors and the bereaved family members. "If you've got four kids and you end up needing a four-bed household, then you have to wait an extremely long time if you're ever going to get a property," he says. One of his clients has been on the waiting list for a council house for 16 years, and he believes the tragedy has made a bad situation worse.

Many of the low-rise blocks at the base of the tower, known as the Walkways, that had to be vacated after the tragedy were larger properties. "So you've suddenly got this extra wave of four-bed households needing to be rehoused," says Western. "It's gridlock, basically, adding more pressure on the system and taking away a lot of the supply."

"The chances are that many families won't ever get a permanent place to call home," he continues. "By the time they're getting to the top of the list, the kids will have grown up and be starting their own families." One of his clients with five kids has had to move his family nine times in the past 18 months.

Dent Coad blames the council. "They've been trying to move people out. There has been absolutely blatant social cleansing," she says.

Nour-eddine Aboudihaj, of the campaign group Justice for Grenfell, tells us that problems with rehousing survivors are impeding the recovery of traumatised people. "Before you can start the healing process, you need to have a home, and if that's not available you cannot move on," he says. "You will be still stuck in a kind of limbo state. You start to think about why you were there in the first place. That brings flashbacks and memories." Aboudihaj talks of the effect this can have. "A lot of people are having problems sleeping; some are taking drugs. They're stressed."

"One of the things that are important is having access to legal aid and having access to the right tenant advice," Aboudihaj tells us. But people have limited options as to where to go for help: "Most of the advice agencies in Kensington and Chelsea have been closed because the council didn't fund them." He knows of the work done by North Kensington Law Centre. "But it's just one small organisation that cannot satisfy the large population that we have," he says.

Start of a new social justice movement

When North Kensington Law Centre first opened in 1970 in a former butcher's shop on the Golborne Road in West London, the Attorney General, Lord Elwyn Jones, and president of the Law Society presided over the ceremony. The Lord Chancellor sent his blessing.

Towards the end of the 1960s the legal aid scheme, then run by the Law Society, was being challenged by a new generation of radical young lawyers inspired by developments on the other side of the Atlantic. The idea of 'access to justice' had been an integral part of President Johnson's war on poverty (see Chapter 10). In 1968, Michael Zander, now emeritus professor of law at the London School of Economics and Political Science, was the first legal academic to name-check US-style 'neighborhood law firms' as a possible model for UK practices, in the Society of Labour Lawyers' pamphlet *Justice for All*.[1] It was not just Labour; the Conservative Party also argued in their paper *Rough Justice* that the legal system had to reach out to the poor in order to remedy 'the failure of many people who need legal advice to ever get to the solicitor's office'.[2]

If anywhere needed this approach, it was the then blighted part of West London. 'It has the problems of most slum areas but more so,' said the narrator of 'Law Shop', a 1970 *World in Action* documentary which tracked a week in the life of the first law centre.[3] 'Some 68,000 people, many of them immigrants, are compressed into probably the worst housing conditions in Britain.'

Michael Zander set out the ambition of the law centre movement back in 1978: 'Nothing less than the introduction of a new public service to operate alongside, and supplement, the private profession would suffice to deal adequately with the problem of providing proper legal services to a section of the public who went short of them.'[4]

Roger Smith OBE, former director of JUSTICE and the Legal Action Group, tried successfully to transfer his articles to North Kensington and later joined Camden, where he worked between

1973 in 1975 before becoming director of West Hampstead. 'The idea was that law centres were going to be about systematic change and not just "band aid" legal services,' he wrote in 2007.[5] 'These were organisations that through their work in the community and work in the courts wanted to change the world. It was highly idealistic.' A generation of committed young lawyers began their careers in law centres, including a number of government ministers and leading members of the Labour Party such as Baron Paul Boateng and Harriet Harman QC, who cut their teeth at Paddington and Brent, respectively.

The documentary programme was called 'Law Shop' to reinforce the notion that law centres would make legal advice accessible to all. So, 'instead of the formality and staid dignity of the typical solicitors' office,' wrote Zander, law centres went out of their way to 'present an informal, casual atmosphere'. 'They are normally at street level in main shopping centres,' he continued. 'Instead of the usual discreet nameplate, they have a large "LAW CENTRE" sign in the window. Shopfronts and interiors are plastered with posters and notices about legal rights, campaigns for racial equality, meetings of local tenants' associations and information as to what to do about bad housing, wife battering or harassment from landlords.' Zander also noticed that the furniture veered towards the 'somewhat dilapidated' and their staff tended to 'wear jeans and unconventional hairstyles'.

The documentary showed terrace after terrace of semi-derelict houses with smashed windows, exposed plasterboard and leaking roofs in the shadow of the newly built A40 Westway. It was broadcast the same year that Grenfell was built – which ironically promised a new life for social tenants built on the bulldozed remains of the slums on the other side of Ladbroke Grove.

The documentary captured the poor queuing for legal advice at Toynbee Hall in Spitalfields, East London, which was described as 'a legacy of Victorian legal charity'. Toynbee Hall was created in 1884 by husband and wife Samuel and Henrietta Barnett, a Church of England vicar and a teacher, to bridge the gap between rich and poor by providing a boarding house for university graduates in one of the most deprived parts of the East End. Their radical vision, part of the settlement movement, was to create a place for future leaders who would first live and work as volunteers among the poor.

The 'Poor Man's Lawyer' service evolved out of that movement, led by Frank Tillyard, a barrister living at Mansfield House university settlement in East London. Tillyard would offer help to anyone who came to the Toynbee Hall with a legal problem. Soon it was 'common practice for County Court judges and police court magistrates to send people who could not afford a lawyer to poor man's lawyers meetings for legal advice'.[6] To this day, Toynbee Hall remains a major player in the local advice sector. In 2018–19 it provided debt advice to some 23,150 people and its Free Legal Advice Centre provided free legal support on 1,121 separate cases.[7]

The *World in Action* documentary revealed that a model of 19th-century philanthropy remained the only option for Londoners in the early 1970s. 'There have been many attempts in the past at "poor man's law services" – and they have nearly always given a poor service. A poor service for the poor man,' James Saunders said in the programme. 'We have been set up to do away with this completely. An absolute first-class marvellous service for the poor man – just in the same way that the businessman in South Kensington gets the same service as the company that puts its legal expenses on the tax form.'

"One of the reasons why we started the law centre was because private practice solicitors were pretty useless," Peter Kandler, the solicitor who set up North Kensington Law Centre, tells us. "They didn't act for tenants. They acted for landlords."

★ ★ ★

How did the mainstream legal profession react to the new law centres? In its 1973 annual report, the Law Society decried the nascent movement as a subversive means of stirring up 'political and quasi-political confrontation'.

The kind of social welfare law advice that law centres were created to provide was also becoming a lucrative income stream for private practice law firms. The Law Society, which ran the legal aid scheme until the late 1980s, allowed solicitors a fee to cover advice and assistance on any matter of English law on the basis of a means test carried out by a solicitor. This became known as the 'Green Form Scheme'. Set up in 1973, by 1975–76 it represented 7% of total fees earned by solicitors, and 11% ten years later. However, by the mid-1980s over half of Green Form spend went on personal injury, crime and family matters. The number of Green Forms in social welfare law grew from 27,000 in 1975–76 to 172,000 ten years later, but as a percentage of the total number of bills from only 11% to 17% over the same period.[8]

'I'd quite happily have seen private practice shut down, with law centres doing both criminal and civil work,' the solicitor and first chair of North Kensington Law Centre, Peter Kandler, said in 2007.[9] 'It would have taken the profit element out of practice, not that there is a profit element any more. I always felt that there was a better way of giving a service to the public than relying upon profits to drive the business.'

The issue came to a head in 1975 following a stand-off between law centres and the mainstream profession over the opening of Hillingdon Law Centre in West London. The Law Society gave in to pressure from local solicitors who had tried to stop the young upstarts by refusing them the necessary waivers required by solicitors to work in a law centre. A deal was struck whereby law centres did not compete with private practice on solicitors' traditional patches (adult crime, matrimonial work, personal injury, probate and conveyancing), in exchange for the regulatory permissions required to practise as solicitors.

By 1989 there were more than 60 law centres. Since the 2013 LASPO cuts, the Law Centres Network reckons its members have lost over 60% of legal aid income and over 40% of total income.

★ ★ ★

When North Kensington Law Centre first opened on Golborne Road it was helping tenants of slum landlords like Peter Rachman, who ran his business from nearby Notting Hill and was infamous for exploitation and intimidation. The need for vulnerable tenants to have access to decent legal advice to deal with dodgy landlords and unfit accommodation has been a persistent feature in North Kensington Law Centre's 50-year history.

Mike O'Dwyer, a housing lawyer who worked at the law centre from 1978 to 1990, lives 200 yards away from Grenfell. "For me the law centre always has been a community resource," he says. He recalls its lawyers taking the judges from Bloomsbury and Marylebone County Court to visit tenants' homes to impress upon them the squalor of North Kensington. "It was a pretty revolutionary thing to do at the time," he says.[10]

The judges in those days were "totally landlord orientated", agrees Peter Kandler. He recalls the former Court of Appeal judge Sir Stephen Sedley being driven by one of their young barristers to West London to see the conditions that tenants were expected to put up with. "From then on, he looked at tenants' applications more favourably," he says. "There were no facilities to help tenants. The Citizens Advice Bureaux, which went on to do a great job as the century developed, were then run by grey-rinse ladies who told you off for being a tenant."

Grenfell was not the only tragedy to take place on the North Kensington Law Centre's doorstep. In 1981 a fire ripped through three large, connected houses in Clanricarde Gardens, Notting Hill Gate, a short distance from Grenfell. Over 100 people, mainly migrants working in the hotel and catering sector, had been crammed into a rabbit warren of bedsits.

"The council had been called in 18 months before," Mike O'Dwyer recollects. "They hadn't carried out any of the enforcement warnings. The fire tore through the building with enormous ferocity and there was no means of escape. It was horrific."

An inquest returned a verdict of misadventure. O'Dwyer acted for 13 of the survivors in a civil claim against the defendants' insurers. He recalls: "They were represented by a City law firm. I was in the backroom of the law centre with a semi-automatic typewriter." The case was settled days before the hearing and the survivors were paid £5,000 each in compensation. "The landlord's representatives had alleged it was arson," he says. "They accepted the cause of the fire was restricted electrical wiring under the floorboards in the context of heavy occupation."

In November 1983 there was a finding of maladministration against Kensington and Chelsea council for not having taken the proper steps to enforce regulations. Nicholas Paget-Brown, the former leader of Kensington and Chelsea who resigned over the council's response to the fire, rejoined the council shortly after.

"My message to tenants at the time was that if you want protection, then look after yourselves," O'Dwyer recalls. "We were so angry with the council. I lived with that case through my entire professional career."

Like mice in a box

A fortnight after our visit to North Kensington, we speak to Maryuri Arboleda. She lives with her partner, their seven-year-old son and 15-month-old twins in a tiny one-bedroom flat in Southwark in South London. The five of them sleep in the living room and have turned the bedroom, the smaller of the two rooms, into a lounge. "My son is seven years old. He needs his own space to do his homework and watch movies," she says.

The previous week the couple had successfully challenged Southwark council, arguing that it had wrongly applied the test for statutory overcrowding as defined under the Housing Act 1985. Overcrowding is calculated according to either the 'space standard' or the 'room standard'. These calculations look at the number of people, their ages and genders, and the number of rooms or size of the rooms they are occupying.

The housing charity Shelter reported in 2018 that there were about 1.5 million people on council waiting lists, only 290,000 social homes were made available in 2017 and more than a quarter (27%) of those on the lists had waited for over five years.[11] More than half of households waiting were currently living in overcrowded or unsanitary housing.

Arboleda and her partner first put their name on the housing list back in June 2017 so that they could move out of their cramped, rented 'one-bed' into social housing and a flat that was more suitable for a growing family. "We have tried everything we could to move. I knocked on many doors, went to many organisations and they all said the same thing," she says. "We kept being told that they wouldn't do anything unless we were homeless. It was very frustrating."

Arboleda's partner is a facilities coordinator for Virgin and gave up her job in a shop to look after the twins. Their tiny second-floor flat is not only too small for the growing family, it isn't suitable. Arboleda struggles to lug her double-buggy up two flights of stairs, and has to leave one of the twins at the bottom of the stairs as she does so. She has been to the doctor because of her back problems and was referred to the Maudsley Hospital in South London because of her depression. She likens living in the flat to being like "mice in a box". "We all live in the same room. I was so stressed that my hair was falling out," she says.

The successful challenge was brought by the Public Interest Law Centre together with a local community group, Housing Action Southwark and Lambeth. "Lots of families in the group are living in a single room, a studio flat or a one-bedroom flat," explains Housing Action's Izzy Koksal. "They can't afford the high rents in the private rented sector for a suitably sized flat. To avoid street homelessness, they have to accept whatever they can find and whatever dodgy landlord will accept them."

Koksal reckons overcrowding is "definitely much worse" in the private rented sector because of "super-high rents", as well as discrimination. "Lots of members in our group say that the landlords they approach do not like that they have children or that they claim benefits – and also people, often migrant families, do not know their rights to access assistance from the council and the housing register. Even when people know their rights, enforcing them is another issue," she says, "as the long struggle Maryuri Arboleda faced with Southwark council shows."

The family put their names on the waiting list in June 2017, when the twins arrived, but only heard from Southwark in February 2018. Initially, Arboleda wasn't hopeful. A friend of hers has been on the waiting list for eight years.

Housing Action Southwark and Lambeth is in touch with families in overcrowded council housing as well. "Because of the huge shortage of suitable family-sized council homes in Southwark, and across London, overcrowded families in council homes are stuck on the same long waiting list alongside overcrowded families in private rented housing," Koksal reckons. "There just aren't the right-sized council homes there. There are so few three- to five-bed council homes in Southwark."

Across the country, statistics show that overcrowding is worse in council housing than in the private rented sector but, Koksal adds: "I think London is the reverse."

Helen Mowatt, a solicitor from the Public Interest Law Centre, explains that Southwark had wrongly applied the statutory test by assessing overcrowding solely by reference to floor area and not considering the number of rooms. She reckons that, had they applied the test correctly, the Arboledas' home would have been deemed statutorily overcrowded months ago.

Mowatt argues that this is not a one-off error on the part of the council. According to freedom of information requests by Housing Action Southwark and Lambeth (HASL), Southwark has been consistently misapplying the law. The council provided information going back only to February 2018 and found that 46 banding decisions had been made which involved assessing whether a household was statutorily overcrowded, and in all cases the test was applied incorrectly, including 13 cases found not to be statutorily overcrowded. According to Mowatt, these cases must now be reviewed. "[But] we are unclear as to how many households may have been affected before this date," she says.

HASL point out that the statutory test has not been updated since 1935, and Izzy Koksal calls it "an outdated and ungenerous law" with an unfairly high threshold. The last Labour government accepted that the statutory test was 'no longer defensible in a modern society'. "Yet we often meet families who do meet the definition of statutory overcrowding, which shows how very severe the overcrowding is," Koksal adds.

"Austerity, the cuts and a lack of housing mean that local authorities do what they can to put people in the incorrect bands. A lot of people don't know their rights. If they are told they are in band four, the lowest band, they might not question it," Public Interest Law Centre's Helen Mowatt continues. HASL approached a number of law firms and housing law specialists before they contacted the law centre. "Housing lawyers don't have the energy or capacity because they have so much on," says Mowatt. "They have so much to deal with, with homelessness and evictions. Considering someone's banding isn't a priority. That's understandable, but actually it can have a massive impact."

Elizabeth Wyatt, from HASL, agrees. Overcrowded housing has a "devastating impact" on people's lives. "We have been raising the problem of overcrowding with Southwark council for years but the council have failed to engage and take meaningful action," she says. "Southwark council should be supporting their residents to access their housing rights and the secure council homes they need. Instead it took a legal challenge before the council would accept that it had been wrongly denying that our families were statutorily overcrowded," she adds.

* * *

House prices in neighbouring Lambeth have risen by 47% and private rents by 27% in recent years. By 2018 the waiting list for social housing in Lambeth has grown to 23,000 people and more than 1,300 families are living in overcrowded homes.[12]

Unsurprisingly, Lambeth's Labour MP, Helen Hayes, ranks 'housing' as the number one issue in her constituency case-work. In February 2019 she introduced the Planning (Affordable Housing and Land Compensation) Bill in Parliament. The Bill sought to overhaul the land value system to enable councils to purchase land to build social housing. When we meet she tells us about the "lack of access to secure, genuinely affordable social housing". "We see people every week who are on the housing waiting list living in a variety of different circumstances, often at the sharp end of the worst of the private rented sector," she says. "People are living with very high levels of overcrowding."

The borough's remarkable transformation has forced many older residents out. According to Karen Brunger, head of advice services at Merton and Lambeth Citizens Advice: "Brixton was probably seen until about 15 years ago as a deprived area but there has been a new generation and money coming in which has meant local people are being priced out of the market."

'Falling through the net'

As a result of the LASPO cuts described in Chapter 1, legal aid is available for housing problems only when a person's home is at immediate risk, such as in possession proceedings or where housing disrepair poses a serious threat to their health. Many landlord and tenant disputes are no longer included in the scheme, nor is there legal aid to challenge problems with Housing Benefit. Early intervention for housing debts before they get to court has also been removed from scope.

In the year after the introduction of LASPO, the volume of legally aided housing cases halved. In 2010–11, 14,401 applications for representation in housing-related cases were made. When we visit Lambeth in 2018 this is down by 45%, to 7,963.[13]

The 2013 cuts have had a catastrophic impact on the threadbare safety net available to the vulnerably housed. The Public Interest

Law Centre was soon to find itself temporarily homeless when, in July 2019, Lambeth Law Centre, based in Brixton, became the latest law centre casualty of LASPO. The two law centres shared premises. Lambeth Law Centre had employed 18 people and was forced to close its doors after 38 years of service. 'Unfortunately, the law centre has faced financial pressures caused by legal aid cuts and increased operating costs,' it said. The Public Interest Law Centre migrated north and was rehoused at Camden Law Centre.

As a result of LASPO, the housing charity Shelter suffered 'a 50% cut in funding for over 50% of our legal services from just over £6m, down to just over £2.8m'. 'An increasingly crisis-driven approach to housing advice in general, and the removal from scope of welfare benefits, and housing benefit in particular, is leaving people to fall through the net,' it said.[14] In its briefing, published the same month that we visited Grenfell, the charity explains why legal aid is 'crucial' in tackling homeless.

Shelter has called for a reversal of the 2013 cuts: restoring legal aid for help with Housing Benefit, Universal Credit or other problems relevant to possession claims or which are likely to lead to homelessness; for disrepair and unfitness claims; and for debt issues relating to the affordability of residential accommodation.

Lambeth MP Helen Hayes tells us how valuable the advice sector is to her community. "We have some brilliant organisations and, every single day, we're grateful for them." That said, the borough's advice agencies were "pretty overstretched" and her office tried "not to overburden them".

We speak to Shelter's legal team. Reflecting on the offices the group has had to close post LASPO, the charity's principal solicitor, John Gallagher, explains that "they were in areas like Milton Keynes and Ashford and Taunton". "Maybe places where there wouldn't be a high volume of pure legal issues but where many of the cases that would come to us would have benefits implications," he says. In other words, cases that were no longer covered by the diminished post-LASPO scheme.

"We used to do welfare benefits advice, debt advice, housing advice and community care, everything," Sadaf Mir, a housing solicitor with the housing charity, adds. "Now that's been scaled back." "If I had a client who had a housing benefit problem, I'd help him with the possession issue, welfare benefits or debt," she continues. "It was holistic." Post LASPO, those areas of advice are out of scope. "So what really happens is I end up doing a lot of the housing benefit appeals pro bono [without charging] in order to help the clients. Who else is going to do it?"

According to the Shelter briefing, more than eight out of ten of their lawyers felt unable to provide the same level of support to the clients they took on as they did before LASPO. Seven out of ten had to turn away vulnerably housed people because their case was now out of scope, while more than eight out of ten lawyers found it much more difficult to find other agencies to help clients in resolving issues Shelter no longer dealt with.

Gallagher reckoned that the impact of LASPO has not been as devastating on housing as in other areas of law, such as immigration, welfare benefits and family. "At least possession proceedings, loss of home and homelessness survived the cull," he says.

"What didn't survive was all that early advice on landlord and tenant problems, which happen constantly: problems with tenancy deposits, low-level disrepair," he continues. The Shelter briefing cited Grenfell as highlighting the problem of disrepair: '[It] is vital that, assuming that the current Homes (Fitness for Human Habitation) Bill is enacted, [tenants] can access free legal advice, advocacy and, where necessary, representation, to ensure that they can enforce their rights to a home that meets the fitness standard not only when, but before, it starts to pose a serious risk to health and safety.' The legislation, introduced to give tenants the ability to take landlords to court if their home was unsafe, came into force in March 2019.

Post LASPO, advice is "only available now where there's a serious threat to health or safety, and you're seeking an order," Gallagher explains. According to 2018 Ministry of Justice figures, the number of disrepair cases has collapsed by 94% since 2010.[15]

On 7 February 2019 we meet with senior solicitor Katie White and solicitor Alison Jones from the legal team at Shelter Cymru's offices on an industrial estate in Fairwater, Cardiff. Both worked at law centres (White at Brent, and at Avon and Bristol, and Jones in the former Cardiff Law Centre). "The really serious cases where people are living in squalor don't seem to be being dealt with at the moment," White tells us.

Disrepair is a major issue. "It's so limited as to what you can do under the legal aid scheme and, particularly in Wales, housing conditions are poor," White says. "People really need that kind of advice, support, help."

"You've got people living in accommodation which does need repair but because you can't show it's prejudicial to their health you can't get any funding to force the landlord to do it," says Jones.

In 2019, Shelter Cymru advised on 813 cases that involved disrepair. This represented just 8% of their total caseload (9,961 cases). It is often difficult to bring stand-alone disrepair claims into scope for public funding.

"It seems to be logical if someone's got a damp condition, or they've got minor problems with their electrics, there's a potential danger there," she continues. They typically get "short shrift" from the Legal Aid Agency, she adds.

★ ★ ★

The Grenfell tragedy prompted a debate about the limits of publicly funded housing law advice. In an interview on BBC's *Newsnight*, the housing activist Pilgrim Tucker asserted that the tower's residents had long had safety concerns about the state of the building and "tried to get lawyers but because of the legal aid cuts they couldn't".[16]

The then Lord Chancellor, David Lidington, insisted that publicly funded legal help would have been available for the residents. 'Under our legal aid arrangements if you are a tenant and you have concerns about safety issues in your flat or house you can get legal aid to take action against your landlord,' he blithely assured viewers.[17] Residents of Grenfell had long been raising their fears about the tower. Emma Dent Coad told us how the Royal Borough of Kensington and Chelsea sent 'cease and desist' letters to those in the block "who were warning of some hideous tragedy".

Lidington also claimed that the Legal Aid Agency had no record of the Grenfell residents ever having made such an application. 'Given the difficulties of having lists of tenants, I do not want to give a 100% guarantee, but the key point is that tenants are eligible for legal aid if there are serious safety concerns about their property,' he continued.

Housing lawyers were quick to point out that, irrespective of the cuts, there is not and has never been legal aid for 'safety concerns'. "It's clear that Grenfell has exposed gaps in our legislation," comments Connie Cullen, services manager for Shelter, which had been working with North Kensington Law Centre, the local Citizens Advice and other groups near Grenfell. She explained that, in relation to housing disrepair cases, tenants could only get legal aid "for things that have gone wrong". "You can't get funding for pre-emptive action," she clarified.

Priced out

North Kensington Law Centre now occupies a vast subterranean bunker beneath the Lancaster West estate. The doors at the rear of the building are just a few feet from Grenfell Tower. The same kind of gentrification that has transformed Brixton means that the law centre can no longer afford to coexist alongside the art galleries and eateries of Golborne Road. If its offices have the ambience of an NCP carpark, that's because, before the area was re-designated the Baseline Business Studios, it was where tenants parked their cars and left their rubbish. Breeze blocks divide the old parking bays to create tiny retail units occupied by the council and rubbish collection points.

The centre's lawyers complain that their cramped basement home is inadequate and inappropriate. In the aftermath of Grenfell they had to conduct confidential interviews with bereaved clients in the brick-paved corridor running between the units, for lack of office space. As a result of the fire most of the small businesses that previously occupied the tiny units moved on, but the law centre cannot afford to move to somewhere more suitable, less cramped and where they can offer client confidentiality.

It is a minor miracle that the law centre is still in business. The 2013 legal aid cuts have led to an alarming unravelling of an already threadbare network of advice agencies, a process exacerbated by austerity-driven local authority cuts. Law centres have borne the brunt of that. Eleven have closed in the five years post LASPO, including Lambeth and Cardiff, and many of those that survive are a shadow of their former selves. The Law Centres Network reckons that over the four years to 2017 their members have lost over 60% of legal aid income and over 40% of total income.

North Kensington's income dropped from £900,000 in 2010 to just £441,251. Historically, North Kensington Law Centre has always been poorly supported by the Royal Borough of Kensington and Chelsea. It presently receives only about £59,000 from the council. This is less than in 2016, the year before the fire (£62,350), and would barely cover the rent on their former home.

Annie Campbell Viswanathan says that the old address is still available. "But they want a commercial rent and we don't have the money," she continues. "We were forced to move. This area has gentrified and what used to be run-down Golborne Road is now prime land location. We just don't have the resources."

In the weeks after the Grenfell fire the centre's then director, Victoria Vasey, said that the last few years had been 'about survival'. She pointed out the irony that in the weeks following the tragedy the law centre had been able to provide the kind of service for clients that it would like to, as a result of the huge influx of pro bono help.

The legal profession's response to the tragedy represented an unprecedented collaboration between a beleaguered not-for-profit sector and the pro bono community in general, and the City firms in particular. Since the fire, more than 650 people, mainly lawyers, had volunteered their help. Specialist advisers from other law centres and Shelter, as well as members of the Housing Law Practitioners Association, had been providing the equivalent of one to two full-time housing advisers every day and experts in immigration, employment and welfare benefits were also on hand. City firms contributed infrastructure support and a constant flow of up to six volunteer lawyers a day from some 25 firms.

In the four weeks after the blaze, the law centre's small team of lawyers, plus a small army of volunteers, advised 150 families affected by the fire; a third of that number were formerly residents of the 24-storey tower block. The reality was that the invaluable work done by the law centre had little to do with legal aid. As Nimrod Ben-Cnaan, head of policy at the Law Centres Network, identified at the time, the work done by North Kensington Law Centre for its devastated community was 'mostly thanks to public donations, charitable grants and pro bono volunteering'. 'Legal aid covers so little of their legal needs,' he noted.[18]

3

On the Streets

There are already more than 50 people at Birmingham's largest drop-in centre for the homeless within 15 minutes of its doors opening on the morning of Wednesday, 18 September 2019. The large, hanger-like structure of the centre – formerly a taxicab depot – occupies an industrial no-man's-land in Digbeth. It is located between the coach station, handy for new arrivals with no fixed abode, and the Custard Factory built by Alfred Bird in 1902 and now a hub for the creative industries.

The centre, known as SIFA Fireside, is within walking distance of the city centre: close, but not close enough for its unruly clientele to scare off shoppers and office workers. Its unwieldy name derives from the union of two charities in 2007: SIFA (Supporting Independence From Alcohol), set up to help street drinkers in Moseley; and The Fireside, a place of respite near the centre set up by two Catholic nuns to cater for the same marginalised group.

★ ★ ★

We are here to shadow Habib Ullah, a solicitor specialising in welfare benefits from Birmingham Community Law Centre who runs a weekly drop-in clinic. The number of homeless people in Birmingham has tripled over the past few years. Around the time of our visit, the housing charity Shelter estimates that one in every 66 people resident in the city is homeless.[1]

One in every 200 people across England is without a home. The London borough of Newham tops Shelter's list (one in 24), followed by Haringey, and Kensington and Chelsea (one in 29). Birmingham is the only city outside of the south-east of England in the top ten. SIFA Fireside typically sees more than 150 homeless people every day who rely on its soup kitchen. This reflects a huge rise in street homelessness – from 157 cases in 2010 to 3,479 seven years later.

The sharp end of the housing crisis

First up is Krzys, a Polish man in his mid-30s wearing a grey shell-suit and matching hoodie, with short-cropped hair and a closed-trimmed beard and moustache. A SIFA regular, Krzys speaks no English and so communicates with Habib Ullah via a Polish project worker, Angelina. About one third of the people who come to the drop-in centre hail from Central and Eastern Europe. Angelina seems to know most of the clients, including Krzys, who is cheerful despite the seemingly overwhelming problems he faces.

The police have confiscated Krzys's passport and papers. Luckily, he has copies, knows the name of the officer involved and has filed a complaint form. His immediate concern is that he has no money and nothing to evidence his benefits claims. He is nervous about an upcoming interview at the job centre.

SIFA Fireside is concerned that misinformation about the recent changes to the benefits system – namely, the chaotic roll-out of Universal Credit – is spreading like wildfire through immigrant communities. "Universal Credit has replaced Jobseeker's Allowance [JSA]," Habib Ullah explains, adding that, as with JSA, Krzys will be expected to look for jobs and attend the job centre at least every two weeks to see a work coach.

Krzys is anxious about the nature of the interrogation that he might face at the job centre. "It's normal to be asked questions," Ullah assures him. "With Universal Credit, they will give you more opportunities to find work and there will be more focus on you getting a job. My experience is that the first few months will be quite intense. There's no limit on how many times they can ask you to attend. If the work coach decides that a person needs a lot of support they might call you in every day. It will become your job to go there everyday."

Krzys is told that if he misses a deadline without a genuine reason, he can expect sanctions, and those sanctions will increase every time the rules are broken. The solicitor also explains that claimants can be expected to travel up to 90 minutes by public transport. "We might think that having to travel to Wolverhampton or to Worcester is too far. Not for the job centre," he adds.

Krzys presents as smart, cheerful and lucid. That wasn't always the case. His life unravelled dramatically after he ended up serving seven months on remand in connection with the death of a man he shared a house with. This was how he came to lose his paperwork and end up on the streets. He currently has a bed in a homeless hostel.

The idea behind SIFA Fireside is to work with the vulnerably homed like Krzys by addressing immediate needs. He can shower, use their clothes bank and have something to eat and drink in the warmth. The charity also helps with longer-term plans, offering support for sorting out problems with benefits and housing, as well as accessing rehab services and help in securing a job. In Krzys's case, they have been helping him to recover the missing paperwork and have sorted a temporary passport through the Polish embassy.

Next up is Stefan, another Pole, with a troubled relationship with alcohol. He's in his 50s, looks crumpled and defeated. He fell off the wagon and ended up sleeping rough after separating from his wife and two children. Stefan apparently had his own successful motorcycle repair business in London before ending up on the streets in Birmingham. "He's a Dr Jekyll and Mr Hyde. I have met both," Angelina says. He has been refused benefits on the grounds that he has failed the 'habitual residence' test needed for European Economic Area nationals to demonstrate that they have the right to reside.

Habib Ullah:	As the rules stand, you cannot get Universal Credit straight away because before your claim, you weren't in employment. When did you last work?
Stefan:	March.
Ullah:	So from March until now, what have you been doing?
Stefan:	Nothing. Just, life ….
Ullah:	You haven't been working? Once you stop working you break the link, and you cannot claim Universal Credit as a 'worker'. If you

claim as soon as you stop being self-employed
or as soon as you stop work, you would still be
treated as a worker. You have lost that status.

As Ullah unpicks Stefan's complicated story, it becomes apparent
that it is the Department for Work and Pensions that is in error.
The solicitor drafts a covering letter for Stefan: 'I believe your
decision is incorrect as I am not subject to the habitual residence
test due to having been granted settled status by the Home Office.
I have provided evidence of my settled status to the Job Centre ...'

Stefan is homeless and uses SIFA Fireside as his home address.
He has recently applied for a job, with the charity's help. Halfway
through the meeting, Angelina brings in his post. "This might
help," she says.

It doesn't. One letter turns out to be from the Inland Revenue,
informing him that his outstanding tax liability of £1,200, the result
of late filing, has increased to £2,600. A second letter contains
details of a fine in relation to a court application concerning
domestic violence. That will be another £360.

"So many obstacles," sighs a sympathetic Angelina. "Every week
there is something new for Stefan."

"Every day," he says.

★ ★ ★

SIFA Fireside represents the sharp end of the housing crisis in
Britain's second city. According to the Labour MP for Birmingham
Edgbaston, Preet Gill, housing problems "account for the largest
volume of case-work we receive" and comprise almost a quarter
of the constituency advice work her office handles (23%). "One
of the issues that stand out for us is the use of hostels and bedsits as
temporary accommodation," she tells us. "Lots of one-child families
end up in accommodation that's not suitable for them."

"Whichever city you go to now, homelessness is so much more
visible. You can see it in terms of people begging and sleeping
on the streets," says Hollie Venn, who works for Trident Reach,
an organisation providing services to vulnerable adults across
the Midlands. "When I drive around for work I see tents in
Birmingham now." Trident Housing provides over 3,400 homes,
as well as hostels and homelessness services.

Our visit to Birmingham takes place 18 months after the introduction of the Homelessness Reduction Act 2017. Theresa May's government was elected in 2017 with a manifesto commitment to 'halve rough sleeping over the course of the parliament and eliminate it altogether by 2027'. The legislation imposes duties on local authorities enabling the homeless, or those at risk of homelessness, to have access to support, irrespective of priority of need status. These duties have been foisted on councils at the same time as they face drastic funding cuts.

A few months prior to our visit to the Midlands, a survey of 151 town halls by the Local Government Association, published in March 2019, found that six in ten councils said they had had more households in temporary accommodation since the Act was introduced 12 months earlier.[2]

Venn is sceptical about the legislation. "It just means the local authority has got longer to make a decision for you," she says. "I can't really see it decreasing homelessness. I'm not convinced. What we're seeing are people with complex needs not getting access to the right services because the threshold has been increased."

★ ★ ★

Stefan and Krzys don't present as street homeless (they are clean, smart and sober), unlike many of SIFA Fireside's regulars, whose various addictions are all too obvious. Chief executive Carly Jones points out that a high proportion of the people they see are in crisis by the time they walk through the doors. "We have such big numbers of clients where, I'm going to use the term loosely, there is 'no recourse to public funds'," she says. The 'no recourse' policy was introduced in 2012 as part of the government's so-called 'hostile environment', preventing migrants from claiming social support (see Chapters 6 and 7).

Jones continues: "If you include people who are on the brink of crisis, I would say that comprises about 70% and those in complete crisis maybe about 20 to 30%." By that she explains that she means "people out on the streets sleeping rough and coming in here for their showers, meals and everything to survive, basically".

In between meetings at SIFA Fireside, we talk to Habib Ullah and Angelina.

How does she stay so cheerful, working with such a demanding client group of rough sleepers and alcoholics? "Well, I have only been here a year. Come back next year," she jokes.

Some days over the winter months when it is cold there can be more than 200 people at the drop-in centre. "It can be very draining. Sometimes there is shouting. Quite recently a guy jumped up at me – he was British – screaming: 'What do you have in your pants?' It was so inappropriate," she recalls. "You have to cope with so many things. Rarely people thank you. I'd say our clients from Central and Eastern Europe are less demanding, generally speaking. They know it's not their country and they appreciate it when you help them."

Ullah is a veteran of the law centre movement. Before Birmingham Community Law Centre, there was Birmingham Law Centre based in Sparkbrook, the poorest ward in the city. "As a direct result of LASPO cuts we had to close down in 2013," he tells us. The closure left Britain's second-largest city without a law centre.

The solicitor had worked at Birmingham Law Centre for 14 years, together with a colleague, Michael Bates. When it closed the two solicitors transferred to nearby Coventry Law Centre, which set up a Birmingham office and became Central England Law Centre. Coventry Law Centre is a first-generation law centre, founded in 1976 by four councillors, and has always been well supported by the city council.

"Michael and I approached Coventry Law Centre and, basically, said Birmingham now didn't have a law centre and that we wanted to carry on the work we were doing," he recalls. Ullah had been running a weekly clinic for a charity in Sparkbrook which had a building but no funding for services. "They trusted us enough to let us use it for free for a couple of years. So we started again, Michael and myself." He describes the new Birmingham service as 'precarious'; just 40% of funding comes from legal aid and the rest from grants, the biggest being a three-year grant from the Oak Foundation, which is now in its third year.

"One of the problems with Birmingham as a whole is that there are very few decent places to go for advice," Ullah tells us. "Three or four years ago we had five Citizens Advice Bureaux and now they've all closed down. There is only one in the city centre, and that's mainly telephone-based advice."

SIFA Fireside used to have a debt adviser from Citizens Advice, but not any more. "Generally when people have no income, debt isn't the issue," Ullah points out. "If they do see a debt adviser, what are they going to do? They can't make repayments." During the four years that he has been running the SIFA Fireside drop-in clinic, Ullah has only seen one person prior to their being evicted. "It's always afterwards," he adds.

Citizens Advice: 'a massive volunteer army'

"We will never, never meet all the demand in this area," reckons Janice Nichols, chief executive of Birmingham's Citizens Advice. She describes demand for their help as "limitless". "We're always striving to find ways and doing more with the resources that we have, but it's a very challenging environment in Birmingham."

Eighteen months before our visit, the bureau cancelled its drop-in service. If you need help, you now have to ring first to make an appointment. "People used to be able to just come to our offices. If you got here and were one of the first 50 or 60, we'd see you." People could be waiting up to five hours to be seen. "That's just not a civilised way to provide services and, frankly, it just wasn't safe," Nichols adds.

According to Nichols, the new system is fairer because "if you couldn't get here, if you were a carer or somebody who can't leave your home, you weren't getting a very good service". She continues: "I'm not professing that people get a very good service now; but, in all likelihood, you've a better chance of being helped since we, sort of, closed our doors."

★ ★ ★

Citizens Advice has had a presence in Birmingham since 1939. The Birmingham branch was one of 200 bureaux that opened the day after the Second World War started. In anticipation of conflict, the National Council of Social Services had looked into how to support the civilian population in its hour of need. It concluded that a network of bureaux should be established throughout the country, but particularly in cities and industrial areas 'where social disorganisation may be acute'.

That network withered in post-war Britain, from a peak of 1,074 bureaux to 416 in the 1960s. However, Citizens Advice subsequently redefined itself by focusing on consumer protection and debt advice. The service expanded as a result of the recessions of the 1980s and 1990s and became an increasingly effective lobbying force. For example, in 2004, after a decade-long campaign by Citizens Advice the government added an amendment to the Housing Bill to include a tenancy deposit protection scheme.

Citizens Advice nation-wide now represents a massive volunteer army. Its volunteer advisers offer generalist advice as distinct from the specialist legal advice that is covered by the legal aid scheme. Some bureaux have legal aid contracts, but not many. Immediately before the 2013 LASPO cuts, it was reported that legal aid constituted 15% of bureaux' income.[3] In the year of our research, more than 21,300 volunteers provided help in some 2,550 locations, supported by 7,000 staff. As a result of such public spiritedness, Citizens Advice claims that approximately 1.3 million people were able to receive face-to-face help and a further 867,000 were assisted over the phone. Citizens Advice is a franchise, and so that is achieved through 270 independent charities which are all responsible for their own funding.

Compared to the rest of the threadbare advice sector, Citizens Advice is, relatively speaking, well supported by government. Of its £110 million income in 2018–19 (up from £77 million in 2013–14), it received £26.5 million to run its Money Advice Service; £16 million came from the Department of Business, Energy and Industrial Strategy (consumer advice) plus £22.3 million (unrestricted 'core' costs); £11.5 million came from the Ministry of Justice (support for witnesses in the criminal court); £9.8 million from the Department for Work and Pensions (DWP) (help for Universal Credit claimants); and a further £9.1 million from the DWP (pension advice).[4]

Birmingham Citizens Advice was almost forced to close in 2013 as a result of the double whammy of legal aid and local authority cuts. At that point it was assisting about 50,000 people a year, as compared to just 23,800 in 2018–19.

In 2010 Citizens Advice published research, drawing on data from the Civil and Social Justice Survey and the Ministry of Justice, into the economic case for legal aid. It reckoned that for every £1 spent on legal aid for housing advice the state could save as much as £2.34; for every £1 on debt advice, £2.98; and for £1 on benefits advice, as much as £8.80.[5] The network itself lost around £19 million of funding as a result of LASPO. Around half of its bureaux previously held legal aid contracts which funded qualified staff to provide specialist advice to people with legal problems relating to debt, welfare benefits, housing, family, employment and immigration.[6] In 2014, Citizens Advice reported that more than nine out of ten of its offices (92%) were struggling to refer people for specialist legal advice.[7]

Citizens Advice is a largely apolitical presence. This is certainly so compared to law centres, which often exist in permanent conflict with the local authorities that they regularly sue on behalf of tenants or employees (and upon whom they may be dependent for funding), as well as engaging in strategic litigation on a national level, attacking government policies when it is in the interests of their clients to do so.

When David Cameron set out his vision for the 'big society' in 2011 he spoke approvingly of how 'some local authorities' were responding 'extremely well' to the challenges of austerity: 'for example ... in leafy old West Oxfordshire they are working as hard as they can to make sure the Citizens' Advice Bureau – an absolutely vital part of the Big Society – doesn't get a cut'.[8]

From April 2019 Citizens Advice received £51 million in government funding to provide advice and support to Universal Credit claimants. It was claimed that the DWP obliged the service to sign up to 'gagging clauses' preventing them from taking 'any actions which unfairly bring or are likely to unfairly bring [DWP's] name or reputation and/or [DWP] into disrepute'.

Copies of the agreement were obtained by a social welfare activist, Frank Zola, under the Freedom of Information Act. "Citizens Advice provides help to large numbers of those punished by Universal Credit, such as disabled people and families who have ended up losing thousands of pounds by claiming Universal Credit, vast rises in debt, rent arrears, evictions, survival crime, five-week delays in first payments and the horror of its inbuilt benefit sanctions and excessive conditionality," Zola says. "Against this background, does Citizens Advice campaign and advocate for Universal Credit to be stopped and abolished? No, it decides to act as a mere duplicitous adjunct of the DWP and even agrees to a grant gagging clause that prevents them from being critical of the DWP."

Citizens Advice's chief executive, Gillian Guy, insists that there was "nothing in the grant agreement" that prevented them from raising "evidence publicly about the impact Universal Credit is having on the people who come to us for help". "Citizens Advice is, and always will be, totally independent from government," she adds.

★ ★ ★

"Citizens Advice have been able to do less and less over recent years," local MP Preet Gill told us. "Constituents can't sit down and talk to them anymore. They have to phone, and it's often difficult to get through. At a critical juncture in the roll-out of Universal Credit, the lack of readily available advice and support risks letting problems spiral and people slide into rent arrears, and often homelessness."

According to Janice Nichols, Birmingham Citizens Advice's chief executive, the bureau can answer only a fraction of calls, which are "running between 8,000 and 9,000 calls a month". "Just to put that into perspective, that's more than all the calls per month in Wales, where there are 19 local Citizens Advice who work together to answer those calls," she says. The phone lines are manned by volunteers supervised by an experienced adviser. "We probably answer less than 10% of the calls," Nichols reckons.

Nichols concedes that "it's very likely people just aren't bothering". "If you can't resolve something straight away you might leave it, and then actually it becomes more difficult. People end up getting into crisis."

An average of 20 people a day come to the bureau in 'emergency' situations; people whose needs are so urgent that "we couldn't turn them away". "People may get to the point where they will just take a chance and turn up here because they don't know what else to do," Nichols says.

"We're the second city and there's nowhere to refer or signpost people to," reflects Linden Thomas, a senior law lecturer at Birmingham University who runs the law school's pro bono programme. Thomas sits on the board of trustees for the Birmingham Citizens Advice.

"Citizens Advice still provides an awful lot of advice," she says, "but it's funded for specific things such as debt advice funded by central government or very specific support for Universal Credit.

The idea that 'I've got a query. I can just go to my local CAB', that's just either gone or it's going."

Thomas tells us that the council is proposing to cut funding for any kind of first-port-of-call advice service. "It's already all by telephone, not open door, from Citizens Advice in Birmingham because of the cuts. It's increasingly desperate." Could pro bono take up the slack? No, she says. "It can't begin to do that, and the lawyers that might want to and the universities that have the goodwill and want to don't necessarily have the expertise."

★ ★ ★

It's the same bleak message from the smaller advice agencies in the city. People are desperate, demand is off the scale. "We've a waiting list of 25 weeks," says Julian Mander, director of operations at Riverside Church, which provides free, face-to-face advice for people in Moseley.

Riverside Money Advice has a team of 13 volunteer advisers who are "absolutely swamped". It is part of Community Money Advice, a network which has in the region of 150 centres around the UK attached to churches. The charity's vision statement on its website talks of a 'God-given mandate' to help the poor in their community, quoting from the Bible: 'If anyone sees a brother or sister in need but has no pity on them how can the love of God be in that person? Dear children let us not love with words or speech but with actions and in truth.'

"Unlike Citizens Advice, which receives statutory funding, the Community Money Advice network is totally voluntarily funded," Mander explains. Their network runs on goodwill. "We survive on the donations of church friends or other people who support what we're doing," he says. "Some previous clients have become supporters." Mander says the agency is "tucked under the church's charity registration". "They're covering the bills and overheads, but then everything that we need – our membership of Community Money Advice, resources, stamps, leaflets, advertising and training – is paid for by donations from people who really like what we do and want us to succeed."

Over Christmas, Riverside received an anonymous donation of £5,000, plus eight other donations totalling about £6,500, making £11,500 in all. "That will keep us going for another half a year,"

Mander reckons. Riverside has enough funding for a part-time administrator for a day a week to support the volunteer team and who fixes appointments, and Julian Mander is paid to work one day a week. "Everything else, we can only do it because everyone is volunteering," he says.

He calls Citizens Advice "brilliant"; but he explains, by an analogy with crossword puzzles, that their approaches are very different. "Fifty years ago, crosswords were built around a large in-depth knowledge of a small number of things: a bit of English literature, a couple of science questions, and a little bit about politics," he says. "Now, crosswords are focused on all sorts of issues. A little knowledge is required in a lot of areas."

Citizens Advice has "wide knowledge of every single issue that someone might have and relies upon being able to deliver it quickly in little bites". "If you do get to see someone, you'll have half an hour and they'll send you away with a piece of paper and you're told what to do. Most people can't do anything more because they need help to get active. Maybe they're not on the internet, or they don't know how to access things. There are often other things in the way that need tackling as well."

Mander reckons that Riverside takes "the holistic measures needed to rescue people". "We go as deep and as thoroughly and for as long as it takes," he says. Riverside follows a three-part strategy: sort out the immediate crisis; deal with the ongoing budget, providing appropriate money skills in order "to stay out of trouble"; and what Mander calls the "more holistic side", identifying other issues contributing to clients' problems and praying for clients. "For some clients, we can do this whole journey in about three months and sometimes it's as quick as about four conversations. For other people, we've been meeting with them for ten years on a sort of annual review."

He gives an example of a family they started working with just before Christmas, "on the verge of destitution and homelessness". "There were a number of problems: cancer, mental health, rogue landlords, multiple debts, electricity not working, boiler broken down, son with Asperger's, father on the verge of alcoholism, and a mother not accessing the GP because of her poor mental health. All combined together into one maelstrom of complete chaos," he recalls.

Mander continues: "There's no way that you can have a sane, calm, and non-urgent conversation about what debts there might be and what you can do about it. It is all of those other things that make recovery completely impossible." Mander says Riverside has been supporting the family on a weekly basis. He even took their son who has Asperger's on a five-kilometre crazy mud run in Shrewsbury over the Christmas period. It was the first day the family had had out together for a year. "They'd just lurched from crisis to crisis from day to day."

For Mander, "they're not just clients now" but part of the community. "We are looking out for them and trying to do everything that's going to make that journey successful for them," he says.

A vast legal advice desert

There are few parts of the country where the fraying fabric of the legal advice sector is stretched more thinly than in Suffolk. The East Anglian county has a population of about 750,000 and covers nearly 1,600 square miles. Its communities comprise more than 480 villages alongside larger towns – such as Ipswich with a population of 133,000.

Suffolk is also home to the newest law centre in the network. The county's image of rural prosperity belies genuine legal need. According to figures from the End Child Poverty campaign published in 2018, in two constituencies (Ipswich and Waveney) almost 30% of children are considered to be living in poverty.

Suffolk Law Centre exists as a tiny legal advice oasis in what is otherwise a vast desert. "As of this moment, there isn't a single housing lawyer in Suffolk. We haven't had once since 2014," Audrey Ludwig, director of legal services, tells us when we visit the centre on 7 November 2019.

The law centre sprang to life in November 2018 out of the Ipswich and Suffolk Council for Racial Equality, known as ISCRE, and its ten members of staff tend to work across the two organisations. "Our ethos is about building a community voice and being the conduit through which the community can communicate their concerns," Phanuel Mutumburi, the charity's operations director tells us. "We have been able to build trust in the community."

Mutumburi calls it "a mutually beneficial relationship" between the two groups. "Whilst the law centre focuses on case-work, we identify trends and so, for example, if there are people complaining about issues in the health service or education, then there is probably a failure in the service somewhere."

As well as ISCRE's long-standing anti-discrimination practice, the law centre has built on a number of volunteer legal advice clinics that have been running for years. There are sessions staffed by local volunteer lawyers in family, employment, immigration, personal injury and housing advice, as well as a form-filling clinic for family clients and a volunteer duty scheme for first hearings at the family court at Ipswich Magistrates' Court.

Audrey Ludwig acknowledges that the law centre can only do so much. "We are a sticking plaster," she says. "We have waiting lists of several months for everything, which isn't great." That there are any new law centres post-LASPO is nothing short of a miracle. However, against the odds, there are green shoots in the law centre movement. Ludwig has been watching the progress of Greater Manchester Law Centre, which opened in 2016 (see Chapter 6). "We really admire what they've done," she says. "They have done it based on their perception of need in their area. That's absolutely the right way to do it. So have we, and, for example, we don't do welfare benefits because there are a couple of charities in Ipswich which do benefits appeals. That's not our priority."

According to the Law Centres Network, its members have lost more than 60% of their legal aid income since 2013, and more than 40% of total income. "Austerity came to us early," says Ludwig. "Our funding was cut a long time before others. Ironically, we have been forced to learn some of those tricks about being tiny, cheap and very good at fundraising."

"We are trying to cover the areas where there are gaps," she tells me. "We want to get into those rural areas." Suffolk also has poor transport links, and the law centre would like, funding permitting, to run a 'coffee caravan' to provide remote advice using Skype to reach its more far-flung parts.

Nor did the Ministry of Justice assist access to justice in the county when it shut down magistrates' courts in Lowestoft and Bury St Edmunds in 2016 as part of its court closure programme. As a result, the county is left with just one courthouse, in Ipswich.

'I have had clients who have told me that they cannot afford to travel from the west of the county to Ipswich and would wait to be arrested on a warrant,' said one defence lawyer when Bury St Edmunds Magistrates' Court was closed down. 'This is the reality of centralising courts and the demise of local justice.'[9]

★ ★ ★

When we visit Ipswich Magistrates' Court, a bright orange tent is pitched on the small traffic island opposite the building. Outside the tent there are a mountain bike and a half-opened pint of milk. We have been told that court users from out of the city are so nervous of missing their appointments that they are now making the journey the night before; however, the court's security guard says that is not the case. "He's always there," he says.

Audrey Ludwig arranges for a meeting with Ipswich Housing Action Group (IHAG), which runs the Chapman Centre for the homeless in the city. "We work every day with at least 25 people and half of them have been on and off the streets for at least ten years," explains director Halford Hewitt, who has been with IHAG since 1992. Its money advice service helped 1,300 people last year.

IHAG was set up in the 1970s with, as Hewitt puts it, emphasis on the word 'action'. It has been involved in the radical 'Housing First' scheme pioneered in New York in the 1990s, which works by housing homeless people immediately, whatever their needs, and giving them direct control over their support. "The traditional journey from the street is that you go into an emergency shelter or a hostel and stay there for a couple of years before you get your own property. All funded by the government with ridiculous constraints," Hewitt explains. "You take people off the streets – they could still be drinking – you give them a bed and say: 'Now you have your bed, you can't do any of that stuff'."

Housing First turns that traditional model on its head. "You take someone and say: 'Here is your property, this is yours forever'," continues Hewitt. "It is not a temporary but a long-term tenancy. You support that person and they determine what their need is." It is an approach underpinned by a set of principles and backed by intensive support for vulnerable tenants. The model has been credited with ending homelessness in Finland.

IHAG's housing team is responsible for supporting up to 55 tenants in 14 shared houses in Ipswich. So far a one-year Housing First pilot with funding from clinical commissioning groups has helped to securely house six people who might otherwise have been on the streets.

Debt advice is essential to IHAG's homeless and vulnerably housed client group. "When you get into debt your world becomes so difficult. Your confidence, your relationships break down, and when the whole world is falling on your head, you just don't have the capability," Hewitt says. "We try and empower people to learn how to sort their problems out. But in the initial stages they cannot do it. They need a lot of hand-holding."

Demand for help is high. Hewitt points to a ward in Lowestoft "where the life expectancy between it and the neighbouring ward differs by 16 years". "You have that in Ipswich too," reckons Ludwig, adding that "the life expectancy difference between one end of Belstead Road and the other is ten years. The Stoke Park and Westgate areas of Ipswich are in the lowest 10% of wards nationwide."

"We take the view that it is not just about the clients in front of us but it's about the system that is causing that to happen," Hewitt says. Audrey Ludwig calls IHAG "a challenging organisation". "From our perspective, that's a good thing", she adds. As well as there being no legally aided housing law specialists, there are no public lawyers in Suffolk. Ludwig cites research findings that in areas where there are public lawyers local authorities perform better and social care services are of a higher standard than in areas without.[10] "There is no culture of challenge in this county," she continues. "We're very much 'a grumble at home but mustn't grumble in public' place."

When we arrive, Halford Hewitt has just been writing a letter to the work and pensions minister, Esther McVey, complaining about the pledge of £51 million for Citizens Advice to assist claimants with their Universal Credit claims. He sees it as a divisive move that undermines other providers in the local advice sector. "At the heart of everything that goes wrong in the advice sector is procurement," he says. "Nothing done separately can't be done better together. We spend a lot of time creating partnerships and networks."

He argues that Citizens Advice isn't a single organisation. "It's a franchise of about 300 independent charities. How are they going to maintain standards?" he asks. Of 107 people IHAG has seen over the last few months, he claims almost half (46%) then came into their mainstream service for debt advice. "Citizens Advice aren't going to be able to do that. We spend an average of 12 hours for every client. Citizens Advice spend half an hour."

A culture of disbelief

In 2011 a single mum from Birmingham, Terryann Samuels, was declared 'intentionally homeless' after she fell into arrears as a result of a £34 shortfall between Housing Benefit and rent. The council argued that £700 a month rent for her home in West Bromwich was affordable because she had 'flexibility' in her income from other welfare benefits, including child tax credits, to cover the gap. She had four children all under the age of 16 years when she was served an eviction notice by Birmingham City Council.

Eight years later and shortly before our visit to the city, five Supreme Court justices ordered the local authority to rethink its decision. 'I find it hard to see on what basis the finding of intentional homelessness could be properly upheld,' opined Lord Carnwath.[11] The question was not whether, faced with that shortfall, she could somehow manage her finances to bridge the gap, but 'what were her reasonable living expenses, that being determined having regard to both her needs and those of the children, including the promotion of their welfare', he added.

It was 'an important judgment for the future of the welfare system', according to the housing charity Shelter. 'When someone is forced to choose between rent and keeping their children fed, they cannot be viewed as "intentionally" homeless when they choose the latter,' commented chief executive Polly Neate. 'Housing Benefit cuts mean it has not kept pace with rents for years – it now doesn't cover a modest rent in a shocking 97% of the country – and cases like this are the result.'[12]

That this landmark ruling almost never happened reveals the fragile state of access to justice. Despite the self-evident importance of the issues at stake, the single mother had been repeatedly refused public funding by the Ministry of Justice.

To qualify for legal aid, you have to be financially eligible, the issue concerned must fall within 'scope' (that is, be covered by what remains of the post-LASPO scheme) and you have to pass a 'merits tests', which means the case has to be deemed to have a reasonable prospect of success. The Legal Aid Agency judged Samuels' chances poor.

Fortunately for Terryann Samuels and many vulnerably housed people like her, her lawyer disagreed. At the end of the case, Mike McIlvaney of the Birmingham-based housing law specialists Community Law Partnership published a detailed chronology of the case, tracking the hurdles that he had had to surmount complete with flowchart. There were more court applications relating to securing public funding for his client than relating to the substantive proceedings. Even after permission to appeal to the Supreme Court was granted, funding was withheld until judicial review was threatened for a third time.

As a result of concerns over the Legal Aid Agency's 'culture of refusal' that was revealed by the case of Terryann Samuels, housing lawyers claimed that they were being forced to take on litigation at their own financial risk. Around the time of the Samuels ruling, figures obtained through parliamentary questions showed that since the 2013 legal aid cuts, legal aid applications for representation in homeless cases had fallen by 34%.

The Ministry of Justice was 'blocking access to justice and making perverse decisions' about the merits of cases, Jo Underwood of Shelter told the *Guardian*. 'Shelter solicitors across the country acting for homeless and badly housed clients experience this kind of bad decision-making from the LAA [Legal Aid Agency] on a regular basis,' she said. 'We work hard to keep cases out of the courts so that our clients can find or keep a home without unnecessary and stressful litigation. However, when we do need to defend cases, ensure a client has a voice in court or bring a legal challenge to unlawful and poor practice, we face huge bureaucratic hurdles and lengthy delays to get our homeless clients the legal aid they are entitled to.'[13]

★ ★ ★

In 2019 the fledgling Suffolk Law Centre scored a notable success in plugging a glaring gap in the local advice sector when it secured a much-needed legal aid contract for a housing lawyer – or so it seemed. In the midst of a housing crisis and with ample evidence of need, there wasn't a single legal aid lawyer in the county to provide publicly funded legal advice.

The Law Society reckoned that almost one third of legal aid areas had 'just one and – in some cases – zero law firms who provide housing advice which is available through legal aid': in other words, they were advice deserts.[14] According to the Housing Law Practitioners' Association, the 2013 cuts had led to a 'substantial reduction' in the number of housing lawyers and the number of cases being undertaken. 'Figures produced by the LAA have shown a reduction in housing cases of over 50% since LASPO came into force, in a period in which rough sleeping, statutory homelessness and evictions from rented accommodation are all on the rise,' the group said.[15]

However, the offer of a contract to the new law centre for a much-needed housing lawyer came with a catch which reveals much about the confused and patchy network of post-LASPO legal aid provision. The law centre had been the only organisation to put itself forward in tenders. The contract was conditional upon the centre being able to recruit a supervising housing lawyer with at least three years' experience in housing law.

Suffolk Law Centre has advertised three times but, so far, still has not managed to secure a candidate.

4

Christmas at the Foodbank

Volunteer Sue is on hand to greet everyone as they arrive at St Matthew's Church, just off the busy Wandsworth Bridge Road, South Fulham. They receive a cheery welcome, a hot cuppa and something to eat as they wait to pick up their emergency food parcels. Sue is on first-name terms with the regulars and fusses over the young mums. "Does baby want milk? I can warm some up. I'll get some toast," she says.

It's less than two weeks to Christmas (12 December 2018) and so, if you have a voucher, you can pick up a Christmas present for the kids. In December 2017 Britain's largest foodbank provider, the Trussell Trust, provided 159,388 three-day emergency food supplies, a 49% increase on the monthly average.

This Christmas will be their busiest to date. The charity blames that on benefit cuts and the unfolding chaos of Universal Credit. Shortly before our visit to Hammersmith and Fulham Foodbank, the government announced its plans for the next stage of the Coalition government's flagship welfare reform unveiled in 2010 by the then work and pensions minister Iain Duncan Smith: 'managed migration'. Until now, only people making a new application have gone onto the controversial new benefit system. The idea is that claimants under the old system will move en masse onto the benefit, and so people currently claiming up to six benefits will move onto single monthly payments.

The advice sector is bracing itself. According to the Trussell Trust, in 2018 there was a 52% average increase in foodbank use in areas that have had Universal Credit for at least 12 months, as compared to 13% in those that have not.

In the six months up to the end of November 2018, Hammersmith and Fulham Foodbank, which opens six times a week in three different locations and is supported by the Trussell Trust, fed 7,342 people, as compared to 6,376 in 2017 and 3,317 in 2016 over the same six-month period.

★ ★ ★

As you walk into St Matthews there is a series of large, white plastic tubs full of fresh fruit and veg, including bananas, melons and pineapples – if you have a voucher, you help yourself. At first glance, you wouldn't know it was a church hall.

The chairs for the pews are stacked to one side, and the lectern and a wonky Christmas tree are partially hidden behind a wall of collapsed seats. A third of the hall is screened off and, out of sight, volunteers assemble parcels. The rest of the hall is arranged like a café and recipients of food vouchers sit at the tables and drink their tea, which is provided by Sue. 'Whilst you are waiting, volunteers are packing a three-day supply of food just for you,' reads the note on each table. Each package allows for ten meals per family member.

We are here to shadow Sophie Earnshaw, a lawyer from Hammersmith and Fulham Law Centre who has a weekly clinic to offer legal advice to those who need it – and, judging by today's experience, many do.

An hour into her advice session we meet Asma. Dressed in a bright blue hijab, the 33-year-old woman from Algeria could be in her teens. We learn that she has three children under the age of 16. Asma is at the end of her tether.

"I haven't received any money for three months. I'm living off food vouchers," she tells Earnshaw. Earlier this year, her husband threatened to kill her, not for the first time. The school was informed and social services arranged for her and the kids to move to a refuge.

The family, who moved to London in 2016, ended up in the middle of nowhere, outside Lincoln. "It was a very rural area. Nothing there, just grass," she recalls. Six days later they were back in London, and for the last two months they have been living in another refuge.

She hasn't a penny to live on: her housing benefit is paid directly to the refuge; her husband receives the child benefit and, the final straw, she has now been refused Universal Credit. The DWP has decided that Asma does not have a right to reside because she and her partner, who is an EEA national, have split up. Sophie Earnshaw advises that, on the facts before her, the DWP are in error and have failed to take into account that Asma is still a family member of an EEA national and does indeed have a right to reside. "Even if you and your husband are not together, you should still be entitled to Universal Credit," she explains.

Asma has requested a review of the decision. The problem for Asma is that it will take months for a statutory appeal, and her situation is self-evidently urgent. Earnshaw advises that one course of action would be to send a pre-action letter threatening to challenge the refusal in the courts, as well as the local authority for its failure to provide financial support. Both of these are public law challenges.

"I need a solicitor," Asma says.

Sophie Earnshaw explains that she is a solicitor and that she works at Hammersmith and Fulham Law Centre. "I looked everywhere but I couldn't find a solicitor," Asma continues. "I called the law centres. They told me they didn't have appointments until January. I don't have anywhere to go with the children." Earnshaw takes her number and assures Asma that she will fix an appointment at her office.

In the Valleys

Some months later we meet Tina Morgan. This time we are at a foodbank in a former steel town in the heart of the South Wales Valleys. It is Tuesday, 12 March 2019 at Ebbw Vale Foodbank and Tina has been referred there by her landlord, Tai Calon Community Housing. Like Asma, Tina is obviously distressed. As well as a food parcel containing nine meals, she will receive a £49 fuel voucher, available in some parts of the country for those who have to choose between 'heating and eating'.

A single mother of three and grandmother of five, Tina has been on disability benefits for years. She suffers from arthritis, fibromyalgia and depression. She recently had her gall bladder removed and suffered a stroke. She lives with her daughter and grandson. Until recently, her daughter was her carer. "We just about managed until my grandson Joe died six months ago," she tells me.

Joe had been diagnosed with leukaemia at 18 months. Tina mentions that his tragic death was covered in the local press. Later we find the article. The headline reads: 'Family celebrate Christmas four months early for dying toddler'. "We had to go to the hospital to see his consultant yesterday," Tina continues, "but my daughter won't leave her bedroom. She blames herself. She didn't leave his side for two years."

Tina Morgan has complex benefit problems that urgently need the attention of a legal aid social security law expert, but she doesn't know where to go for help. Deductions are being taken from her benefits because of an advance made to cover the five-week wait for her first Universal Credit payment. The new benefit was rolled out in the area in June last year. Shortly before our visit to South Wales, Citizens Advice called for an overhaul of Universal Credit because delays in the payment of the benefit were causing havoc. 'Half the people we help with Universal Credit are still struggling to keep a roof over their heads while they wait for their first payment,' said Gillian Guy, the chief executive of Citizens Advice.[1]

Tina's daughter is also repaying child tax credit that was erroneously paid for eight weeks after the death of her young son. It is a loss of income that has tipped a grief-stricken family into crisis. "We live from day to day, hand to mouth," says Tina. "People have helped, but everyone's in the same situation."

Ebbw Vale is an hour by train from Cardiff, a journey through the Welsh valleys that offers reminders of the town's rich industrial past: the redundant pithead at Cwm, the last deep mine in the area, and Ebbw Vale Parkway station on the site of the world-famous steelworks that once employed 13,000 but closed in 2002.

In Ebbw Vale, the largest town in Blaenau Gwent, there are no legal aid lawyers, there is no Citizens Advice Bureau and no law centre. The railway's passenger service reopened in 2008 after a 46-year gap. In Wales there were 31 providers of publicly funded benefits advice before the 2013 LASPO cuts: when we visit there are three. The number of firms providing legal aid has fallen by 29%, compared with 20% in England.

★ ★ ★

In October 2019 a former head of the judiciary made the case for Wales to have its own fully devolved justice system. An independent commission headed by Lord John Thomas of Cwmgiedd, previously Lord Chief Justice, unanimously concluded that the people of Wales were being 'let down by the system in its current state'.[2]

Government spending on the justice system for Wales had collapsed by a third since 2010, to £723 million in 2017–18. It would have been 'far steeper' had it not been for 38% of the total justice budget in Wales being made up by the Welsh Government and local councils, the inquiry reported. 'Legal aid is in a considerable mess,' Lord Thomas said. 'Wales is different from England demographically. Because there is greater deprivation, it would be much more sensible if the overall budget was directed to where needs are greatest, such as on housing and employment and welfare.'

We discovered, as a result of Freedom of Information requests submitted to the Ministry of Justice during the course of our research, a 40% reduction in legal aid firms across the country since 2010. Where there had been 201 firms, there were 119 in 2019. This makes Blaenau Gwent one of the most underrepresented parts of the UK in terms of legal aid. We reckon there is one firm for every 17,400 residents.

Consequently, and as reported by the Commission on Justice in Wales, there has been an increase in the number of people representing themselves in court and exponential growth of 'advice deserts'; and increasingly 'high street' law firms have been going to the wall as a result of legal aid cuts. It found that the Welsh Government had been forced to spend its own funds on advice services but this had failed to bridge the gap caused by the 2013 legal aid cuts. According to the Commission, if policy were 'determined and delivered in Wales' there would be 'overall coordination of the provision of legal aid and advice services to meet the identified needs of people in Wales'.[3]

One of the biggest problems identified by the inquiry was the proliferation of advice deserts in Wales's rural and post-industrial areas, of the kind seen in Chapter 3. There was a serious risk to the viability of the legal profession all over the country, but especially in the kind of traditional 'high street' legal services that are generally considered to dominate in Wales.

A month after our visit to the Valleys, a leading law firm specialising in social welfare, TA Law, gave notice to the Legal Aid Agency and closed its doors after a decade of advising people in the area from its Swansea base. 'As a firm, we endeavoured to fight the cuts year on year to try and stay in business so that we could continue to help in welfare benefit and housing cases,' said solicitor Helen Williams. 'I am sorry to say that we have lost our battle and are about to become another victim of the LASPO cuts.'[4]

She also pointed out that the firm's problems predated the 2013 cuts, explaining that a move from hourly rates to fixed fees under the New Labour government had meant that a welfare benefits case, no matter how complex, could pay no more than £208. In 2012 there were 31 providers holding welfare benefits legal aid contracts across Wales. After the demise of TA Law, there are now two.

★ ★ ★

"You walk down the high street and you see the boarded-up shops, testimony to a town that's suffered greatly and changed out of all recognition over the last 20 years, and since the steelworks closed," says solicitor Glyn Maddocks, who is based in Crickhowell.

A member of the Law Society's human rights committee, Maddocks reflects on the devastating impact the legal aid cuts have had on access to justice for the community. "The reality is that access to publicly funded legal advice has always been massively variable and provision patchy," he says. "There has never been much by way of legal aid in the Valleys and the quality of that advice, often from one-man bands, hasn't always been great. In the days of coal and steel, people were looked after by their own communities, through local groups, churches and their unions. All gone. There is nothing in its place."

We also meet with Mick Antoniw, Labour Member of the Senedd for Pontypridd, which is at the junction of the Rhondda and Taff/Cynon Valleys some 20 miles down the A470 from Ebbw Vale, and similar in size. "The loss of legal aid is massive," he tells us. "The people who really need some advice and advocacy are some of the most desperate people, particularly those on welfare. They don't understand the system or how it works, and sometimes our role is to just try and clarify it for them."

We visit Antoniw at his high street constituency office in the heart of the town. He was previously a partner at the trade union solicitors' firm Thompsons, where he regularly represented workers from the Nantgarw and Cwm collieries as well as the massive South Wales forgemasters plant. He was a member of the Welsh Government and most recently Counsel General, the government's chief legal adviser.

The biggest issue for his constituents is problems with benefits. Antoniw talks about "the demise of advocacy, support and legal advice". "There's a whole chunk of people out there. The ones who are less educated, with learning difficulties and so on, and who just accept whatever is told them," he says.

Antoniw talks about the difficulties of a diminished local advice sector where a heavily circumscribed legal aid scheme means that caseworkers are left to cherry-pick those cases they are prepared to take on. "That's the trouble," he says. "The more marginal or complex cases tend to be the ones that get pushed to one side, focusing what resources there are to get the best results."

★ ★ ★

Ebbw Vale Foodbank occupies what used to be the magistrates' court and is now the Christian Centre. In the old police cells, three volunteers sort, weigh and date new donations. "We weigh everything in," volunteer Jenny tells us. "Every week we pick up from Tesco's and this week we have received 127 kilos." Foodbanks were pretty much unheard of in the UK prior to the 2008 credit crunch. Ebbw Vale has had one for a decade.

There are presently nine tons of food on the premises which serve as a warehouse for six distribution centres in Blaenau Gwent. "There are times we do get worried about the levels of food, if we drop down to four to five tons," says Wayne Evans, a retired bank manager and a pastor at a local Baptist church, who helps run the foodbank. Today, they have a glut of Fray Bentos tinned pies. "Normally, it's beans," says Sue, adding that at one point an entire cell was devoted to housing baked beans. When the manager of the local Tesco visited the foodbank, he reckoned that they had more cans than his supermarket.

Great generosity is matched by great need. The population of Blaenau Gwent is about 65,000, and so far this year the foodbank has helped 4,576 people, which makes it the busiest year to date, and there is still one month to go before year end. Last year it helped 4,200 people. By far the largest sources of referrals are the job centre and Tai Calon, contributing a total of 468 referrals last year, as compared to just 28 from Citizens Advice. "Dare I say it, but I don't think a lot of the agencies are touching the root problems," says Evans. He adds that they are not allowed to use the word 'referrals' in relation to those who come via the job centre. "We're supposed to say 'signposted'."

Ebbw Vale's foodbank, like Hammersmith and Fulham's, is part of the Trussell Trust. According to the Trust's guidelines, voucher holders can have three food vouchers in a six-month period. "That isn't going to work, because we know with Universal Credit that for the first five weeks they haven't got any money at all," says Evans. "We don't want anybody to go through the door without having food. That's the bottom line."

Life isn't just food

During our time at Hammersmith and Fulham Law Centre, Sophie Earnshaw met one of her regular law centre clients, a Turkish lady in her 50s. They arranged to meet at the foodbank to go through her paperwork. Clearly in pain from major neck surgery, the client has been incorrectly assessed by the DWP in relation to her Personal Independence Payment (PIP) and failed to qualify for the mobility component.

There is very limited publicly funded legal advice for welfare benefits as a result of the 2013 legal aid cuts. The only legal aid that remains is for appeals to the Upper Tribunal, for which there is just a flat fee of £208. Earnshaw calls that "a token gesture". "You might well have spent ten hours on a client before legal aid even kicks in," she says.

Earnshaw will refer her Turkish client to a clinic that the law centre runs with a global commercial law firm, Debevoise & Plimpton, which has an office in the City but has its headquarters in New York. The firm's lawyers, who volunteer at the law centre, will draft a submission in support of her appeal and attend the hearing at the first-tier tribunal. As Earnshaw explains the scheme, her client mentions that she has spent £450 cash on a lawyer. His advice turns out to have been nothing more than filling out a form which, Earnshaw says, "takes no time at all. Frankly, it's blatantly exploitative." As the client leaves, she struggles to lift herself from her seat and has to be helped to her feet.

Earlier, we were interrupted, very politely, by a woman in her late 40s with a headscarf. She wanted to have a word with Earnshaw and to retrieve her cup of tea. It turns out we had inadvertently been sitting in her place. She had come to the UK from Afghanistan 12 years ago with her sister, having been the victim of an acid attack. She has severe burns down one side of her body and scarring all the way to her scalp. She is constant pain and continues to have surgery to try to make life bearable.

She attends the foodbank twice a week. Her Employment and Support Allowance (ESA) was stopped after the DWP assessment, predictably, found her fit for work. Citizens Advice has referred the case to Earnshaw for the appeal to the first-tier tribunal.

Shortly before our visit, the Labour Party had promised to restore legal aid for benefit appeals, should it come to power. Labour in government had a poor record on legal aid (as discussed in Chapter 9), and even in opposition was not vocal in its opposition to LASPO; however, Jeremy Corbyn, the party's leader when we visit West London, is a doughty champion of unfashionable causes and a long-time supporter of legal aid. According to his shadow justice minister, Richard Burgon, more than two-thirds of appeals against decisions on PIP and ESA are successful. Labour reckons that in the five years since the LASPO cuts came into effect in 2013 the number of people receiving legal aid to challenge benefit decisions has fallen by 99%; meanwhile, it points out that the Ministry of Justice spends more than £100 million a year on tribunals disputing appeals against benefit decisions.

Towards the end of the morning session, we have a chance to talk to Asma. She tells us she was just 17 years old when she entered into an arranged marriage with her abusive and violent husband in Algeria.

She moved to France, where her husband is from. She recounts how her kids were taken into care by social services after her husband attacked her son. What happened? He hit her son in the face with a bottle. "His face was covered in blood," she says. "I spent months trying to get them to return my children. I would have done anything to get them back."

She told the judge "everything was OK". "I didn't want to lose my kids. I was crazy," she says. "I didn't want to separate from him. I wanted him to change. I wanted to provide a good place with him for my family."

The family later moved to the UK. The violence continued. After the husband threatened to kill their mother, the son told his teacher at school that he no longer felt safe living at home. That led to the intervention of UK social services. The family now share a refuge with other women and their children in a neighbouring borough. She says her son is "worried all the time. He wants to know when we will have some money and when will we be secure."

Asma is not receiving any financial support from her ex-partner. "I don't know about the future," she says at one point. "I am very scared."

This is Asma's second trip to the foodbank. "Life isn't just food," she says. "The children have so much they need and they see the other kids in the refuge with things." Before she leaves, she is given two Christmas present for the kids.

When I say it must be reassuring to have received some proper advice from an experienced specialist lawyer like Sophie Earnshaw, she says: "Yes," before adding: "Do you think she will ring?"

The rise of the foodbank

London has an established not-for-profit legal advice sector, meaning that those people in crisis like Asma who find themselves needing to rely on foodbanks can (if they are lucky) find help. That is not the case in the Valleys.

Sophie Earnshaw did ring Asma. A few days after our visit to Hammersmith and Fulham Foodbank, the solicitor provided us with an update. She had met with the mother and her kids at the law centre soon after the foodbank clinic. She had challenged the local authority's failure to provide financial support, and weekly payments were now being made by social services and would continue until Asma's Universal Credit was resolved.

★ ★ ★

The day after our trip to Ebbw Vale we spoke to Warren Palmer, the centre director at the Speakeasy Advice Centre in Cardiff.

The recent history of the advice sector in Wales's capital city has been fraught. Cardiff Law Centre, one of the first law centres, was forced to shut in 2016, largely as a result of the LASPO cuts, and its departure left the country without a law centre. Prior to that, Cardiff's Citizens Advice Bureau had been forced to close for a year after being declared financially unviable in 2011.

The Speakeasy itself dates back to 1992, when members of the Glenwood Church set up an advice centre because of concerns in the congregation that, increasingly, people in their Llanedeyrn community were trapped in debt. Shortly after our visit the advice centre joined the network of law centres. Its legal aid funding has dropped from 70% to 20% of its income post-LASPO, and it is increasingly reliant on charitable grants and donations.

Warren Palmer, a specialist benefits adviser, ran an advice clinic from the information shop on Ebbw Vale high street for six years, up to 2013. "I would drive up. This was before the railway and the bypass," he recalls.

A huge amount of investment had gone into the town since it was devastated by the closure of the steel works, including the new railway line and a bypass. "Much of it came from Europe, of course," Palmer notes. It has been reported that more European Union (EU) money came to Ebbw Vale than to any other part of the UK. More than six out of ten of its residents (62%) voted Leave in the 2016 EU Referendum.

"It wasn't like anywhere else I knew," says Palmer. "There were so many boarded-up shops, so little opportunity, so little for people to do and so few job prospects."

★ ★ ★

"There were never any foodbanks," says Karen Taylor of Citizens Advice Rhondda Cynon Taff in Pontypridd. "Over the last couple of years we've definitely seen a rise in priority debt issues. So previously you'd see people with sort of high credit debts; now people are finding it difficult to afford their basic expenditure: gas, electric, rent and council tax."

The 2013 legal aid cuts, followed by the introduction of Universal Credit, have created a perfect storm. "We lost the legal aid contract and all of a sudden people weren't able to afford to buy food, people weren't able to afford their day-to-day expenditure," she says.

People come to Citizens Advice for food vouchers. "It's awful when someone comes in and says, 'I've got four kids at home and I can't afford to feed them.' What we try and do then is say: 'Right, let's look at what the debt problem is, let's try and sort that, apply for benefits, look at what your income is. Can we help you and save any money?'"

Citizens Advice Rhondda Cynon Taff has a second office in former mining town Mountain Ash, further up the Cynon Valley and just 19 miles outside Cardiff. "A lot of the banks have closed and statutory services have moved to Aberdare," Taylor says. "There was a town hall and a police station; now, in Mountain Ash, we are one of the only organisations that are open five days a week. We see people coming in, outside of opening hours, desperate for help in really vulnerable circumstances."

Citizens Advice runs from the local library, so it's accessible to residents in a town where even the job centre has been shut down. The branch runs two dozen outreaches across the local authority. "Our advice is supposed to be free. But if you have to travel from down to Ponty it'll cost you – so actually it's not free. We need to be spread around all of the valley to make sure people are getting properly free advice."

"We had somebody walking four miles to get to us. It's 4.45 pm and we've been there all day but we'll try and sort them out and get them the help they need," Taylor says. Residents have also been affected by court closures. "It was centralised in Port Talbot," Taylor says. "All of a sudden, people weren't paying their fines because they couldn't get to the court to pay the fines." She accepts the business case for centralising public services at a time of austerity. "But sometimes removing it from the community has a massive ripple effect. How can somebody who is on £75 a week afford to get to Merthyr and pay their £10 fine?" she asks.

★ ★ ★

As we leave the Ebbw Vale foodbank we meet Detective Constable Paul Pritchard in the car park as he arrives to pick up a food parcel for a soon-to-be-released prisoner. As a manager in Gwent Police's integrated offender management unit, his job it is to manage offenders in the community.[5]

He works with a cohort of some 30 prolific offenders whose criminality is largely driven by their drug habits. He explains: "The reason why I pick up food parcels is that a lot of my guys are heroin addicts; if they're given a voucher when they come out of prison, that voucher becomes a commodity. They go down to the dealer and say can I swap the voucher for a bag of heroin? There is a lot more than £10 of stuff in a food parcel."

The prisoner he is picking up the food parcel for is due to go directly onto Universal Credit. Delays on first payments are making Pritchard's job even more difficult. "Thankfully, we have the foodbank to fall back on. I have guys released from prison and all they have is the clothes they're stood in." That is quite a challenging situation, he says.

This is another vivid illustration of the vulnerability of newly released prisoners. Two of the dozen people we saw appear in court at the Stratford Hearing Centre had just left prison and had fallen into arrears while serving sentences (see Chapter 1). Their debt had been exacerbated by the roll-out of Universal Credit with its five-week wait before the first payment. The judge had been sympathetic. "I have seen the situation before," he said to one. "It's one of the consequences of prison people don't understand. He deserves the benefit of the doubt."

Paul Pritchard points out that the men he works with ("98% are males," he says) are typically waiting four to five weeks before they have a payment. "You can imagine a heroin addict coming out with no money and nowhere to live," he says. "He's going to start offending pretty quickly."

He mentions one of his ex-prisoners who is a one-man crime wave committing up to 15 offences a night. Heroin and Valium are the two main problems here. There are two types of Valium: that which is "manufactured by somebody with a cement mixer probably in the Philippines" and which is "quite cheap", and prescription Valium. A side-effect of taking the fake Valium is delusions and, in particular, the belief that you can't be seen. "You can imagine someone who's pretty good at breaking into garages and sheds and then they think they're invisible," Pritchard says. "We can come in in the morning and find out we have a lot of work to do."

'A sticking plaster on the wound of systemic inequality'

Carol and Paddy Henderson set up the Trussell Trust in 1997 with a legacy left by Carol's mother, Betty Trussell. Their work began in Bulgaria, helping children sleeping rough at a railway station.

Three years later, Paddy Henderson received a call from a mother in Salisbury, Wiltshire, where the couple live. She was struggling to feed her children and having to send them to bed hungry. His response was to set up a foodbank, which he ran from his garden shed and garage.

In April 2019, 58 academics, activists and food writers published an open letter warning against foodbanks becoming 'institutionalised' in the UK. Charitable food aid was 'a sticking plaster on a gaping wound of systemic inequality in our societies', they wrote.[6] At the time of writing in 2020, the Trussell Trust supports over 1,200 foodbank centres across the UK.

Daphne Aikens founded Hammersmith and Fulham Foodbank in 2010. It was one of the first foodbanks in the capital and now opens six times a week in three different locations: Fulham, West Kensington (opened in 2012) and White City (opened in 2016). When the Fulham branch opened, only a handful of foodbanks existed. "We originally started just offering food parcels, as well as a listening ear and a bit of signposting," Aikens explains.

Aikens soon realised that "it wasn't a question of people coming in once or twice, picking up a food parcel and – suddenly – everything's fine". "We began to notice that people started to need the foodbank more regularly," Aikens says. "By the time people come to a foodbank they aren't just hungry, there is usually something else going on."

We also speak to Adrian Curtis, founder of the Blaenau Gwent Foodbank. He tells us that the Hendersons designed the charity "to complement the safety net of the state, not replace it". "What you've seen over time is the safety net slightly withdrawing in terms of the amount of people and the type of support that is given to people," he says.

We meet Curtis in Pontyclun, a village further into the Valleys than Ebbw Vale, where Bethel Baptist Church doubles as a foodbank. He explains that the idea behind foodbanks was to refer people back into the support to deal with the issues behind the crisis, but that support was often no longer available. "What we're finding is some of those services no longer exist and are oversubscribed, as the safety net has been tightened," he says.

"The interventions that happen in a foodbank are about much more than just food," he continues. "It's becoming emotional support, advice services such as debt advice. The amount of work that foodbanks are doing is deepening." Foodbanks were building extra services: community cafes and parent-and-baby classes. "Charities that run foodbanks are introducing debt advisory services," Curtis says. "Rather than just signposting someone to Citizens Advice where there is a waiting list, or other services where they might be oversubscribed. It's much easier to have a debt adviser sat here."

This avoids vulnerable people being passed from pillar to post. "When someone has plucked up the courage to walk through the door and ask for emergency food aid, to say, 'Well, now you need to pluck up the courage and go to this other charity to deal with the debt issue, and then pluck up the courage to go to this housing charity to deal with your housing problem,' people are sometimes embarrassed."

Hammersmith and Fulham Foodbank runs holiday clubs for families with children who would get free school meals, and cooking and budgeting courses; and the week before we visited it started a mental health project offering up to 20 clients up to six free sessions with a psychotherapist. Of the seven people we see, at least three appear to have obvious and long-term mental health issues. "About 50% of foodbank clients, not just in Hammersmith and Fulham but across the country, do," Aikens tells us.

The foodbank provides debt and legal advice. It first developed a debt advice scheme with a local agency (Crosslight Advice), until that ran out of funding; then it had two advisers from Citizens Advice, but now has just the one, who, Daphne Aikens notes, is "deeply stressed". Hammersmith and Fulham Foodbank have been working with the law centre for three years but the drop-in clinic at this particular branch is relatively new.

"I don't want it to be a place where people come every week. That was never the intention," Aikens says. She reckons that dependence on the foodbank has grown since the introduction of

Universal Credit. "We were one of the first boroughs to pilot it and it has been with us a couple of years," she says. "The impact has been very significant – life-changing in a very negative way."

Sophie Earnshaw agrees. She used to work at the charity Child Poverty Action Group before moving to the North Kensington Law Centre, where she worked with Grenfell survivors, bereaved family members and local residents. Her role as child poverty solicitor at Hammersmith and Fulham Law Centre is funded by the City Bridge Trust.

The problems with Universal Credit are manifold and the lawyer offers a "top five": the minimum five-week wait for first payment "that can put people instantly into arrears"; the disproportionate impact on disabled people, who can end up receiving less under Universal Credit as noted by the House of Commons work and pensions committee in the week of our visit ("a huge issue"); and then there are the kind of "right to reside" problems faced by people such as Asma.

Then there is the possibility of up to 40% deductions from someone's allowance for rent arrears and debt. "Where deductions are taken, people are now surviving on £35–£40 a week," Earnshaw says. "How can anyone afford to live in London, or anywhere else?" Finally, she points to the general complexity of Universal Credit. "The DWP approach tends to be 'computer says no' and close the claim. It is only if you have advice that you will know how to challenge that effectively."

* * *

On the day we visit Ebbw Vale Foodbank, volunteer Stuart Winstanley is running the fuel voucher scheme. Ebbw Vale is one of four locations in Wales where fuel vouchers are given out. The scheme is run by the energy provider Npower together with the Trussell Trust and pays out £49 for those on prepayment meters who are struggling to keep the lights and heating on. The scheme is funded from a fine imposed on the power company by the energy regulator, Ofgem.

Winstanley uses Wayne Evans' iPhone to process the vouchers, which requires the latter's fingerprint to release the phone's passcode. Winstanley was born and raised in Ebbw Vale. "Many people who come here are already tied in with other support agencies such as the Wallich [a Welsh homeless charity], Women's Aid, or social workers from various teams. It is heartening in a way that people are getting support; but then a lot of support is needed," he says. "Many of them have multiple problems and they have been continuing for some years. They appear to be beaten down by it."

Winstanley has spent a career working in the advice sector. He was at the Welsh Refugee Centre in Cardiff in the seven years before he retired, and prior to that was a substance misuse worker. He quotes from William Blake's poem 'London', where the poet wanders through 'each charter'd street' noting in every face he meets 'marks of weakness, marks of woe'. "You can see it here in people's faces. I don't want to get too literary but they're lined and etched like the valleys around here from the industrial scars of the pits. Blaenau Gwent is towards the top of the tables in poor health."

Winstanley calls the last three months' experience running the fuel voucher scheme in his home town "humbling". "Like many who were born and grew up in the town in 1980s, the changes have been astonishing. There was a clearly identifiable community when I grew up as a boy, based upon the old industries. Most families would have at least one family member working in one or other," he says.

His father worked in the Waunlwyd Colliery. The job security "and vision for the future" that he grew up with has long gone. "Now it is all floating zero-hour contracts," he says.

Winstanley claims to have had "no illusions" when he began volunteering at the foodbank. He continues: "I was aware of the impact of Universal Credit and how it operated. I know the problems with Blaenau Gwent and the multi-layered nature of the problems people face. We have had year upon year of austerity and local authority cuts. It is humbling to see people can survive and manage that with a smile and be so grateful for the bit of help you can give."

"But foodbanks in the 21st century," he sighs. "At a time when we have astonishing tech like iPhones, yet we still can't find sufficient jobs and people still can't have a feeling of well-being, peace and a certain amount of dignity. The loss of social cohesion is that thing that is almost irreplaceable and kids growing up almost not knowing it. That is sad."

5

Meeting the Real
'Daniel Blakes'

Walton is the only UK constituency to boast two football clubs: Liverpool and Everton are half a mile apart at the opposite ends of Stanley Park. When we visit on 21 September 2019, outside local MP Dan Carden's office on Priory Road there is a transit van that is usually seen on match days parked up outside Anfield and Goodison Park. It bears the motto 'Hunger Doesn't Wear Club Colours'.

Fans Supporting Foodbanks is an initiative set up by Dave Kelly and Ian Byrne to tackle food poverty in their city. "Dave's the Evertonian and I'm the Liverpudlian," Byrne tells us. The idea first came to the pair when they spotted a queue of people just down the road from where the MP's office is situated. "I thought it was for the bingo," Byrne says. "It was an independent foodbank run on donations from the community. But the community hasn't got nothing. We saw the pantry. It was just pitiful."

As well as being a fan activist, Ian Byrne is Dan Carden's office manager. As he explains, every other week some 60,000 people pour into Anfield and 45,000 into Goodison to watch their teams play. "We thought if football fans brought in one tin, then that would make a huge difference," he says. "Now one quarter of all food donations coming into 13 foodbanks in North Liverpool comes from fans." The cause has been adopted by the teams and the van was bought with a donation of £30,000 from Liverpool's chief executive, Peter Moores.

Fans Supporting Foodbanks brings food to donate to rival fans' foodbanks during away fixtures, as a show of solidarity; and an idea that began with "a couple of wheelie bins" (as Byrne puts it) outside the two grounds has spawned similar initiatives outside football stadiums up and down the country.

The initiative featured in an article in the *New York Times* quoting Philip Alston, the UN's special rapporteur for extreme poverty, describing food poverty in the UK as a 'social calamity'.[1] 'And so, across the country … soccer, and in particular its fans, has stepped into the breach,' the article continued. 'In front of stadiums filled with multimillionaire superstars, fans have taken it upon themselves to help those who need it most.'

When we explain the idea behind our project (that is, to monitor the impact of the 2012 legal aid cuts and the undermining of the advice sector) to Byrne, he says: "Food poverty is about those who haven't the power to fight the things that they had taken away from them. Taking away human rights and access to justice is stripping away a basic tenet of what this country is about. It's another strand of austerity."

Walton stretches all the way from Fazakerly to the city centre and has a population of 30,000. "And we haven't got a CAB," says Byrne. "It was shut down. You can only imagine the pressure we're under as a constituency office."

★ ★ ★

Dan Carden was elected to Parliament in 2017, having won 86% of the local vote, and, in doing so, seeing off the competition, Liverpool mayor Joe Anderson. In his maiden speech the 30-year-old MP talked about his pride in Liverpool ('one of the great port cities in the world'). 'My dad and my grandad worked on the docks when it was the engine room of our city's economy and social life,' he said, before describing 'the agony that this government has inflicted through welfare and disability cuts' on constituents. 'It is no wonder that people who visit my surgeries are as often as not in tears before they are able to utter a single word,' he said.

One of the first tasks the MP's new office undertook was to build connections with the advice sector, such as Vauxhall Law Centre, a short walk away in Kirkdale, and Merseyside Law Centre, based on Bold Street in the city centre, with local law firms and with Liverpool University, where law students take part in constituency advice clinics. "Straightaway we identified the lack of specialist legal advice in the area," case-worker Valerie Beach, a former welfare rights adviser who works in the office three days a week, tells us.

Why? "Locally an MP doesn't have any power to do or change anything," Dan Carden says. "All I can do is write letters and add my support. If a constituent comes to us and says: 'I have this problem with access to benefits or to do with the health service', I can just send them to Citizens Advice or wherever. We don't know what happens next. Too often we find out later that nothing gets resolved and the blame lies with everyone. They will say: 'I wrote to my MP and my MP fobbed me off with Citizens Advice'. If we bring the advice in-house, then they know they get the best they can from us."

Ian Byrne, who is also a councillor in the ward of Everton, describes the area as "a complete desert for many services", and certainly for advice. "We have used every penny to pay for Citizens Advice to go into four community centres in Everton," he says, adding that they have also put all they can into Vauxhall Neighbourhood Law Centre. "It's possibly the only place in all Liverpool where you can get proper representation. We put £8,000 in, that's everything we had, to kick-start funding. If that goes under, there is nothing."

Pared to the bone

For the past four and a half years, Vauxhall Law Centre's three part-time staff have been on notice of redundancy. "It's precarious to say the least," fundraiser Alan Kelly explains. Five years previously nearly all its regular funding came from legal aid or the local authority ("about 40% from each"). The familiar double whammy of legal aid and local authority cuts has pushed a law centre set up in 1973 to the edge. Historically, Liverpool City Council has been the main funder. "For the last three years we haven't had any core funding," he says. That has changed in 2019 when we visit, as the Law Centre has just been awarded a £28,500 grant.

When the law centre was set up in the 1970s, the main issue was housing. "The area was, for want of a better word, a slum," Kelly says. The housing isn't too bad anymore, he adds. "Everything else is. The big issue now is poverty."

Kelly reels off a grim list of statistics. Kirkdale has the highest mortality rate in the city (715 per 100,000), as compared to Liverpool (497) and nationally (335). Life expectancy is also worst in the city: 74 years, as compared to 78 in Liverpool and 81 nation-wide. "Average income in Britain is £37,000; in Liverpool it's £27,000; and Kirkdale it's £24,000," he says.

"This is one of those areas where anyone who can, gets out," says Kelly. "You're left with a population that tends to be older than average and tends to consist of a lot of people who are vulnerable for a large variety of reasons. It might be evictions, but more often than not it's sickness, disability, old age and infirmity."

David Taylor, a stalwart of the law centre movement and a respected figure in Liverpool's advice sector, has been at Vauxhall for 30 years. His first job was at Salford Law Centre, which he remembers as being "a bit bogged down in staff meetings and navel-gazing". "Everyone was on equal pay," he says. "I was quite happy with that; but they had to work out why they wouldn't offer equal pay to the cleaner. It was apparently because she didn't attend the staff meetings, which would have been quite a good deal if she didn't have to."

A job came up at the then new law centre in Vauxhall. "I jumped at it," he says. "I was the only candidate, just as I had been the only candidate at Salford, and they were more or less stuck with me." Taylor was the law centre's first solicitor. "As a law centre you are meant to have two solicitors but we've never had two. We could never stretch to it," he says.

This was in the days before legal aid, and Taylor did his welfare rights work and some housing on the Green Form scheme (see Chapter 3). Was it effective? "It was just another funding stream. I was never adept in terms of maximising the income from Green Form work, which subsequently got a very bad reputation. Quite rightly so. The way that some people misused the scheme was shocking."

In 2018 Vauxhall Law Centre achieved a remarkable success rate for its welfare rights tribunal work. In April 2018 it represented 111 people before the tribunal: 13 cases were adjourned, and 95 were successful at first instance and three won on appeal. "For the first time in our 45 years, we won every tribunal," says Kelly.

Kelly continues: "Now, that sounds good. But I used to be a welfare rights adviser myself. I always used to think, if I was winning all my appeals then I wasn't doing enough appeals."

The changes to the welfare system have had a brutal impact on people living locally. "You can't walk a hundred yards without bumping into people sleeping in doorways. These are the visible signs, and then there are the less visible signs. People in houses without any gas, electricity or water." These are the people who rely on the support of Vauxhall Law Centre. "They're being ground into the earth," he says.

★ ★ ★

The future is just as perilous for another long-standing member of the city's advice sector, Merseyside Law Centre. "We've had year-on-year 50% cuts from the local authority going back before LASPO," newly appointed assistant director Janet Coe tells us. It is one of the more recent additions to the law centre network. Until recently, the advice agency was known as Merseyside Welfare Rights, which was established in 1988 although it has been helping Liverpudlians with their benefits problems since the 1970s under a variety of names (for example, Check Rights and the Money Advice Centre).

Prior to the 2013 legal aid cuts, the law centre had about 30 members of staff and was well supported by the local authority. "Our funding was up to £250,000 a year from the council at one stage, with a similar amount from legal aid work," Coe says. "We had a turnover of around £1.5 million."

The law centre had been funded through a local authority grant initially for five years; it was then cut to three years and finally to two. "We thought we had a grant for another year at £60,000 and then they decided they were going to open up for bidding again," Coe says. In 2019 the law centre has received just £25,000 from its local authority. It is down to 10 staff with two solicitors and two dedicated welfare rights advisers.

The service has been pared to the bone. Mary Heery is senior solicitor and full time; Coe works three days as assistant director and two days as a solicitor; and Lorna O'Reilly, volunteer supervisor, works one day a week. "We've moved from Merseyside Welfare Rights to Merseyside Law Centre, without any management posts to speak of," says Coe. Their director works for a different organisation which donates his services one day a week to oversee strategy. They have an office manager who works three days a week as well as an 82-year-old administrator working nine hours a week. "That's the only administrative support we have," explains Coe.

"Legal aid probably barely covers a salary at the moment," Janet Coe says. There are two trainee solicitor positions funded by a charity known as the Legal Education Foundation through its Justice First Fellows scheme, which funds trainee solicitors working in social welfare law. In 2012 the College of Law, formerly the market leader offering vocational legal education training, was sold to a private equity company and the proceeds went to establish a £200 million foundation. The foundation has since appointed 88 'fellows', many in the not-for-profit advice sector, to 'create the social welfare law leaders of the future'.

Merseyside Law Centre's two fellows "massively increase capacity," Coe adds. However, the fellowships cover the costs of the posts for only two years and there are no guarantees a fellow can stay in the agency where they train (or even the sector). The law centre has approached local solicitors' firms to contribute to trainee salaries. "We are a bit disappointed thus far not to have had a collective contribution," Coe says.

The law centre receives a small amount of money from Dan Carden's office and hopes other MPs might similarly offer support in return for help with constituents' legal problems. It was also the recipient of a £14,000 grant from the *Guardian's* 2018 Christmas Windrush appeal, distributed through the Law Centres Network.

Janet Coe and volunteer coordinator Lorna O'Reilly are sanguine about the impact of the local authority cuts. They point out that they have enjoyed a good relationship with Liverpool City Council since the late 1980s. "There just isn't the money there anymore," says O'Reilly. "Years ago we would have all been out marching but we now know how strapped they are."

The law centre is based on busy Bold Street in the city centre and, as we talk, a demo makes its way noisily down the road protesting the end of free TV licences for the over 75-year-olds. "Nothing like pensioners getting militant," O'Reilly quips.

Merseyside Law Centre applied for law centre status in 2016. Why? "As welfare rights work became a bit stigmatised, we saw the benefits of rebranding as a law centre," says Coe, a housing solicitor who first volunteered with the service in 1996. "Being

Merseyside Welfare Rights doesn't explain the work we do and we were finding it increasingly difficult to attract funding."

O'Reilly was originally an adviser with Merseyside Welfare Rights. "I left in 1989 to go to the local authority and came back as a solicitor in 2001; and then left again in 2013 as a result of LASPO," she says. "There wasn't enough funding for two solicitors. I took redundancy. I now organise the volunteers."

What was the ethos of the organisation when she first joined at the end of the 1980s? "Challenge everything," she replies. "It really was. One of the things that strikes me is the nature of debt workers I come across now: negotiate repayment, do not challenge liability. In our era, the debt workers we knew challenged everything."

The law centre, like Vauxhall, has a very high success rate for its welfare rights tribunal work, about 90%. O'Reilly reckons about 80% of its case-work is done by the volunteers under her supervision, including what are known as 'mandatory reconsiderations' (where claimants disagree with a DWP decision about benefits, they can ask for that decision to be looked at again). The law centre provides representation for clients who have to attend a tribunal. "A lot of organisations provide written submissions, which isn't as good," says O'Reilly. "People come to us who have been let down by all kinds of organisations. A lot of the written submissions we see are ridiculous." One member of staff handles between six and eight appeals every week. "We try not to turn anyone away. We don't cherry-pick cases," says Coe.

Universal Credit is essentially an online benefit. It is 'digital by default', as the DWP has put it. An application needs to be made online and prospective claimants need to provide an e-mail address. It is a requirement that the UN special rapporteur on extreme poverty in his UK report has called 'a digital barrier that effectively obstructs many individuals' access to their entitlements'.[2]

The system's dependency on claimants having access to a smartphone or computer to manage their accounts online is a major barrier for people who rely on Merseyside Law Centre. Coe and O'Reilly estimate that possibly a quarter of their clients have neither a smartphone nor a computer.

O'Reilly continues: "I always say that the National Debt Line is a great service for middle-class people. Middle-class people who get into debt can just access that service and use it – you don't need anything else. You can barely get our clients to open an envelope."

Coe says their staff rely on a benefit calculator application. "We are often flabbergasted by the changes in people's income when you move from one benefit to another. We try and steer away from Universal Credit. Have you heard of anyone better off?"

The law centre also runs a community advice clinic in Dovecot, where it has had a presence for about 20 years ("a big ex-council estate where people don't leave for advice"); and outreach services in Old Swan and Princes Drive. It has legal aid contracts for housing advice in Liverpool and Dovecot and, as of 2018, in St Helens and Halton, as well as a small welfare rights contract. The Legal Aid Agency invited the law centre to bid following a lack of interest from potential providers because, as O'Reilly puts it, "you can't make any money out of legal aid". A requirement for a legal aid contract is a permanent presence in the area. "Almost immediately we found that difficult to do because we only have two solicitors," she adds.

Coe and O'Reilly agree that the business case for taking on legal aid contracts is slight. "We are trying to open more certificated cases," says O'Reilly, adding that they haven't had capacity to do that because of the bureaucracy and, in particular, the chaos being wreaked by Legal Aid Agency's new digital billing system.[3] "It's so cumbersome," she says. "You spend all the time filling in the application form. That's time we could be helping clients."

"I feel like we're doing everything that we can. But the LAA [Legal Aid Agency] is sitting back and waiting for us to fail," she says. "To the extent that the contract manager has turned up unannounced in the office." In Halton, the law centre even struggled to find clients. "There is that myth that housing isn't within scope of legal aid and so people don't actually look for it," says O'Reilly. "Because that's what they have been told, sometimes by their landlords. Housing advice is available under the legal aid scheme if there is a risk of homelessness."

At a housing advice drop-in at Dovecot last week, none of the people they saw fell under what remains of the scheme, and often tenants do not qualify because they are just over the income threshold of £733 a month disposable income. "It's really quite low," says O'Reilly.

A 2018 report written by Professor Donald Hirsch of Loughborough University, a former poverty adviser to the Joseph Rowntree Foundation, found that people on incomes 30% below minimum living standards were being excluded from legal aid.[4]

According to the academic, the legal aid system generally required working people to pay their legal costs, either in full or by making a contribution that most low earners would struggle to pay. While the unemployed were generally covered by legal aid, they might be excluded if they owned their homes. This was based on the assumption that someone could sell their home to cover their legal bills. That was an assumption which, Professor Hirsch pointed out, was out of line with other state means testing, including, for example, help with care costs, where the value of a house was ignored if the applicant or a partner was still resident.

It was also out of line with the courts. As the Law Society, who commissioned the study, pointed out, in 2017 the Supreme Court had declared that employment tribunal fees of up to £1,200 were unlawful because households on low incomes were 'expected to sacrifice an acceptable living standard to afford legal costs'.[5]

A similar effect was being imposed by 'an excessively restrictive formula' to determine whether someone was entitled to civil legal aid, the solicitors' group argued. 'No-one in modern society should have to choose between accessing the justice system and a minimum living standard,' commented the Society's president Joe Egan. 'The financial eligibility test for civil legal aid is disqualifying people from receiving badly needed legal advice and representation, even though they are already below the poverty line.'[6] The group was calling on government to restore the means test to its 2010 real-terms level, arguing that the position had been getting progressively worse because the means test thresholds had been frozen since then.

A Kafkaesque nightmare

In September 2018, Dan Carden spoke in the House of Commons about the devastating roll-out of Universal Credit on his constituents. 'I am here because of the people I have met in my surgeries and foodbank visits, and because of the harrowing stories I have been told,' he told MPs. 'I am here because of the people

I have seen. People who are broken and who feel worthless and trapped in a cycle of poverty that they cannot escape.'

Universal Credit was 'only the latest onslaught from a benefits system that is stuck in Victorian times'. 'It is just the latest instalment of austerity for our city,' he said. 'A city that has borne the brunt of eight years of cuts that have hit the most deprived areas the hardest. Our local authority budget has been slashed by 64%, £444 million since 2010, and 40% of children in my constituency are growing up in poverty.'[7]

Carden cited a local letting agent in his constituency who told him that all of the agency's tenants on Universal Credit were now in rent arrears. 'Every one of them,' he said.

★ ★ ★

The award-winning 2016 film *I, Daniel Blake*, winner of the Palme d'Or at Cannes, pitched its eponymous hero against an indifferent welfare benefits system. During the course of our research the Ken Loach film was frequently invoked by politicians and commentators.

For example, in January 2019 the Labour MP Rupa Huq compared the case of a constituent who was almost left with £10 a month to live on to the fictional character. 'We're told everyone gets an advance; she was told to go to a foodbank,' she said to the then work and pensions secretary Amber Rudd, adding that *I, Daniel Blake* was 'becoming reality'.[8]

In the film, Daniel Blake is forced to rely on state support for the first time in his life when he is laid off as a result of a serious heart attack. To receive help, the 59-year-old carpenter needs to go through a DWP work capability test. Inevitably, he is deemed fit to work.

At his local job centre, Daniel Blake meets a single mother-of-two, Katie, who is struggling to make ends meet after her benefits are sanctioned. After two years in temporary accommodation in London, she had been moved 300 miles away to Newcastle because, she is told, there is no housing in the capital.

As a condition for receiving Jobseeker's Allowance, Daniel Blake must keep looking for a job, but he refuses a job at a garden centre because his doctor will not allow him to undertake physical work. When the job centre work coach tells him he must work harder to find a job or be sanctioned, Daniel daubs 'I, Daniel Blake, demand my appeal date before I starve' on the building.

On the day of his appeal, Katie accompanies a clearly anxious Blake to court. He dies of a heart attack ahead of his hearing. At his funeral, Katie reads the speech Daniel would have read at his appeal.

> I am not a client, a customer, nor a service user. I am not a shirker, a scrounger, a beggar nor a thief. I am not a national insurance number, nor a blip on a screen. I paid my dues, never a penny short, and was proud to do so. I don't tug the forelock but look my neighbour in the eye. I don't accept or seek charity. My name is Daniel Blake, I am a man, not a dog. As such I demand my rights. I demand you treat me with respect. I, Daniel Blake, am a citizen, nothing more, nothing less. Thank you.

★ ★ ★

As a result of our time in Newham, described in Chapter 1, the housing lawyer Simon Mullings introduced us to one of his clients. Tony Rice had been repeatedly described in the press as 'a real-life Daniel Blake'. 'Three years ago, Tony Rice was forced to stop part-time sales work after being stabbed in the thigh and face,' one newspaper report began. 'Tony is about to be evicted from his home in North London, and for the first time in his life, has found himself reliant on foodbanks. Like so many others, he's fallen victim to the failed roll out of Universal Credit.'[9]

The then 51-year-old from Waltham Forest had been assessed as unfit for work by his doctor on account of a mix of physical and mental health difficulties, including depression and post-traumatic stress disorder. As far as the DWP was concerned, he was fit for work.

Waltham Forest Council wanted him out of the council flat where he had lived for the last six years. On 12 December 2016 his barrister, Mary-Rachel McCabe, managed to persuade a judge to give him more time.

'Today in the county court I represented a real-life #DanielBlake,' tweeted McCabe. The barrister explained that her client had been repeatedly sanctioned for failing his 'claimant commitment' of job-searching for 35 hours per week. He wanted to challenge the assessment that found him fit for work, but he couldn't until he had what is known as a 'mandatory reconsideration' (when a claimant disagrees with a DWP decision they can ask for that decision to be looked at again). 'He has chased this many times, to deafening silence from the #universalcredit department,' McCabe continued. 'The result of this Kafkaesque nightmare? [My client has been] living off £114.33 a month (that's £26 a week) and has been relying on foodbanks. His rent arrears are now £10,000.' His lawyers challenged the sanctions placed on his Universal Credit claim and he was then able to pay off some of his arrears. It was McCabe's Twitter account that prompted the media coverage.

We speak to Tony Rice a year after the media coverage. "I am still having problems," he tells us. "I am too ill to go out to work. I can't go out and earn money and I can't rely on the DWP. I am really worried about losing my place. I love it here. I've been here all my life."

"I was stabbed three times," he recalls. "The DWP sent me for a medical and said I was fit for work after three months. As long as you can move your arms and legs, they think you are fit for work. If I went back working on the forklifts I'd end up killing someone because I'm on so much medication for pain. I can't concentrate."

When he went to court, what was at stake? "Everything," he said. "I risked losing everything. I have my sisters but they have their families. I wouldn't ask them for help."

★ ★ ★

"I went down to the job centre and I told them: 'If I get evicted because of you lot, then I'm going to buy a tent and pitch it outside. I and the dog are going to come in and sit in the warmth of your offices all day.' They said: 'You can't do that,' and I said: 'Just you watch me.'"

Anthony Smith didn't need to pitch up outside the job centre in Wrexham, North Wales; instead, volunteers at his local CAB came to his rescue on the day of his eviction. That was eight weeks prior to our visit to Flintshire Citizens Advice on 22 February 2019, where we were first introduced to Smith. Things were looking up for him then. He wasn't sleeping on the streets but had managed to find a job working in nearby Connah's Quay as a garage mechanic.

Flintshire is situated in the north-eastern corner of Wales, with the River Dee to the north. Once devastated by the closure of the steelworks where Smith was once employed, it is now home to both Toyota and Airbus. It was one of the first counties in the UK to pilot Universal Credit. When we visit, Flintshire County Council, as well as many of its tenants, is struggling to come to terms with unexpected consequences of the problematic roll-out of the new benefit.

According to a 2019 BBC *Panorama* investigation drawing on data from 129 councils, the average amount in arrears owed by tenants claiming Universal Credit was £662.56, as compared to only £262.50 for those on housing benefit.[10] Flintshire County Council tenants on Universal Credit owed on average six times as much rent as those on the old benefits.

In November 2018 Anthony Smith was £4,000 in arrears to his council landlord. He could not see a way out of his predicament and so he purchased the tent from a friend for £5. "It was a nightmare. I went to Wrexham County Court. I was going to be evicted by 11 am the following morning," he recalls. Flintshire Citizens Advice was a lifeline. "If it wasn't for them, I would have just walked out of the door of my house, put the key through the letterbox and moved into my tent. My mate said to me: 'You're not going to do anything stupid.' I said 'No.'"

The previous year he had rescued a dog, a large German shepherd. "She's kept me going. She's had a rough life and I thought I need to keep going for her. We are best mates." Smith had been struggling with the online process.

'Digital by default' is not going to work for Anthony Smith. He doesn't do computers, nor does he possess a smartphone. He ended up sinking further into debt as a result of sanctions. He claims to have had his benefits docked because, he explains, "I couldn't attend the job centre when I was in hospital with pneumonia; even when I went for a job interview at Shotton Steelworks, they said I should have let them know." "Perhaps I should have, but I didn't have credit on my phone," he continues. "That's how hard it was." The DWP signposts claimants without access to computers to public libraries. However, nearly 800 public libraries have closed since 2010.[11] Smith would go to the Citizens Advice to check the status of his account. "God bless them," he says.

According to the BBC *Panorama* investigation, Flintshire County Council had outstanding rent arrears of £1.6 million and was £450,000 worse off than the previous year as a result of the introduction of the new benefit. The amount of debt written off by debt relief orders, a simplified form of insolvency introduced in 2009 for debtors with few assets (like Anthony Smith), has risen threefold over the three years since the investigation. In Flintshire, out of 550 Universal Credit claimants, some 480 were in arrears and the average arrears were £1,200, as compared to £210 for claimants on housing benefits. The month before we visited Deeside, its Citizens Advice helped more people with Universal Credit than it had ever done before.

"We have had Universal Credit since 2014, for nearly five years now, and you can see how it has affected people. We have been full service since 2017, and one of the first areas to go full service," Julie Griffiths, operations manager at Flintshire Citizens Advice, tells us. The service, which has offices in Holywell and Mold, had seen 108 Universal Credit claimants in the month before our visit.

We asked "What are the big problems that you see?" "Trying to manage until that first payment," Griffiths replies, echoing the point that Sophie Earnshaw made at Hammersmith and Fulham Law Centre. "If you have someone who has nothing, how can you expect them to wait five weeks until their first payment? What are they supposed to live on? The government say they have given people advance payments; but that's not the answer because that is just more debt; they have to pay that back and then they're worse off for the next 12 months."

On the day we meet Julie Griffiths at Citizens Advice's Deeside office, she had spent the morning running an advice clinic based in Shotton Job Centre. On a single day in 1980, 6,500 jobs were axed at Shotton Steel. It was reckoned to be the biggest single redundancy in Western Europe. "Can you imagine thousands of people becoming unemployed overnight? It's had a massive impact," says Griffiths. "Airbus is a massive employer for us and it's talking about leaving because of Brexit. They've just had a big order cancelled. It's always a constant threat. If that goes that will destroy the economy here."

Flintshire Citizens Advice is part of the community and has a lively cafe which was set up with money from British Steel. "They left a legacy fund which paid for the refurbishment of the building, which was derelict," Griffiths says. "Money from British Steel funded this." At the time of our visit the prospect of a 'no deal' Brexit threatened not only Airbus but Toyota's Deeside manufacturing plant, which employs 600 people.

Flintshire Citizens Advice invited the UN special rapporteur on extreme poverty to visit, and his team of investigators ended up speaking to a number of its clients. In a submission to the inquiry, the bureau explained that they did not have 'a specific definition of poverty'. 'However, we would generally consider clients who do not have enough money to cover essential expenses (food, rent, utilities and broadband, and essential travel) to be living in poverty,' it continued. 'We would consider those who are unable to access funds sufficient to cover these expenses to be living in extreme poverty. We often have clients with no income and a need for immediate cash to pay essential bills.' In such cases, the bureau issued food vouchers and helped clients to access emergency funding such as the Welsh Government's discretionary assistance fund scheme.

The report highlighted the vulnerability of those without internet access or basic computer literacy. 'Many do not manage to get what they are entitled to and face stoppage of their Universal Credit payments because they are unable to respond to posts in the online journal,' it stated. Advisers reported 'extensive errors on the part of the DWP, many in ways that would not have been possible under legacy benefits'. 'This seems to be because of the complexity of Universal Credit and confusion over the way its different elements interact on the part of DWP staff. It is not clear whether these errors will decline with experience or are systemic,' the report continued.

Nowhere else to go

On 21 February 2019 we visit Wrexham, North Wales, 11 miles down the A550 from Deeside. The town's Labour MP, Ian Lucas, tells us that there are "virtually no sources of advice available locally now". "We are the biggest town in North Wales," he says. "We don't have a law centre. I'm not sure we've ever had one and we have a CAB that's currently threatened with closure."

Days before our visit to his constituency office, Wrexham Citizens Advice had received a last-minute reprieve from the council. In 2015 the council's executive board, a coalition of independent councillors and Conservatives, had announced a phased reduction of 50% per year for Citizens Advice over the following two years. There would be nothing in the third year: a funding cut from £99,000 a year to zero in just three years.

Lucas had been backing the local campaign to save a service that deals with about 21,000 enquiries a year. 'Wrexham is now the only council in Wales which cannot find money to help fund its own Citizens Advice service,' the MP told the local press at the time. 'This is simply not acceptable and, in fact, I believe it is highly irresponsible.'[12] According to Lucas, the community came out in support for its Citizens Advice. "Some only have £1 but it all helped," he tells us. One of the volunteers, Gwyn Evans, a 73-year-old suffering from pancreatic cancer, raised over £7,000 through the Just Giving website when he shaved his hair into a Mohican haircut.

"I was determined to embarrass them into keeping it open," the MP tells us. "If the CAB had closed, we'd have lost the main source of advice in town." According to Lucas, the council was "supposedly going to send out a contract for advice services more broadly"; but that did not happen. No tender took place. The council runs its own welfare rights unit. Lucas explains: "The only provision of advice services that was going to be funded was the council's welfare rights department within the council, which obviously leads to initial conflict of interest problems, but also it's means tested now."

"We are the only agency providing free advice and information on every subject, A–Z," Gaynor Roberts, chief executive of Citizens Advice Wrexham tells us, adding that "there are agencies doing bits here and there but not holistic service". "After 24 years of working here, I'd say austerity has increased poverty, left some people behind technology-wise and for the most vulnerable, where literacy and understanding has made a big impact on their personal circumstances, quality of life has gone down." What would the people of Wrexham do if the service had closed? Roberts pointed to research based on the experience of 200 clients, in which 171 clients said 'no idea where else they would go'.

★ ★ ★

It is well documented that in the absence of publicly funded legal advice, constituents have been taking their legal problems to MPs like Ian Lucas and Dan Carden in increasing numbers. 'If I did every housing issue I would be dealing with about 500 people a week. I could not do it,' Jeremy Corbyn said back in 2015. He was speaking as MP for Islington North, before he became Labour leader, and as a member of the House of Commons justice committee.[13] Corbyn was responding to a comment made by fellow Labour MP and colleague John McDonnell, who reported that 'most MPs, particularly London MPs' were becoming 'swamped' with welfare benefit cases.

A 2017 report by the All-Party Parliamentary Group on Pro Bono into unmet legal need in London found that almost nine out of ten of appointments at MPs' surgeries raised legal issues.[14] The biggest issues were housing (37%), immigration (23%) and welfare benefits (13%). The study drew on observations of 40 surgeries held by 21 MPs (15 Labour, 5 Conservative and 1 Liberal Democrat), comprising 325 constituents' appointments. Housing benefits cuts and changes to housing association policies have led to 'an untenable situation' and were causing 'confusion among constituents', said the cross-party group.

That research followed a 2012 study by the Young Legal Aid Lawyers which found that 38% of MPs' case-work involved legal issues and the vast majority (87%) of constituents expected their MP to 'take action to resolve these issues following the surgery'. The pre-LASPO research reported that more than seven out of ten MPs (71%) had needed to refer constituents to a legal adviser: 67% of MPs had referred constituents to Citizens Advice for generalist help; 64% had referred constituents for specialist advice from a dedicated not-for-profit organisation such as a law centre; and 60% had referred constituents to legal aid solicitor firms.

★ ★ ★

"I understand the frustration of those who cannot get advice," Ian Lucas tells us. He reports that one of the biggest areas of legal advice sought by his constituents post-LASPO relates to family break-up. "It's mainly men," the MP says. "They tend to be very angry and cannot get any assistance then to deal with what are very emotional issues. It is indefensible."

In the week we visit Wrexham the Conservative government publishes its long-awaited and much delayed five-year post-implementation LASPO review. According to the Ministry of Justice, the government's legal aid reforms are on track to achieve their aims, defined as taking 'the legal aid system back to its initial intention – to ensure public funding would remain sustainable by refocusing resources on those who most need it'. Ministers promised £5 million for IT aimed at 'making sure that people can access the right help'; plus another £3 million to help litigants-in-person to navigate the system. The Ministry of Justice also announced that they would pilot face-to-face early legal advice and review the impact of the means test.[15]

The Law Centres Network offered the following context: the government had cut nearly a third of the legal aid budget, about £751 million, through LASPO. "The help lost, tens of thousands of cases, could have mitigated against massive welfare reforms, or helped uphold workers' rights, or prevented the Windrush scandal," commented Nimrod Ben-Cnaan, the group's head of policy. The promise of "just 1% of what was lost" (that is, £8 million) to non-legal support, tech development or innovation offered "precious little to bridge the immediate, yawning justice gap".

Ian Lucas calls the review "a sop". The MP, a former personal injury lawyer, is not uncritical when it comes to his own party's 'access to justice' track record. Back in 2000, New Labour scrapped legal aid for routine accident cases and replaced it with the insurance-based arrangements known as 'no win, no fee' or, by lawyers, as conditional fees. "The personal injury system is terrible," he says. "I hate conditional fees. They have been a disaster and really diminished the moral worth of lawyers – if they ever had it."

Legally aided personal injury had proved a reasonably efficient public service. It was reckoned that in its last year (1999/2000) the then Legal Services Commission paid out £178 million and recouped £125 million from unsuccessful defendants.

The changes introduced what Lucas calls "a commercial element" into lawyers' practice. 'No win, no fee' is a deceptively simple phrase. On one level it means (as the name suggests) solicitors are paid nothing for their work if they lose; however, they can also charge more if they are successful.

"When I was a personal injury lawyer, damages were calculated on the basis of need," he says. "You now have a system where a proportion of damages are taken away from the person who needs it so that the lawyer gets a cut. I thought that was very wrong."

★ ★ ★

Ian Lucas's constituents are helped by senior case-worker Matthew Parry, who has been in the MP's office for 12 years, and Adrienne Jeorrett, a former psychiatric nurse who works three days a week. "We have always had an open door policy," Parry explains. "People can just walk in and speak to someone. So if someone says: 'My ESA [Employment and Support Allowance] has suddenly been stopped, my assessment went really badly and I have no points,' we can unpick that and have a mandatory reconsideration appeal."

Unsurprisingly, the government's ongoing welfare reforms are the mainstay of the office's workload. "We're getting a lot of EU nationals coming in because they can't access Universal Credit: a lot of Poles and Portuguese people," says Jeorrett. "They're really struggling."

There are limited sources of help locally – as well as Citizens Advice, there is Bawso, a grassroots group that offers support to Black and minority ethnic people throughout Wales, and which has an office around the corner from the MP. "People get to the point where they can go no further," says Parry, adding that "there are a number of not very good organisations springing up and charging a lot of money because people don't talk the language".

Exploitation of people with immigration problems is a theme of the work they see (see also Chapters 6 and 7). "There are an awful lot of chancers who take money off people with no realistic chance of being allowed to remain in the country. It is fraught with difficulty," Parry says.

Jeorrett reports that the MP's office sees "large amounts of people with 'no recourse to public funds'". "They cannot access the night shelters, they are homeless, but what happens to these people?" asks Jeorrett. The MP is involved in a voluntary project where churches provide rough sleepers somewhere to sleep for four months over winter. "It's only a 10-week project and finishes on 17 March," says Jeorrett. "Everything is insufficient. It feels like everything has been taken away."

Talk turns to concern for the welfare of a Portuguese constituent who has been in Wrexham for over a decade. She has been to prison twice for assaulting someone in a job centre, which the two case-workers regard as a totally inappropriate outcome for someone with obvious mental health problems. "She is an extremely vulnerable adult. We just wonder where the hell she is," Jeorrett says.

The woman, who had worked for the best part of ten years, had been evicted. "She couldn't get housing benefits, Universal Credit or anything," Jeorrett says. "Citizens Advice was giving her food vouchers. But if you are homeless, what do you do? You can't just open a tin somewhere."

According to Parry, the woman is stranded by "this pocket of the benefits and immigration system" where they say: "We won't force you to leave but, because you have no realistic possibility of being employed, you do not have habitual residence or right to reside so we will not give you benefits." "What does she live on?" he asks. "She ends up homeless."

"You could see it happening," continues Jeorrett. "We were waiting for the moment when she became street homeless. We saw her shortly after and now nothing. She could have been trafficked."

★ ★ ★

When we visit Liverpool, like any other day in the last few months there is little news other than Brexit. It is announced that Boris Johnson and Jeremy Hunt are to face each other in the Tory leadership campaign to replace Theresa May.

What's it like being a new MP representing a constituency like Walton in Westminster at a time like this? "Frustrating," says Dan Carden. "All everyone wants to talk about is Brexit. If you were to ask what is the biggest issue in my constituency, Brexit isn't even in the top ten: poverty, ill health and all the issues that flow from that, so crime, addiction and surviving. We're not talking about those issues. Westminster is a ridiculous place."

The busiest category of work for his case-workers in the month when we visited the MP's office is identified as "foodbank vouchers". The office "should" run on an appointments system, case-worker Valerie Beach tells us. "But it's not. Someone knocks on the door and says 'I have just gone over onto Universal Credit, I am on week four and I've got no money'. These are not the type of people you can turn away. We try and do what we can."

Liverpool City Council has been "fantastic", she adds. The council has already committed £1.7 million of its own money to fund discretionary housing payments, stopping families from becoming homeless by preventing rent arrears. A 2018 council analysis of the impact of Universal Credit in the city reported that the budget was under 'significant strain'. 'There are a number of reasons for the high level of expenditure: the most basic of these is the continued impacts of welfare reforms,' it said.[16] Mayoral lead for fairness and equality Jane Corbett told the *Liverpool Echo* that the situation was 'absolutely shocking'. 'Across the board what is obvious is that all of our schemes are coming under exceptional pressure, particularly as a result of Universal Credit.'

"The benefit system is a total ★★★★ing disaster in this area," Dan Carden tells us. "We have the council going above and beyond and putting millions of pounds in. But it's a sticking plaster. A sticking plaster applied by a council that has had hundreds of millions of pounds a year cut from it." Universal Credit has had a "staggered roll-out" in the city and, the MP points out, "at the same time we have had four job centres over the last two years close across Merseyside".

In his September 2018 speech in the House of Commons, Dan Carden spoke about the experience of a constituent whom he had seen in his surgery the previous day. Ann had gone onto Universal Credit when she lost her job as a cleaning supervisor. She phoned the DWP to register her claim and was advised that she would need to go online to register.

Ann did not have access to a computer, nor did she know how to use one. She went ten weeks without receiving any payments and was directed to her local foodbank. There followed three consecutive months of sanctions because of, according to the MP, 'bewilderment at the system, and lack of understanding of the digital diary'. She was told to travel to look for jobs without financial support.

Carden told MPs that the experience for his constituent was 'humiliating, degrading and utterly confusing':

I am sick of living in a society where we punish people because a broken economy does not provide them with decent jobs. What looks good to Ministers on paper is in reality asking a 60-year-old woman who has worked all her life to spend hours each day walking around a city handing in CVs in shops, begging for jobs. I do not think it is humane or worthwhile for society to be in that position. I am here today to ask the Minister to apply the brakes to stop the roll-out of Universal Credit in Liverpool and fix the flaws in its design and delivery.[17]

6

Caught in a Hostile Environment

"No matter what I do or what I say, no matter how many passports I've got, people will say to me: 'You're a Paki'," Fazal Karim explains. "Me, I feel Asian British. I don't know anything different apart from the life I've had here. When people go to America and France on holiday, I look at Pakistan like that. I haven't been there for 60 years. I have never been back. I never could get back. I had no passport."

We meet Fazal Karim on 18 October 2018 through Bolton Citizens Advice. He came to the advice agency after his benefits were stopped. "He has been screwed over left, right and centre by everyone: the Home Office, his previous solicitors, and the benefits agency," the bureau's immigration services manager, Gail Lyle, tells us. "You name it; and he's had a slap off each and every one of them."

Karim came to the UK from Pakistan in 1969 at six years of age. His mother had died, his father had remarried and the family had left for England. Karim was left behind because he was ill and unable to travel on the date of departure. When he finally joined his newly reconstituted and resettled family, he discovered he didn't fit in. "I felt pushed out, excluded, and so I ran away from home," he remembers. The boy ended up in a children's home and remained in care in various homes in the Peterborough area until he was 19 years of age. "I was looked after by the state," he says. "My life has been documented since the day I came here."

But this was not good enough for either the DWP or the Home Office. Karim had been in receipt of tax credits, and was advised to switch to Universal Credit. After an eight-week wait, the DWP refused his application on the grounds that he didn't have a right to reside in the UK. He had always worked; however, he lost his job over his newly disputed immigration status. He ended up losing his benefits and was left with no right to work. "I spent a year and a half with no benefits, no job. Nothing," he recalls. Karim reckons to have spent "£20,000 to £30,000" on lawyers and Home Office fees trying to resolve his immigration status.

Thanks to Gail Lyle, he has now received confirmation that he was issued with indefinite leave to remain when he arrived first in the UK more than half a century ago. "She is a miracle worker," he says.

Lyle explains how Fazal Karim came to Bolton Citizens Advice after he and his family were evicted from his house. "He was massively in debt because his benefits had stopped eight weeks earlier and he couldn't keep up with the rent or his loan payments," she recalls.

Lyle explains that her client had "no issues" until the Home Office issued him with a biometric residence permit for those here for more than six months from outside the EU.

Windrush generation

In May 2012, Theresa May declared in an interview with the *Daily Telegraph* that she wanted to create a 'really hostile environment' for irregular migrants in the UK.[1] That 'hostile environment' found political expression through a shopping list of measures introduced under the Immigration Act 2014 and the Immigration Act 2016 limiting access to work, housing, healthcare, bank accounts and more.

In 2014 the maximum fine on employers for employing a person working illegally in their business shot up from £5,000 to £20,000 per employee. Fazal Karim lost his job because he couldn't evidence his immigration status. He ended up seeing a number of immigration lawyers in Bolton in an attempt to sort out his status. "None of them picked up on the fact that he had indefinite leave to remain because he was a Commonwealth citizen when he entered the UK as a minor: now known as the 'Windrush generation'," Lyle explains.

Problems with his immigration status impacted on Karim's 18-year-old-daughter, who had a place at university. They asked to see her passport. "She hadn't got one," says Lyle. "She had never left the country." On the incorrect advice of his lawyer, Karim had put in an application under the ten-year 'family and private life' route for himself, his wife and his daughter. She was born British in the UK. There was no legal aid for Karim and his family. The family was advised by Bolton Citizens Advice on a pro bono basis. His case has now been accepted under the government's Windrush compensation scheme.

The passenger liner *Empire Windrush* docked in Tilbury Dock, London on 22 June 1948 bringing some 500 hopeful settlers from Jamaica, Trinidad and Tobago and other Caribbean islands to help fill labour shortages in the aftermath of the Second World War. Some 70 years later the so-called Windrush scandal broke, leading to the government having to apologise for deportation threats made to Commonwealth citizens and their children. Despite having lived and worked in the UK for more than half a century (like Fazal Karim, who is of Pakistani heritage), many were told that they were here illegally because of a lack of paperwork. Some were detained and deported, others lost their jobs or homes or were denied benefits or medical care.

One shocking feature of the 'hostile environment' has been the ratcheting up of the costs of making immigration applications. The fee to apply for indefinite leave to remain rose 119%, from £1,093 in 2014 to £2,389 in 2019, despite the cost of processing an application being just £243. According to an investigation by the *Sunday Times*, that fee hike netted the Home Office a £203 million profit in 2018. Rupa Huq, a Labour MP, said that the level of Home Office profits exposed by *The Times* was 'shocking but not surprising'. 'Every week I see people who have been ripped off by exorbitant application fees for a substandard service while being fleeced by money-gobbling solicitors,' she said.[2]

Fazal Karim had been misadvised by his lawyers to put in applications to the Home Office on the basis of long residence. The fee is paid per person, so Karim had to find that sum for himself, his wife and his then 18-year-old daughter. The Home Office rejected his application and gave him leave under the ten-year route to permanent settlement, which requires a decade of lawful residence. That route comprises four 'blocks' of two and half years (30 months), with each block incurring a fee of £1,033 plus an immigration surcharge contribution of £500. Applicants need to amass 120 months before they can get indefinite leave to remain.

"No one from the Home Office picked up that Fazal is a Commonwealth citizen with settled status from the day he arrived," recalls Gail Lyle. The experience had a devastating impact on his family, including on his daughter, who was due to begin university the previous year but lost her place because she was told she did not have a right to reside.

★ ★ ★

"How can they sit there and say you're not entitled to a family life?" asks Hilary Brown, a leading immigration lawyer who was helping Windrush clients in South Wales when we speak with her. "It's all about this 'hostile environment' regime. They think it's acceptable to take away legal aid from parents who just want to be with their children. It's disgraceful."

We meet Hilary Brown at the office of her law firm, Virgo Consultancy in Barry, nine miles south-west of Cardiff on 30 October 2018, a couple of weeks after our trip to Bolton. Before the LASPO cuts, solicitors would have been paid the flat fee of £234 to help clients to disentangle the complexity of a typical Windrush case.

LASPO ended even that modest contribution. In 2014, Shailesh Vara MP, then junior minister at the Ministry of Justice, blithely assured MPs that the immigration process was 'designed to be straightforward and easy to navigate'. 'Therefore people in immigration cases should generally be able to deal with their own application and not need a lawyer,' he continued.[3]

In May 2018, Hilary Brown told BBC News that many of her clients, migrants from Commonwealth Caribbean countries who settled in Wales from the late 1940s to the 1970s, were 'living in fear' of a knock on the door.[4]

Brown has more than 20 Windrush cases, including Leighton 'Joe' Robinson, who ended up stranded in Jamaica for 21 months after going there on holiday. He had made the trip for his 50th birthday, which would have been the first time he had been back to the Caribbean since arriving in Britain at six years of age.

He was stopped at the airport and told that he could not return home to Northampton on the Jamaican passport he had brought for the trip.

Brown told the reporter that her clients were 'terrified of being identified and are too suspicious to come forward'. 'They don't trust the system or that they won't be removed,' she said.

On the Operation Black Vote website, Hilary Brown is described as 'a one woman force of nature'. 'Hailing from one the oldest black communities in the UK, Cardiff, all who know her affectionately refer to her as "Ms Brown" in that typical Caribbean tradition of someone held in high regard,' wrote Lee Jasper, the former deputy mayor of London.[5]

In the same article, Jasper described his own experience of 'the tragic consequences' of 'shyster lawyers who fleece money from people facing immigration difficulties'. 'Case after case comes my way of people seeking help after they have been robbed of their money and left to face the consequences, that can literally on occasion result in imprisonment, deportation and even death,' he wrote.

In the 1990s, Hilary Brown used to run both Butetown and Grangetown Citizens Advice Bureaux in Cardiff. "Two areas with a rich, diverse history of immigration into the UK, and I, by default, became a specialist in immigration and asylum," Brown recalls.

"The world was always an unsafe place," she continues. "We saw lots of Somali people coming here in the 1980s through to the situation with Kosovo in the late 1990s. It was very obvious that there was a need for specific advice around immigration and asylum."

When she was with Citizens Advice, Brown insisted on setting up a women-only waiting room, which was a first for the network. "Women are far less prepared to come forward. They'll often ring, give a breakdown of their situation without revealing their names or where they're from," she says. "You kind of build up a relationship with a woman over time, and you know everything about her bar her name. It's only when she feels that she can trust you will she then come and present herself as a client."

Brown cites the example of one client, a young mother, making an application for leave to remain. "Whilst the application was under consideration, she received notification saying that she couldn't work," she explains. The client had no entitlement to benefits. "She had a British child born in the UK whose father was British, and the little girl was able to be registered as a British citizen," says Brown. "But Mum wasn't able to access benefits, she wasn't able to work. She relied on handouts."

The client was then diagnosed with breast cancer while the Home Office considered her application. The lawyer contacted the department in an attempt to reinstate her welfare benefits. She never received a response. "We watched her go through chemotherapy treatment," she says. "I remember her coming in to bring me documents and telling me she was going off in two days' time to hospital to have a mastectomy, and how she was ashamed that she didn't even have any slippers to take into hospital."

The solicitor bought her client a nightie and underwear out of her own money. "You know the things a lady needs to go into hospital," she says. "She had nowhere to go and no one to turn to without disclosing the fact to lots of people that she had an irregular immigration status. She didn't want to bring that type of embarrassment to her daughter."

Six months before our trips to Bolton and Cardiff, the Labour MP David Lammy delivered a blistering analysis of the government's responsibility for the Windrush debacle in Parliament. The then home secretary, Amber Rudd, found herself unable to say how many Caribbean immigrants had been deported 'in error'. 'Frankly some of the way they have been treated has been wrong, has been appalling, and I am sorry,' she apologised to MPs.

Lammy branded it a 'day of national shame'. 'Let us call it as it is: if you lay down with dogs, you get fleas, and that is what has happened with the far right rhetoric in this country,' he continued. 'Will the Secretary of State apologise properly? Will she explain how quickly the team will act to ensure that the thousands of British men and women who have been denied their rights in this country on her watch in the Home Office are satisfied?'[6]

One Tory MP, Roger Gale, wanted to be clear about the limits of the government's culpability. 'Will she make certain that it is made very clear, very publicly, that there is no need to hire an expensive lawyer to put this right – we can do it?' he wanted to know. Rudd duly obliged. 'It is my firm belief that the individuals who will be able to access this group in the Home Office will not need legal advice, because the process will be simple and one in which my team will try to assist,' she said.

According to Hilary Brown, "the Windrush hostile environment and the problems that that has created" left people "failed by this oppressive immigration regime". Something has to change, she tells us. "There needs to be a new look at the whole immigration rules. There needs to be a new look at the Legal Aid, Sentencing and Punishment of Offenders Act. It just isn't working."

The numbers game

"Manchester is diverse. We speak over 200 hundred languages," says Afzal Khan, Labour MP for Manchester Gorton in south Manchester. "Diverse in the sense of ethnicity but also in the class idea as well," he adds.

Immigration is the number one case-work issue for his constituency office. "The 'hostile environment' and the policies that the government has introduced have caused lots of difficulties for so many people," says Khan, who was the first Muslim Lord Mayor of Manchester. "People who have been here 50, 60 years, given the best part of their lives, contributed in all sorts of ways, people who are British; and yet, because of the 'hostile environment', they've found themselves in deep waters."

The MP tells us that the government is "driven by a numbers game". In 2010 David Cameron, then leader of the opposition, pledged that 'net migration', the difference between the numbers of people entering and leaving the country, would be reduced to the 'tens of thousands'. It is an elusive and contentious target that his and successive governments have never come close to achieving. As a consequence, Khan says that "the government's starting point is to say 'No'."

Government ministers talk of the simplicity of the immigration system; in reality it is notoriously convoluted and complex. "The law is different in immigration," the MP says. "The burden is on the individual and not on the state, so they can just sit back: 'No, you prove it.' It's difficult if you don't know the system, if you don't have the means and you don't have legal aid."

When the Immigration Rules were introduced in 1994, they ran to eight pages but now they weigh in at over a thousand.

The sprawling legislative mess that is immigration law has become a theme of recent court rulings. So, for example, Lord Justice Jackson in a Court of Appeal judgment reflected that the law had 'achieved a degree of complexity which even the Byzantine Emperors would have envied'.[7] The Supreme Court quoted the Master of the Rolls describing the law as 'an impenetrable jungle of intertwined statutory provisions and judicial decisions'. 'It is difficult to disagree, although on this occasion the judiciary must share some of the blame,' the court added.[8]

A senior immigration tribunal judge spoke out about the consequences of this complexity for court users navigating the courts without a lawyer, and even the judiciary in an unguarded moment. 'Immigration law is a total nightmare,' Judge Nicholas Easterman told a legal conference in 2017. 'I don't suppose the judges know any more about it than the appellants who come before them.'

He went on to describe some Home Office presenting officers as 'good and fair', but others as 'worse than useless'. 'We cannot manage in many cases without proper assistance and we rarely get it from the Home Office,' he said.[9]

The length of time taken to resolve issues to do with immigration status means many of Afzal Khan's constituents are left "hanging in no man's land". "Many are capable individuals," he says. "They are professionals and consultants and yet the immigration system is designed so they can't use their skills. We're crying out for experts and yet immigration law makes sure that they can't do anything."

★ ★ ★

We visited Greater Manchester Law Centre, which is based on Stockport Road in nearby Moss Side, one of the most ethnically diverse parts of the city and a centre for immigrants for over 100 years.

Twenty-year-old law student and volunteer Awar Graf was front-of-house on the day we arrive. Graf is in her third year at Manchester Metropolitan University studying law and has been volunteering from the start. She wants to be a barrister specialising in social welfare law and says she is committed to "trying to stay in legal aid". She is hoping to secure a scholarship to pay the eye-watering fees for Bar school. In 2019 the average fee for the Bar Professional Qualification Course is £16,239.[10] "I am determined," she says. "I like the idea of being an advocate, an advocate for justice."

Why? "I've lived the reality of having a constant struggle with benefits," she answers. "I come from a family who knew exactly how hard it is." Graf describes her upbringing as "constant anxiety about money and housing". Her parents fled Libya in the early 1990s and met in Manchester, a magnet for exiles fleeing persecution under dictator Muammar Gadhafi's regime. Her father was studying Islamic Studies with his father in Libya. "He was like an elder in the tribe and fled because my father's family were against Gadhafi and he then was eliminating the resistance," she says, adding that her uncle had been captured and remained in prison for 12 years.

Her father arrived in Manchester in 1991 and her mother shortly afterwards. "They had to start from nothing, and so benefits was one of the ways they could support themselves," Awar recalls. Her English was better than her parents' and she ended up translating correspondence with the DWP. "Google became my best friend," she says, adding that she was "literally thrown into the world of benefits".

When Graf was 16 years old the family found themselves badly in debt as a result of a ten-year overpayment of income support. "It was just horrific," she remembers. "We didn't know what was going on. We relied on foodbanks for a long while and we nearly lost our home."

Awar Graf and her mother had to navigate the benefits system alone. "Dad was busy with his work," she says. Her father, Mustafa Graf, is the imam at Didsbury Mosque, which is the heart of the Libyan community in South Manchester.

The law student recalls going to the welfare benefits tribunal with her mother: "We didn't have an interpreter. We didn't understand anything to do with the system," she says. She recalls the "look of pity" on the face of the tribunal chair as he reviewed the paperwork that she and her mother had collected for the hearing. He explained that they needed proper help. She says: "I was close to tears. The only reason I held myself together was because of Mum, who was close to a panic attack."

A trip to a Sure Start centre in Manchester for her little sister led to the family being directed to a debt adviser at Shelter who took the case on. Graf recollects the experience as "traumatising". "It doesn't leave you, especially those moments when you're gripped with fear," she says.

When we visited, Greater Manchester Law Centre had been open for two years and, in that time, had recovered over £1 million in benefits for people in this deprived inner-city community. That money has been recovered by its entirely volunteer case-workers, a mix of experienced advice workers and law students trained to provide representation.

Not just a law centre but a campaign for justice

That Greater Manchester Law Centre exists at all today is a striking illustration of the triumph of hope and idealism over any practical considerations, not least the grim realities of funding. A business plan prior to its 2017 launch recognised the stark odds it faced: 'We are establishing ourselves in the harsh conditions of the international recession, without prospect of financial support from either central or local government, and with harsh competition for support from the charitable funding sector.'[11]

'We're not just a law centre. We're a campaign for justice,' said John Nicholson, chair of Greater Manchester Law Centre on its launch. In an interview with the *Guardian*, the 62-year-old barrister spoke about the devastation of the local advice sector in the area that he has lived in since he was a teenager.[12]

Nicholson watched his local Citizens Advice shut its doors, and the wider region become what he calls 'a desert for legal advice', the journalist Frances Ryan wrote. 'Neighbouring Salford's welfare rights and debt advice services was cut four years ago,' Ryan continued. 'When the South Manchester Law Centre closed in 2014 – the last free legal service in central Manchester and Salford – for Nicholson and others in the community, it was the final straw, and the impetus to do something. They had no funds or premises, but within a year they'd built up enough support to found the Greater Manchester Law Centre: a place where anyone can go for help.' 'You've seen *I, Daniel Blake*?' Nicholson asked Ryan. 'We're the people representing Daniel at tribunal.'

'This is a "community" law centre,' John Nicholson told us in 2016.[13] 'We will get the support from the commitment of the community. It will be owned and run by the community, for the community.' The barrister has a long history in the voluntary sector in Manchester; for example, he was involved in setting up the George House Trust, initially known as Manchester AIDSline, at the end of the 1980s. He was practice manager of Bury Law Centre and presently practises in immigration law at Kenworthy Chambers.

'We will have a people's law centre,' he told us. He flagged up the People's History Museum and the 'people's football club', FC United of Manchester. Both managed to attract the support of their communities and both, Nicholson pointed out, were founding supporters of the law centre.

The law centre made its pitch to the public in the following unique way:

> Law centres and the people power that has been their backbone are doing fantastic things across the country in ensuring that access to justice is maintained. This is why you are so important. You are going to be a part of a movement, from its very beginning, to create a new law centre. You'll be a part of a history that will defy the odds.[14]

Denise McDowell, director of Greater Manchester Aid Immigration Unit, is a trustee and one of the small band of activists who, alongside John Nicholson, campaigned for a new law centre. "The money we have had in the last two years has either been money we have raised ourselves, or from grants and the people who have been behind us," she says.

Greater Manchester Law Centre has not received a penny from either its council or the legal aid fund, which are the two traditional sources of income for law centres. There was a certain amount of soul searching about whether to even apply for a legal aid contract. "They are such a nightmare in terms of the bureaucracy involved," says McDowell. "But it's still public funding for legal advice. We are campaigning for public funding for legal advice; and therefore we need to be applying for it."

The law centre decided to go for legal aid work and when we visit has just secured a couple of small-scale and very specific contracts (100 housing cases; four debt cases; and 30 welfare benefit cases) and, separately, a public law contract comprising 30 cases.

The law centre had been looking towards the city's own business community to back it. In an open letter to Andy Burnham, the mayor of Greater Manchester, they outlined plans for 'a levy on Manchester's corporate sector to fund free legal services for people in poverty and vulnerability'. 'We share your belief that radical forward thinking is needed to build a new future for Greater Manchester,' the letter read. 'To survive, we need to be creative. Let's fund our free, face-to-face, high quality legal advice and professional legal representation by imposing a levy on commercial law firms.'[15]

There is a long history to the idea. Back in 1994, the veteran human rights lawyer Sir Geoffrey Bindman, as part of a Law Society pro bono working group, attempted to persuade fellow solicitors to support such a scheme. Back in 2012 Paul Im Thurn, a solicitor on Greater Manchester Law Centre's steering group, proposed adding £25 to the practising certificate fee that all solicitors have to pay to fund the legal not-for-profit sector. Greater Manchester Law Centre have also suggested that local firms pitch in 0.5% of their monthly earnings through a 'Lawyer Fund Generation Scheme'. This was reckoned to work out at £12.50 a month for lawyers earning £30,000. Such schemes have always been fiercely resisted by the mainstream legal profession.

In the absence of such funding solutions, the law centre makes do on grants and individual donations. According to McDowell, the law centre has received "a couple of big cheques" from solicitors' firm and a barristers' chambers. "Whether they will do it again we don't know," she adds. The single largest one-off donation was for £50,000 from an anonymous benefactor.

Is this model sustainable? "I don't know," she says. "The fact that we are doing it at all is the most significant thing because along the way we have had so many conversations with people; we have inspired people. Doing that, for me, is a measure of our success." That, she adds, "and the £1 million of unclaimed benefits that people would otherwise not have got."

Not quite the Brexit capital of England – but not far off

Shortly after 9 am on the day of our trip to Bolton Citizens Advice there are already 15 people in its waiting room, and just two are White. Its chief executive, Richard Wilkinson, reckons that it is not uncommon for White clients to complain of being in the minority at their local CAB. "We have comments when people walk in and say: 'It looks like a London Underground train'."

Nigel Farage, the former UKIP leader, was in town just ahead of our visit at the first 'Leave means Leave' rally.[16] Sharing a platform with former Tory Brexit secretary David Davis and Labour Brexiteer MP Kate Hoey, Farage was reported to have addressed 'a thousand cheering supporters'.

"Bolton is not quite the Brexit capital of England, but we're not far off," says Wilkinson. He describes the North-West town, half an hour's drive from Manchester, as "a bit Stoke-like in that respect". Stoke-on-Trent voted by 70% to leave the EU in the 2016 referendum and Bolton voted 58% to leave.

We had previously visited Bolton eight years earlier in 2011 as the LASPO Bill was going through Parliament and reported that if the cuts went through as planned that would be the end of the bureau, which at that point was struggling.[17] That year the Bolton Citizens Advice helped 14,000 people, and the year before our visit it helped 10,807.

"The numbers coming in might not be dissimilar, but what they get now is one-off advice," Richard Wilkinson tells us. "They don't get deeper case-work and they don't get representation in courts or tribunals. People are disappearing through the cracks. What tends to happen is that because waiting times go up, people can't wait, they don't wait and they simply give up."

Bolton Citizens Advice may still be there, but it is a shadow of its former self. In 2011 they had 55 staff, now they have just 24. They had four funding sources and 70% of income was from legal aid. "Now we have half the income and five times the number of income streams; but they're all tiny," Wilkinson says. Bolton Citizens Advice still has legal aid contracts for community care, housing, immigration and some benefits advice. Back in 2010, under its legal aid contract, the bureau had 1,700 cases for welfare benefits. "All gone as a result of LASPO," says Wilkinson.

★ ★ ★

In 2017 it was reported that more than a third of the refugees who arrived in the UK the previous year under the United Nations High Commissioner (UNHCR) for Refugees' Gateway Protection Programme ended up in the same northern town: Bolton.

Under the programme, the UNHCR identifies the most vulnerable people in long-term refugee camps. They are given international protection before they travel, and a full package of support on arrival in their new home.

It was reported that Bolton had 'welcomed 255 refugees from countries including Somalia, Sudan, and the Democratic Republic of Congo', which was 34% of the total number that came to the UK under the Gateway programme, which assists up to 750 people a year.[18] 'It is common decency that we do not turn our backs on these refugees, many of whom are children – this is the least we can do,' said the council's leader, Cliff Morris.

'The disparity in the number of refugees taken in by Bolton over the years, compared to the rest of the country and particularly the South, is staggering. The current system is unfair and in need of significant reform and we will remind the Government of our concerns.' Bolton signed up to the scheme and claimed £500,000 to put back into local services, which was 'less than £2,000 per refugee', according to the council's Conservative leader, David Greenhalgh.

Shortly after we were in Bolton, Andy Burnham, the mayor of Greater Manchester, threatened to withdraw from the dispersal system. 'It cannot be right that towns in Greater Manchester have more asylum seekers clustered in a handful of wards than entire regions in the rest of the country,' he said.[19] Data released by the Greater Manchester Police under a Freedom of Information request submitted by the *Guardian* revealed that race hate crime in Bolton had increased significantly from 21 reports of race hate crime in June 2013 to 90 in June 2018. David Greenhalgh told the paper that many of the new arrivals were too often placed on 'deprived estates with nationalist tendencies'.[20]

★ ★ ★

Bolton Lads and Girls Club was set up 130 years ago by two church leaders and three industrialists. They wanted to do something to improve the lives of young people working in the mills, and so they bought an old warehouse and opened it as a hostel so that they could wash, eat and sleep in peace. Its volunteer manager, Sarah Randall, tells us that this local institution was "not all about young people". "Cuts to all the services have impacted on everything: social care, schools, mental health, NHS," she tells us. "Very few people have been not touched by it."

What the Club see across their work is "lots of very poor families living on the breadline", including an influx of refugees. Since 2017, the Club has been running its RISE project: Refugee, Integration, Support and Engagement, which includes employing a refugee engagement officer to connect refugees with agencies across Bolton. "Often those families are struggling to understand all sorts of issues around what support they can receive, and they will often have very little English," says Randall.

She says that the Club are effectively filling the gaps that exist in the town's advice sector, helping refugee families with their welfare benefits claims and access to housing. "You know, anything from sorting out help refugees might need with benefits claims, school and help with housing."

More often than not, the younger generation has a better grip on English than their parents and end up dealing with problems to do with their parents' correspondence. "They get the bills and don't know what to do with them. They don't even understand it's a bill," she says.

Legal aid has gone but people need still help

Greater Manchester Law Centre in Moss Side exists to serve the needs of a deprived and diverse inner-city community. That it exists at all is in spite of, not because of, our system of publicly funded law. The problems faced by the advice sector in the North West have a long history and well predate the 2013 LASPO cuts and the onset of austerity (see Chapter 9).

At Greater Manchester Law Centre we met its three staff members: supervising solicitor Ngaryan Li, head of housing and homelessness Kathy Cosgrove, and trainee solicitor Siobhan Taylor-

Ward, upstairs in the law centre's bright blue boardroom. Li's post is funded for three years by the Legal Education Foundation and the AB Charitable Trust; Taylor-Ward's is paid for through the Justice First Fellowship scheme (also the Legal Education Foundation); and Cosgrove's salary is covered by a variety of grants.

"We are a campaigning law centre. We look at the issues," says Li, a social welfare lawyer who moved to head up the law centre from leading legal aid firm Stephensons, which has offices in Warrington, St Helens and Wigan. When the 2013 legal aid cuts came in, her department "shrank from about 30 people to just one, myself".

Li went to her partners and said (in her words): "Legal aid has gone but people need still help." "Luckily, they were crazy enough to set up a pro bono department," she recalls. "We carried on helping people with benefits issues. I would travel across Manchester visiting foodbanks and Sure Start centres still providing the advice for clients; however, the advice provision had been decimated by the cuts." It is not just for reasons of altruism that some local solicitors' firms run pro bono schemes; as Li points out, firms can pick up valuable paid work. Li ran the pro bono department for three years prior to the launch of the new law centre. In Leigh, near Wigan, where she was based, "it was just about us or the local CAB that would deal with cases; and suddenly Citizens Advice started referring cases back to us."

Siobhan Taylor-Ward says that as a young lawyer embarking on a career she wouldn't do anything other than social welfare law. But she reflects that "there aren't going to be any social welfare lawyers left unless something massive changes soon". "There has to be some kind of assistance from the government," she says. "It can't just rely on grassroots organisations like this because there aren't enough funds to fund us all."

Taylor-Ward is also a trustee of Vauxhall Law Centre (and the daughter of David Taylor, whom we met in the previous chapter). "You just can't be working under the threat of redundancy every year like they are at Vauxhall," she says. She reckons that the law centre can't recruit. "Who is going to work there?" she says. "It's full time but you only get paid 18 hours a week. There is no future."

Kathy Cosgrove has been a housing law specialist since 2003. Her old firm, Platt Halpern, was part of what became the Manchester Community Legal Advice Service. In 2010

Manchester City Council and the Legal Services Commission decided to reconfigure legal advice provision in the city through a competitive tender.

That contract was won by Citizens Advice in partnership with private law firms and an independent advice centre. It was a move that was fought by many in the local advice sector and had a calamitous but entirely predictable impact on those agencies and firms that didn't win the tender (see Chapter 9). They immediately lost two of their main sources of funding.

"As a result of the austerity cuts, the people we see who are facing eviction aren't the same as the people we were seeing 20 years ago," Kathy Cosgrove tells us. "It's no longer the people with the really serious mental health problems who have been in and out of prison with alcohol and drug problems; we are seeing women in their 50s and 60s who have worked as dinner ladies and brought up their kids who are now 19 and 20, and they're caring for elderly parents who have anxiety and depression. It is a different demographic."

Cosgrove makes the case for law centres advocating on behalf of vulnerable clients and promoting a 'rights-based' approach to her clients. That's an approach that "might be threatening" to local authorities, she says. By contrast, Cosgrove calls Citizens Advice "the Judi Dench of the advice world". "It is a national treasure. People see it as very respectful, very trustworthy, a very British organisation."

The housing lawyer flags up the new duties imposed on local authorities through the Homelessness Reduction Act 2017 (see Chapter 3). Cash-strapped councils can't afford to live up to the newly imposed statutory obligations. "Their answer is to say: 'Let's get a partnership working with the voluntary sector.' That sounds good; until you realise that the statutory services are just acting as a huge referral point for voluntary sector provision rather than deciding they have a statutory duty to house this person who's missing out on their rights. Quite often people involved say: 'This is partnership working at its best'."

Cosgrove argues that there are not many organisations left that are prepared to advocate on behalf of the vulnerably housed for "a rights-based approach to homelessness rather than merely a charitable one". "Homeless people actually do have rights," she says. "There are very few organisations that take that approach at this moment."

Shortly before our visit, Manchester City captain Vincent Kompany pledged to donate all profits from his testimonial season to help the city's homeless in support of a campaign by the Manchester mayor, Andy Burnham, to 'end homelessness by 2020'.[21]

"That's lovely," says Cosgrove, "but it's not a rights-based approach." She says that the 'beds' will be made available through local churches. They aren't 'beds', she says, but thin mattresses rolled out on a floor by church volunteers. "There will be 47 men with varying degrees of drug and alcohol problems," she says. "They will then mix with people like my client referred there by the council despite being only 19 years old, a care leaver and a Syrian refugee. He couldn't have had 'statutory duty' more tattooed upon his forehead: a care leaver who came to the UK as an unaccompanied asylum seeker."

★ ★ ★

We spoke to MPs up and down the country. Many reported a sharp rise in immigration advice in their constituency caseloads. For example, Sandy Martin, Labour MP for Ipswich, told us that people were "coming to us because the Home Office is not really fit for purpose". On the South Coast, Peter Kyle, Labour MP for Hove, said that immigration advice was a large part of their case-work because the Home Office seemed to be "in disarray, understaffed and very resistant to helping anyone at all". "We definitely experience a hostile environment," he told us.

Sandy Martin pointed out that MPs had "a specific role because the Home Office will accept representations from MPs that they won't accept from anyone else". He said: "Basically what the Home Office has done is its recruited MPs as unpaid – or paid from a different source – Home Office advocates."

Martin flagged the impact of the 2013 legal aid cuts, and the Gorton MP, Afzal Khan, saw them as "all part of the hostile environment". They had led to a further contraction in a much diminished local advice sector. "There are less places you can go to get advice and more and more areas not covered by legal aid," he says. "People have been hit in all sorts of different directions."

7

Deserts and Droughts

Mary worked for 25 years at the World Health Organization in Cairo before retiring in 2011. We meet her in a foodbank for refugees and asylum seekers in Brighton (14 June 2019). The 68-year-old grandmother is immaculately turned out (smart trouser suit and gold hoop earrings matched by gold-rimmed glasses), as though it was another day at the office.

She tells us that the only money she has to live on is a weekly £20 handout from the Red Cross. That she has a roof over her head at all is thanks to a grassroots campaigning group called Brighton Migrant Solidarity and, in particular, the generosity of one of its supporters who lets her stay rent free in a room in her house in Hove. "She a widow, such a nice lady," she says.

Mary was refused asylum at the beginning of 2018 and since then she has had to take the train to Croydon to attend the Home Office's Lunar House every month. She now has to check in only every eight weeks, on account of her failing health. She is diabetic, takes medication for depression and anxiety and suffers chronic knee pain. She tells us that she's on 18 tablets a day. "I suffer so much," she says.

Mary strikes us as a proud woman not given to self-pity. When we mention her age, she quickly says with a smile, pointing at our notepad: "I think I said 21." When she takes the train from Brighton to Croydon she is accompanied by a volunteer from another Brighton charity called Voices in Exile which supports refugees, asylum seekers and vulnerable migrants with no recourse to public funds in the area. We meet at its busy Friday destitution service and foodbank situated at Brighton's old table-tennis club in Kemp Town.

City of Sanctuary

Voices in Exile was set up in Brighton in 2005. "Brighton was a dispersal town then but it had no infrastructure and not everybody was getting the help they needed," the group's director, Mel Steel, tells us. The charity began as a volunteer-led destitution project and set up the first independent foodbank. "Predating the Trussell Trust; it provided a safe social place for people to meet, although nobody involved at that time was accredited to give advice," she continues.

In 2015 Brighton became a 'City of Sanctuary', with Brighton and Hove City Council passing a motion with support from all the main political parties to welcome '*the good work going on in the city to make it a welcoming, inclusive and supportive community which offers safety to those who need it*'.[1] The affluent seaside city has established communities from Sudan, Egypt, Iran and other countries. A 2018 report from Brighton and Hove council estimated that at any one time there might be in the region of 200 asylum seekers in the city.[2] The same study recorded that the number of asylum seekers with ongoing claims who were receiving 'Section 95' support from the Home Office under the Immigration and Asylum Act 1999, and who would otherwise face destitution, had 'steadily decreased', from 126 in 2003 when the data was first published, to 16 in 2017.

That report's authors noted 'serious concerns' about the 'lack of all types' of immigration legal advice, not only in Brighton and Hove but across the South East. 'At the time of writing there is only one provider of legal aid funded immigration advice in the city,' the report continued, adding that the provider (Brighton Housing Trust) was prioritising advice to unaccompanied asylum-seeking children. It reported that those eligible for legal aid, including 'vulnerable people such as victims of human trafficking', needed to go to London or even further afield for help, 'bringing difficulties for those households and support services who then need to fund travel and sometimes staff to accompany such clients to these appointments'.

★ ★ ★

Mary tells us that the last time she went to Croydon, immigration officers tried to force her onto a plane back to Egypt. "There was a policeman in front and one behind me," she recalls. "They marched me by the hand and took my watch off me." Mary suffers from hypoglycaemia on account of her diabetes, and felt dizzy. "I told them I was going to vomit and fell down. They put me a room, locked it with a key and said: 'We will get you a ticket and deport you to Egypt.' I told him if I went *they* would kill me."

'They' are the Muslim Brothers. Mary has a discrete and fading three-decades-old tattoo of a cross on her wrist, which, she explains, is common among Coptic Christians. According to the charity Open Doors, which compiles an annual league table of persecution of Christians, 128 Christians were killed in Egypt for their faith, and more than 200 were driven out of their homes in 2017.[3] The charity's annual report highlighted the plight of Copts and, in particular, a spate of killings over the summer that led a Cairo priest to describe it as 'the most aggressive campaign' against the religious community in the history of modern Egypt. It also reported that in February that year the Islamic State group vowed in a propaganda video to 'wipe out' Egyptian Copts and 'liberate Cairo'. Mary claims that the immigration officer was unconcerned, saying: "Don't worry we will get you a ticket back home". "From that time, I am scared to go alone," she says.

In 2015 Mary, a widow, found herself living alone in Cairo after one of her two sons married and emigrated to live with his wife in the US. "The Muslim brothers knew I was alone," she says. "They wanted to get rid of me and started threatening me by telephone." She recalls two men breaking her door down, entering her flat and shouting at her. "I was scared to be alone, so I stayed with a neighbour until I made contact with a friend who lived far away," she says. "Her brother came at midnight and took me."

Brighton has a Coptic Christian community based around St Mary and St Abraham Coptic Orthodox Church in neighbouring Hove. They are 'her community', Mary says; but the congregation did not assist when she needed money. It was Migrant Solidarity who organised the fundraising of £240 for an expert witness report to support her asylum application.

Mary turns translator so that we can talk to another Egyptian, Mohammed from Alexandria. He arrived in the UK in 2016, was initially refused asylum but was given refugee status in 2018. However, his wife and two kids are stranded in Alexandria. "They want the original birth certificate from one of his daughters in Egypt," Mary explains. "But when you go and ask for a birth certificate in Egypt, they print out the original which has a date of birth and date of issue," she explains. The Home Office has, she translates, confused the two and interpreted this as a discrepancy. "It is very mad," she adds.

Mohammed and Mary have become friends. He will ring her up and update her on the latest developments in Egypt, and they meet at Voices in Exile at the Friday drop-ins. They also share lawyers. They both had the same legal aid lawyer – or "government lawyer", as Mary puts it. "When Mohammed used to go and see the lawyer she never told him anything useful. She just said, 'Don't worry. If you give me money I will work hard for you'."

Did he expect to have to pay for a legal aid lawyer? "No," Mary replies. "She is on legal aid. The government will pay her. She must not take from Mohammed." Mary reckons Mohammed claims to have paid £2,000 in lawyers' fees. "Every time he sees her, he gets so nervous and depressed. His heart is hurting him."

Mary means this literally. He has recently had a stent fitted to regularise the blood flow to his heart. "He was sitting there in this hall with us and suddenly said, 'I feel a horrible pain'. He ended up in intensive care."

Sitting just behind us are Afran and Robert, Kurds from Iran and Iraq, respectively. Afran is in black: baseball cap, short jacket zipped up to his neck and skinny jeans. He is wearing a small backpack. He has been in Brighton on and off for eight years. He is currently making a fresh claim for asylum with the support of Brighton Housing Trust and has an appointment in September.

How did he end up in Brighton? He explains that he arrived in the UK at Newhaven docks, nine miles down the coast. "At the moment, I don't have a penny," he tells us. He stands up and turns out his pockets. The only money he receives is a £10 charity handout. For one and a half years he lived in a hostel but he can't get work to scrape together the £70-a-week rent for a bed in a shared room. So he alternates between sofas and the streets. "Friends help a lot but you can't keep asking. Sometimes I sleep outside. It's easier, I prefer it."

"My life is terrible," he says flatly. "I can't carry on like this. I have been doing this for three or four years." He used to work as

'KP', kitchen porter. "I wouldn't get minimum wage, I'd get £4 an hour," he says. Now the restaurants have tightened up and he can't manage to scrape together the money for a hostel.

"This gentleman," he says pointing at Robert, "is the same as me." The two last saw each other at the drop-in seven days ago. "I have been here for 12 years," Robert tells us. "I keep applying and they keep telling me your country is safe. It makes me crazy."

Afran left the country twice, in 2013 and 2016, ending up in Norway and then the Netherlands, because he wanted to escape winter on the streets in Brighton. On the second occasion, he ended up in a shelter for refugees in Holland ("one room for seven people"), and he recalls being woken up at midnight by immigration officers, taken to the airport and put on a plane and flown back to Heathrow. He had no money and was stranded at the airport. "I stayed there for two days asking people for money to get the ticket to get the train to Brighton," he says.

★ ★ ★

Many of those relying on Voices in Exile end up on the streets of the seaside town. In 2017 it was reported that Brighton had the highest number of rough sleepers outside of London – surprising perhaps for a city with a population of approximately 280,000 people.[4] "Asylum seekers are on the streets but they aren't part of the mainstream homelessness community," Mel Steel, the charity's director, explains:

> "Nobody knows how many there are. Some fetch up and once they have been here a little while start to establish communities. They don't want to be dispersed because they like it here over other places. So some go for subsistence-only asylum support; some decide not to claim at all and just scrape by. Some disperse to other parts of the country and migrate back, breaching the conditions of their asylum support, sofa-surfing and staying with mates."

What's the attraction? Brighton has "most of the good things that go with being a seaside town: a slightly more cosmopolitan vibe, more welcoming and more liberal," reckons Steel, as compared to towns on the south coast which are "a bit more (U)Kipperish". "Even compared to Portsmouth, which is an asylum dispersal town but where there's little infrastructure and very little warm welcome."

Mel Steel has worked in the sector for almost 20 years, mainly in London with the Refugee Legal Centre, which became Refugee Migrant Justice (see Chapter 9), and Asylum Aid, which merged with Migrant Resource Centre. She joined Voices in Exile 18 months prior to our visit, having spent the previous five years working with a charity based in East London called Praxis supporting migrants and refugees.

When we visited Voices in Exile it had ten staff (six full-time equivalent), which was up from five at the start of the year. That included two case-workers: one 'level 1' generalist adviser and one 'level 2' immigration case-worker for more complex work short of appeals; and three volunteers registered as trainee advisers with OISC (the Office of the Immigration Services Commissioner). The charity has also increased its volunteers "from a core of five or six to 40-something".

"A lot of people want to volunteer and work with refugees," Mel Steel tells us. "By that they mean professional Syrian families, but not so much the kind of destitute street homeless families we see." The charity had started working with Sussex University, which is setting up a migration law clinic headed by an immigration and asylum specialist, barrister Will McCready.

How does Steel feel about students dealing with asylum seekers? "Some are great, really keen and smart and they get it," she replies. "They understand they will be filling in forms for a long time, which is what this work is; and they are not going to get to interview clients to ask them about their 'stories', which is what they're imagining they might do."

How, we ask, would she describe Voices in Exile's funding situation? "So precarious, I can't begin to explain," she says. About "20% to 30%" of their funding comes from the local authority "and the rest is all up in the air". Voices in Exile is subcontracted to provide resettlement support in Brighton and Hove through the vulnerable persons resettlement programme.

Traditionally, Steel says, funding has "largely been faith-based and donations. A steady trickle to keep us going." However, the migrant crisis of 2015 and 2016 had led to an "explosion of demand, interest and goodwill from potential volunteers – demand from clients". "The pope told everybody to give refugees their money and so did the archbishop of Canterbury," Steel says. "One unexpected upside of that whole hideous couple of summers was that we got funding. Now we're looking down the tunnel at the other side of that: funder fatigue, media fatigue, compassion fatigue."

Steel reckons that in the last 12 months the charity has provided advice for about 600 cases. This is mainly one-off advice, but there is ongoing case-work in over a hundred cases. "Some asylum, some refused asylum looking to make fresh claims and some reasonably straightforward travel document and family reunion applications," she says. "A vast and increasing number are stuck on the ten-year route on the basis of private and family life."

That requires huge fees of £1,033, plus an immigration surcharge contribution of £500 at 30-month intervals. "So it's ten years of constant anxiety and not knowing whether or not you're going to be able to extend it again the next time," says Steel. "Those who can't raise the money can easily find themselves overstayers. It's like snakes and ladders. You've suddenly gone back to the bottom."

Market failure

It is no surprise that many of those who rely on Voices in Exile's Friday destitution advice drop-in have urgent legal needs. They are unlucky to find themselves in a legal advice desert of the kind described in Chapter 4. Jacob Berkson of Brighton Migrant Solidarity describes the process of finding a lawyer as "soul-destroying", involving a usually futile ring-around of the small number of London law firms that specialise in a difficult area of law.

As explained previously, an advice desert is defined by the Law Society as an area where help is not available through legal aid or where there is only one provider locally. When we visit Brighton, there is just a single provider with an immigration/asylum legal aid contract in the city, Brighton Housing Trust. There were two local Brighton firms that did legal aid work, but both gave up post-LASPO. Now Brighton Housing Trust covers not only Brighton but the entirety of Sussex and Surrey.

The phrase 'advice deserts' is misleading. It suggests that people who are lucky enough to live outside of advice deserts can find advice or representation. Quite clearly, that's not true. Even if someone manages to find a living and breathing legal aid lawyer they have to be eligible, and their legal problem has to fall within what remains of the post-LASPO legal aid scheme. But that's not the end of the story.

When we were in East Sussex, Brighton Housing Trust was not taking on adult asylum seekers. Just prior to our visit, Dr Jo Wilding, a barrister based at Garden Court, had published new research into the dysfunctional 'market' of publicly funded legal advice in immigration and asylum advice as set up under the New Labour government.[5]

The barrister, a research fellow at Brighton University, argued that there was a market failure, despite the government's assertion in its 2019 LASPO review that the market, in fact, was 'sustainable'. According to Wilding, that failure was 'both in terms of geographical availability of services and the ability to ensure adequate quality'.

Under the market-based legal aid system there is a single buyer (the Legal Aid Agency) and many sellers. Economists call this a 'monopsonistic' market, in which the buyer controls the market by setting prices and controlling work volumes. Wilding argues that the 'supply side of the market' (that is, firms and advice agencies) is 'precarious', despite robust demand, because of the problems inherent in the contract and fee regime. 'Urgent policy action is required if this is not to become a catastrophic market failure,' she says.

The barrister set the scene for her research with the reflection that neither legal aid lawyers nor their clients enjoyed the highest levels of public sympathy, 'perhaps least of all' those practising in immigration and asylum. According to Wilding, since the 1990s legal aid policy had been dominated by the notion that suppliers 'induced' demand for their services either by doing more work at public expense than the client needed or else by treating problems as 'legal' when an alternative solution might have been more appropriate.

'Alongside this, to justify cuts, some politicians have publicly described legal aid lawyers as "fat cats" who are "on a gravy train", backed by misleading claims about lawyers' income and the cost of the legal aid system compared with other countries,' Wilding continued. 'In immigration, politicians have also accused lawyers of "playing the system" when acting appropriately in the client's interests, while clients are derided as "bogus" and "abusive", all in the context of very limited public understanding of who gets asylum, why, and how many "layers of appeal" there are.'

Jo Wilding's notion of market failure in publicly funded immigration and asylum work is wider than the Law Society's advice deserts. Away from the deserts, the Ministry of Justice could blithely assert that there were legal aid lawyers with unused matter starts (that is, a firm has not used all its allocated cases), and so all was well.

Such an assertion wouldn't be much of a boast, given the extent of the 'desertification' of England and Wales; but nor would it mean that the market was functioning adequately outside of these barren expanses. The reason is that firms and not-for-profits are compelled to make what Dr Wilding calls 'financially rational' decisions.

The LASPO reforms cut public funding for all immigration work except asylum. It was the system of fixed fees introduced in 2006 to fund legal representation for individual units of work, as opposed to paying representatives at an hourly rate, that incentivised lawyers to spend less time on people's asylum claims.

The Wilding research explains that the standard fee for asylum work is actually lower than the amount it costs for a lawyer to do the work properly. Solicitors reckon the average cost is as much as double the fixed fee. So those firms committed to providing a quality service to vulnerable clients risk losing money on every single standard-fee case they do.

This causes problems across the board, so that recent evidence suggests that social welfare lawyers are voting with their feet. In 2018 the Legal Aid Agency had to reopen tenders for legal aid contracts to plug gaps in 39 procurement areas for housing and debt advice because there wasn't sufficient interest, as well as in six access points for immigration and asylum advice covering 26 councils and seven procurement areas for family work. Richard Miller, head of the justice team at the Law Society, called it a 'told you so' moment, as the profession had repeatedly told the Ministry of Justice that the civil legal aid contracts are not viable.[6]

Law firms or advice agencies still in the game make 'financially rational' decisions. For example, they might prioritise or cherry-pick cases and focus on cases that are less complex or else are either paid at hourly rates or sufficiently complex to escape the standard-fee scheme. It's not a criticism. From a business point of view, they would be mad not to.

Legally aided work is effectively subsidised by private client work or charitable funding. In barristers' chambers, high earners might effectively subsidise legal aid work of other members through disproportionately high contributions. According to Wilding, at least one chambers has folded after a small number of high earners quit for that reason.

It is a highly flawed market model that drives quality out of the system. Committed practitioners refuse to compromise the services they offer but are forced to reduce market share so as to limit losses to the amount they can afford to subsidise. Meanwhile the sharks (in a sector that has historically attracted more than its fair share) take the fee and provide a substandard service for vulnerable clients. Clients in this area of the law don't 'shop around', nor are they likely to complain. Many can't speak English.

Legitimate lawyers also have to deal with the Legal Aid Agency's auditing regime, which is described by practitioners interviewed by Wilding variously as 'hostile', 'punitive' and 'having lost all pragmatism'.

Jo Wilding's report is a damning indictment of legal aid policy. She reckons that for an adult first-time asylum applicant there is presently 'virtually no chance' of being taken on by a high-quality legal aid lawyer because they can't afford to do the work. Not a single not-for-profit provider interviewed for the research had used all their matter starts in a year, and yet all were turning away potential clients.

For example, in Manchester prospective clients were unable to find a lawyer and tribunals were forced to adjourn, despite the fact that there were supposedly providers with matter starts available. According to Wilding's analysis, demand 'far outstripped functional supply' even in a part of the country where the data indicated ample supply.

★ ★ ★

How did this play out in Brighton? Voices in Exile's Mel Steel described to us what she called the charity's "really perverse hierarchy of needs".

"In our skewed and grim view of the world people who are eligible for legal aid are in a much better position than those who aren't," she says. "In the same way that people who are able to get £35 a week to live on are in a much better position than the people who we work with who have nothing. We are talking about bottom-of-the-barrel hierarchies here. For those who are eligible for legal aid, we might try and do some front-loading on a case so that we can 'sell' it to a solicitor, but we would focus on trying to refer them rather than trying to do the work ourselves."

Jacob Berkson, of Brighton Migrant Solidarity, also spoke about working on cases to "make them a more attractive client for a lawyer". "To be fair, that's also about helping people as much as we can," he says.

As noted before, Brighton Housing Trust has the only legal aid contract in the region. When we visit Brighton, it is only taking on unaccompanied minor asylum seekers as clients.

Of course, cases involving lone children seeking asylum are "deserving", Mel Steel agrees. "But also they're an easier win when compared to fresh claims for asylum seekers who have previously been refused, where there are credibility hurdles and potentially poor immigration history," she says. "You are simply not going to get that done in five hours of an initial assessment. You're going to have to find fresh evidence, write a witness statement and unravel poor previous representation. That's going take a lot of hours and you won't get any of that back through legal aid. So it's partly about deserving cases but it is also about economic pragmatism, basically."

If the Ministry of Justice were to argue that there was coverage because there was a provider in an area with an allocation of cases yet to be used, how would she respond? "Absolute rubbish," says Steel. "Even people with an initial asylum claim, which, frankly, should be a shoe-in for legally aided support, we struggle to refer them and have to try and find providers in London and then think about how we can afford to get them there."

The least-bad way forward

When we visited Bolton CAB (see Chapter 6), the immigration advice services manager, Gail Lyle, explained to us the business case for providing publicly funded advice – or, more accurately, the absence of one. "The legal aid contract doesn't pay for itself," she said. "If you're in it to make a profit, I would say it just isn't worth doing."

Bolton Citizens Advice effectively subsidises its legal aid contract with other sources of income. It also introduced a fee-paying service for immigration advice in 2014 after the LASPO cuts, which it reckons was a first for Citizens Advice. Of 278 live cases its immigration team had on the books when we visited, Gail Lyle estimated that it was "probably 60/40" in favour of legal aid over the private work.

Chief executive Richard Wilkinson admits to us that the provision of a private fee-paying service did "not sit entirely comfortably, to say the least" with their ethos. "But it is the least-bad way of doing it," he adds. As he puts it: "Protecting the rights of immigrants is not the most popular cause at the moment. We try to make sure it is at least 25% cheaper than any other private practice."

Lyle also tells us that clients whom they had helped successfully to resolve their immigration status would inevitably return with related issues; however, she would then have to point out that they couldn't help them any more because their case was no longer in scope. "I was turning people away and sending them off to private solicitors who would do the case for, say, £2,000, nor did they need to be accredited because the work was no longer under legal aid," she says. "They'd end up with solicitors doing conveyancing who dabbled in immigration but didn't know the law."

She continues: "If a client comes to a drop-in here they get a 20-minutes slot with an accredited adviser. They might say they want to bring their partner over from Somalia. We can advise them exactly what they need to do without even signing the case up. A lot of the private firms charge a consultation fee. What we do for £750, you would not get anywhere else for under £1,500."

According to Lyle, the move to fixed fees for immigration work, which replaced the old system of hourly rates in 2007, has hit the agency hard. "You used to bill for what you did. For example, if it took me so many hours to deal with an asylum claim, then we'd bill at £48 an hour; now you can bill only £413 per case. In other words, it suddenly didn't matter whether you did £800-worth of work on a case."

For barristers on an asylum appeal, the fee in 2019 was £302, which allowed for three hours of preparation and attendance, including a discussion with a client before court; one and a half hours' travel and waiting and an 80-minute hearing, amounting to £303.92.

Lyle cites the example of an asylum seeker "who might be a victim of torture":

> "We might have to take a statement from them, which the Home Office expects us to do, and it's in the best interest for the client to sit with me for four or five hours to explain what has happened. How can we do that for £413? The alternative is they go straight to a Home Office interview where they sit for one and a half hours and have 200 questions fired at them."

The immigration barrister Colin Yeo recently wrote about the complexity and sensitivity required by lawyers when interviewing asylum seeker clients in preparation for a Home Office interview.[7] 'We know that a client is unlikely to have perfect recall of the events about which they will be questioned, and we know that even if they can remember, they will be reluctant to disclose such horrible traumas, even to a sympathetic interviewer – which many are not,' he wrote. 'Good solicitors will spend many hours in multiple meetings with clients to try to piece together an account of what happened and when. The idea is that by answering questions, over time the client might, in a modern-day process of Socratic dialogue, eventually settle on what he or she considers, on reflection, to be a single version of the truth of what happened.'

The greatest human rights issue of our time

During our time at Bolton, Gail Lyle talks about the horrific experience of one client, a 32-year-old Albanian woman who has been refused asylum by the Home Office. "When she arrived here, she was traumatised, not knowing what was going on," Lyle says.[8]

She had ended up in the UK after her father was diagnosed with lung cancer. He had approached a supposedly reputable organisation for a loan to cover his medical costs and ended up in a deal in which his daughter would work in the UK. "She arrived thinking that she was going to be working as a nanny, to pay them back for paying for the father's treatment that saved his life," Lyle says.

Her father died shortly afterwards and the daughter was taken to a house in Birmingham, where she was told she would have to sleep with men to pay off the debt. "She was put in a cellar, drugged and raped for 72 hours. She was tortured, fastened to a concrete post and told to do what she was told, until she agreed to sleep with men for money," Lyle says.

The woman had been held in this house with other women for almost two years before she contracted chickenpox and was moved to a second property. She managed to make her escape. She didn't go to the police but fled to Manchester after randomly bumping into a fellow Albanian at Birmingham New Street. She somehow ended up at Bolton Citizens Advice.

Theresa May described modern slavery as 'the greatest human rights issue of our time' and pledged in her first month as prime minister to 'make it a national and international mission to rid our world of this barbaric evil'.[9]

Her flagship legislation, the Modern Slavery Act 2015, was brought in between the Immigration Acts of 2014 and 2016 which built the so-called hostile environment – as though making life more miserable for undocumented migrants had nothing to do with such exploitation.

Referrals to the UK's system for identifying and supporting victims of trafficking, the National Referral Mechanism, have increased year on year since it was created in 2009. Some 6,993 potential victims were submitted to the National Referral Mechanism in 2018 – a 36% increase on the 2017 total of 5,142 referrals.[10]

Lyle dealt with the Albanian asylum decision up to court. She referred her client through to the National Referral Mechanism and the woman was put in touch with a Liverpool charity called City Hearts which supports the victims of modern slavery. The Home Office has a two-part decision-making process to determine whether someone is 'a victim of modern slavery'. The woman passed the first 'reasonable grounds' hurdle but failed the second, final 'conclusive grounds' decision. She challenged that refusal in court but, again, was not successful. She is presently on the 10-year route to settlement, requiring a decade residing in the UK continuously and lawfully.

We encountered a number of people who had been trafficked in the course of our year's research. For example, in Birmingham we briefly met 'Will', a Polish support worker at the SIFA Fireside homeless shelter (see Chapter 3). He had ended up homeless and sought refuge at the shelter. Previously he had been taken in by a Czech couple in Walsall and enslaved for two years. He spoke to the BBC about his experience: 'Can you imagine being woken up at two o'clock in the morning, because some drunk Czech person is ranting at you to go and get some vodka for them? Or being woken up at four in the morning and told you have to clean the garden. Just because they are drunk.'[11]

SIFA Fireside see around 60 victims of modern slavery a year, homeless as a result of their experience, including ten who were already homeless when they were exploited. A number of these clients have received a positive decision through the National Referral Mechanism. "Many of the people we support do not realise they have been exploited and often will not disclose," SIFA's chief executive, Carly Jones, tells us.

On the day we visited, we met a case-worker from the anti-slavery charity Hope for Justice who regularly attends the homeless shelter. For the purposes of his work, he didn't want to be identified. A few weeks prior to our visit, the largest-ever modern slavery ring uncovered in the UK was broken up after a three-year investigation. Some of its 400 victims had been working for as little as 50p a day. According to the Crown Prosecution Service (CPS), the traffickers made their victims claim benefits and kept the money. Those who tried to leave were assaulted or threatened. 'Meanwhile their abusers used the fruits of forced labour to purchase high-end cars and other items,' the CPS said.

The gang was reckoned to have made around £2.46 million from wages and benefits not passed on to the victims. West Midlands Police began its investigation in 2015 after a tip-off from Hope for Justice, which noticed an increasing number of Polish people attending one of its soup kitchens. Fifty-one victims eventually made contact through the charity's outreach services at two drop-in centres.[12] According to the West Midlands Police, there were 400 modern-day slavery active investigations from December 2016 to December 2017, as compared to 137 the previous year.[13]

★ ★ ★

Despite Theresa May's seeming commitment to defeating the 'evil' of modern slavery, front-line campaigners were forced to challenge the government's refusal to allow victims access to publicly funded legal advice. In April 2018 a legal charity called the Anti-Trafficking and Labour Exploitation Unit successfully challenged the Ministry of Justice in a judicial review court case after their client, a young woman ('LL'), was brought to the UK and sexually exploited as a child.

The charity issued a statement noting that it was 'bitterly disappointing' that their client had been forced to pursue a case against a government with a prime minister who 'recognised the horror and inhumanity of the crimes suffered by victims of trafficking and slavery and pledged, that "these crimes must be stopped and the victims of modern slavery must go free"'.[14] 'It is bitterly disappointing this government decided to spend taxpayers' money contesting LL's case only to change its mind on the eve of the hearing, leaving our client without access to advice, her life on hold, unable to plan for her future or recover from the horrific abuse she has suffered for almost a year,' the group said.

When we visit Bolton Citizens Advice, Gail Lyle's immigration team has eight trafficking victims on its books from "Vietnam, Albania and Zimbabwe via South Africa". That number includes two children. "They had been brought by an unknown individual to the UK and left at Victoria Station with a mobile phone and a number," Gail Lyle tells us. "That person went to the toilet and they were told to press call. It was the police. They say: 'We've just been left here. We don't know where we are'."

★ ★ ★

In May 2019, Appeal judges ruled that Home Office guidance on young asylum seekers was unlawful and created 'a real risk' of children being wrongly detained.[15] The guidance stated that unaccompanied asylum seekers would not be accepted as children if 'their physical appearance and demeanour very strongly suggests that they are significantly over 18 years of age and there is little or no supporting evidence for their claimed age'.

Lawyers for an asylum seeker from Eritrea, known as BF, argued that assessing someone's age based on appearance was 'inherently unreliable', and so the guidance was unlawful. 'Given the evidence that the margin of error may be as much as five years, the word "significantly" is so vague as to give rise to a real risk that young people under the age of 18 will be wrongly identified as adults,' said Lord Justice Baker.[16] 'We got involved in this case because every day we see children who have been deemed adult under this Home Office policy, leaving them feeling unsafe, frightened and unsupported,' said Helen Johnson, head of children's services at the Refugee Council.[17]

We spoke to Sian Pearce, an immigration solicitor at Bristol and Avon Law Centre. She was running a project funded by Children in Need for young asylum seekers across the South West of England and South Wales. She spoke about the difficulty in advising such a vulnerable client group. "Particularly if you have young people who've travelled through Europe, been in camps and been through very dangerous situations. They will eye you up and judge any adult they come into contact with."

Pearce says that the "stereotypical solicitor–client model" doesn't "really work for anybody, certainly not in social welfare law". "In particular, it doesn't work for young people," she says. "Look, this young person has been through hell. They don't trust their social worker. They don't trust their lawyer. Fair enough. Let's see if we can work a bit harder to help them do that, rather than blaming them for that."

A 2019 BBC *Newsnight* investigation shortly after the BF case identified 137 child asylum seekers wrongly classified as adults who, in a 12-month period, ended up in unsupported and often highly inappropriate adult asylum accommodation.[18] They included Burhan (not his real name), who arrived in the UK in the back of a lorry, aged 16. 'I was in the lorry for three days. I had no food and only a little water, which ran out quickly,' he told the BBC. Classed as an adult asylum seeker, he was sent to live in a room in a house with other asylum seekers, older than him. It was there, Burhan said, that an older man kicked his bedroom door down and attacked him. 'He brought out a knife and lunged at me,' the teenager said.

Greater Manchester Immigration Aid Unit (which we met in Chapter 6) work with unaccompanied asylum-seeking children. They have a legal aid contract covering all forms of public law challenges; however, according to solicitor Laura Gibbons, 'almost all' their cases were related to age disputes. The charity has just one full-time public law solicitor and had taken 18 age-dispute cases since their legal aid contract started in September 2018. 'We have represented children who have been described as being old men with grey hair and wrinkles in situations where that has not been the case and where professionals working with the children have given evidence to the contrary,' she wrote.[19]

★ ★ ★

At the end of our time at Voices in Exile in Kemp Town, we meet a 33-year-old Hindu man from South India called Radut. He doesn't look a well man. It's a warm day and he wears a zipped-up anorak and a pink knitted bobble hat. He tells us he has been coming to the drop-in since December. "I am a gay man from India," he explains. "I am a homosexual who faced persecution. My family abandoned me because of my sexuality."

Is it dangerous to be gay where he comes from? "Yes," he replies. He tells us that his partner was murdered. "After I left my family I was living with him. Religious groups beat us both. I escaped," he says. "He got killed." He fled India in 2010 immediately after his partner's murder and moved to Manchester, where he studied construction before dropping out.

"I couldn't understand the language," Radut says. Was he interested in a career in construction? Not really, he replies. "My friend completed the form. He said I'd like Manchester. I used to work in construction but I lost my job because of my sexuality."

He stayed on in the UK after his student visa expired. "I didn't know about asylum so I just went into hiding," he says. In 2017 the Home Office caught up with Radut and he was detained. It was at that point that he claims to have discovered that he could apply for asylum based on his sexuality. "I thought asylum was something that they only gave for people from countries like Afghanistan," Radut tells us.

It is estimated around 2,000 people seek asylum in the UK each year on the basis of sexual orientation, which comprises about 7% of total claims. It has been getting harder to win asylum in Britain based on sexual orientation, with only 22% of claims approved in 2017, down from 39% in 2015. To be recognised as a refugee, a gay asylum seeker has to effectively prove their sexuality. Unsurprisingly, the Home Office's culture of disbelief that characterises much of its dealing with migrants is very much in evidence in its treatment of those claiming to have been persecuted because of their sexuality.

A 2014 report carried out by the Independent Chief Inspector of Borders and Immigration found that a fifth of interviews with gay and lesbian asylum seekers included assumptions or questions based on stereotyped views about homosexuality.[20] For example, questions included: 'Why did you feel the need to have sex every day when you were on vacation?' and 'What do you believe a relationship with a man may provide that is absent from a heterosexual partner?' One gay man was asked whether he had more or less than 100 lovers, which the report found 'could be seen as being based on a stereotype of gay male promiscuity'.

Radut made an application for asylum from the immigration removal centre where he started to receive support for his mental health problems. He tells us that he suffers nightmares, hears voices and "sees visions".

Does he mean flashbacks? "When I was in India, I was repeatedly raped by two people," he says. "When I sleep it feels like it is happening again. I only sleep for three hours at a time."

Radut is currently staying at a hostel, which he says makes him "feel very scared". He is clearly very vulnerable. The volunteer on tea duty tells us later that he has resurfaced after two or three weeks' absence and that she is relieved to see him again.

Successfully navigating the asylum process without the support of a specialist lawyer seems nigh on impossible. Happily for Radut, his asylum claim is being handled by a solicitor in London from one of the largest legal aid firms (Duncan Lewis).

His time in the UK seems to have been very hard. Why, we ask, does he want to stay? "Here I can be open about my sexuality," he says. "I can proudly talk about my identity." What plans does he have for his future? "If I get status, I'd like to stay and live my life here. Until now I have been very scared. I want to build a life and start again."

Activist lawyers

In September 2015 the dead body of a three-year-old Syrian boy, Alan Kurdi, washed up on a Turkish shore. A photo showing his body lying face down in the sand drew the world's attention to the harsh reality of the migrant crisis. A few weeks later Theresa May, then home secretary, made an uncompromising speech at the Conservative Party conference.

'What I'm proposing is a deal,' she told the Tory faithful. 'The fewer people there are who wrongly claim asylum in Britain, the more generous we can be in helping the most vulnerable people in the world's most dangerous places.'[21] It was a reference to the government's net migration policy, and proposed what the immigration barrister Colin Yeo has called 'a compassion quota'.[22] May continued:

> And my message to the immigration campaigners and human rights lawyers is this. You can play your part in making this happen or you can try to frustrate it. But if you choose to frustrate it, you will have to live with the knowledge that you are depriving people in genuine need of the sanctuary our country can offer.

Yeo admitted to some confusion as to how the home secretary expected that he and his fellow human rights lawyers could 'play their part'. 'Perhaps we should have been out patrolling the coastline, shooting the bottom out of dinghies for those we assessed as wrongly claiming asylum?', he opined.

Contrary to tabloid myth and the insistence of some politicians, immigration cases were not a significant component of legal aid expenditure pre-LASPO. A report by the Hague Institute for the Internationalisation of the Law in 2014 showed that the proportion of the legal aid budget spent on these cases was highest in Belgium (17%) and the Netherlands (13%), and lower in Ireland (7%), Scotland (3.1%) and England and Wales (2%). The average costs per case were in the range of €1,000 in all countries, with England and Wales being at the low end.[23]

In August 2020 a short video posted from the Home Office Twitter account blamed EU regulations for 'allowing activist lawyers to delay and disrupt returns' of migrants. The government had been thwarted in its plans to put 23 migrants who had arrived in the UK on small boats back on a charter flight to Spain. The video, described by one newspaper as resembling the opening sequence of the BBC sitcom *Dad's Army* with arrows indicating

'British forces attacking Nazi-occupied Europe', was swiftly taken down.[24]

Matthew Rycroft, permanent secretary at the Home Office, admitted that officials should not have used the phrase 'activist lawyers'; however, the home secretary waded in, asserting people who had arrived in the UK in small boats had no 'legal right' to be in the country. 'Removals continue to be frustrated by activist lawyers, but I will not let up until this route is unviable,' Priti Patel tweeted.

An obliging 'government source' continued the attack on 'loudmouthed lawyers and barristers' who seemed to 'spend more time on social media than representing their clients' and who think 'even the mildest criticism of their profession will bring about the destruction of democracy'.[25]

The idea of activism being demeaned by government ministers as a professional flaw incensed lawyers and many commentators. Wera Hobhouse, justice spokesperson for the Liberal Democrats, wrote to justice secretary Robert Buckland and attorney general Suella Braverman urging them to condemn such language as 'completely inappropriate' and which 'undermined' the rule of law.

The 'activist lawyer' is a familiar and pernicious refrain. It was deployed by the then home secretary Theresa May to attack lawyers who 'harangue and harass' the 'bravest of the brave: the men and women of our armed forces' at the Conservative Party's 2016 conference.[26]

It is grimly ironic to be used against a sector that has been decimated by her own government. A survey of 92 groups working with asylum seekers, undertaken by the No Accommodation Network together with Refugee Action in the first half of 2018, reported that more than three-quarters (76%) found it 'difficult' or 'very difficult' referring people on to legal representatives, and 87% said it was more difficult than six years earlier.[27]

The same study recorded that, on the Legal Aid Agency's own data, more than half of all providers in immigration and asylum law dropped out between 2005 and 2018. The not-for-profit sector bore the brunt; almost two-thirds (64%) had shut down. By March 2018 there were 26 local authorities with more than 100 people seeking asylum where there was no local legal aid provision.

8

Heading for Breakdown

We speak to lorry driver Trevor Stephens as he negotiates the M4 on a return journey to visit his children. His former partner of almost 20 years is applying for a court order preventing him from seeing her. His life, he tells us, has turned into a logistical nightmare. He has been homeless for the last 18 months after his ex-partner applied for his name to be struck off the tenancy for their council house.

So Trevor lives in his lorry. At the end of each day he parks in a lay-by or on an industrial estate outside Bury St Edmunds, where his children live with their mother. He has three of his four children for eight nights a month and the eldest lives with her boyfriend. When it's his turn, he books a family room at the nearby Travelodge "or wherever's the cheapest". Up until last month, he had been using a friend's caravan behind a pub, an arrangement apparently sanctioned by social services. However, the caravan has been requisitioned by its owner, who has just split with his wife.

The father of four has complex legal needs. Over the last 12 months he has had two six-week spells in prison for breaching bail. "My ex makes up false allegations and the police tried to stitch me up. Nobody gets to hear my side of the story," he tells us.

The man insists he is not violent. On his account, his ex is an alcoholic with long-term mental health problems. He readily admits to breaching bail; but only because, again on his account, she initiated contact by text message begging him to come over because she was scared of being beaten up by her new boyfriend and, on a second occasion, threatening suicide by driving her car into a wall.

He has the texts on his mobile phone as well as messages from his kids calling on dad for help because of concerns about their mother's condition. But he claims no one has been sufficiently interested – not the police, nor social services nor the courts – to bother to check out his side of the story.

Until recently the only legal advice Trevor Stephens had received had been from a duty lawyer when he was remanded. "She told me that they weren't going to charge me with assault as there was no evidence but they were going to charge me with harassment without violence," he says. "She said: 'You can do it one of two ways. Plead not guilty and wait for a court date or plead guilty and be home today.' I pleaded guilty. I was out the same day."

It was advice he has come to regret. As a result, he was subjected to a restraining order, and breaching that order landed him in prison. "Everyone tells me I was stupid. I agree. But what am I supposed to do?"

More recently his probation worker directed him towards Suffolk Law Centre, that tiny oasis in an otherwise barren expanse of legal advice desert, as described in Chapter 3.

★ ★ ★

Carol Ward is a solicitor with a background in childcare law and works at the law centre on Wednesdays and Thursdays, offering discrimination law advice. She also volunteers in a family law clinic on Tuesdays, which is where she met Trevor.

She has been helping him draft a statement in connection with legal proceedings over a non-molestation order, which is issued by courts to prevent domestic violence. "He is homeless," Ward tells me. "His ex has called the police on him any number of times and he's ended up going to prison despite the children contacting him in desperation, complaining that their mother had treated them badly. He has now learnt not to go back to the house."

It's an extreme case, but not unusual:

> "I get a lot of dads coming in where a year or two has passed without seeing their child and I ask why. Most often it's the prospect of going to court by themselves. They are too anxious to do it. It's about trying to reassure them and explaining that it's really important

not to leave it too long because the court will then say: 'Where have you been?' The relationship with the child is damaged hugely by such a long gap. But I understand why it happens."

It is a phenomenon we see up and down the country (as we reported in Chapter 5). For example, Ian Lucas, the Labour MP for Wrexham, reported that one of the biggest areas of legal advice sought by his constituents post LASPO was men seeking advice after a relationship breakdown. "They tend to be very angry and cannot get any assistance then to deal with what are very emotional issues." It is "indefensible" not to allow for legal aid in such cases, he said.

Unrepresented litigants 'flooding' courts

The LASPO cuts removed legal aid from most private family law cases, including those involving divorce and child contact, unless there happened to be evidence of domestic violence (although see later).

As a result of the controversial legislation, the family courts have been deluged by what are known as 'litigants-in-person', who are forced to go through the courts unaided. Post LASPO, the work of the Personal Support Unit (PSU), a charity that helps people going through court without legal help, has increased five-fold, and in the year of our research it helped such unrepresented litigants on over 65,000 occasions across England and Wales.[1]

In the year after the cuts, Citizens Advice reckoned to have helped over 284,000 people with relationship issues, including 107,000 (38%) with divorce issues; almost 97,000 (34%) with child maintenance issues or other issues with children; and 7,500 with problems relating to domestic abuse.[2] 'In the past, many people represented themselves through choice,' Citizens Advice commented at the time. 'Now a larger proportion of people represent themselves because they feel they have no other option.'

The year after LASPO, the National Audit Office reported a 22% increase in cases involving contact with children in which neither party had legal representation and a 30% increase across all family court cases.[3] Eight out of ten family court cases starting in

2013 had at least one party who did not have legal representation, and over half of those without representation had legal help at some stage.

Our courts may perform a 'public service', but they make little concession to the public. According to the Ministry of Justice's own research, 'only a small minority' of unrepresented litigants were able to represent themselves competently, and even those with 'high levels of education or professional experience' struggled.[4] 'The great majority of LIPs [litigants in person] were procedurally (and, where relevant, legally) challenged in some way, with some having no real capacity to advocate for their or their children's interests,' noted the researchers.

The failure of courts to cater for their primary users can very easily spill over into frustration, aggression and even violence. Ministry of Justice researchers floated seemingly without irony the idea of 'some form of publicly funded legal assistance' in order to 'perform a protective function for the court, the other party and any children involved'. They said: 'The appointment of a guardian and children's lawyer in such cases would address difficulties with evidence gathering and provide a buffer between the violent/ aggressive litigants-in-person and the other party.'[5]

These inevitable consequences of LASPO were trailed in advance of the cuts. For example, in 2011, as the then LASPO Bill was going through Parliament, a working group set up by the Civil Justice Council, noting that unrepresented litigants were about to be 'the rule rather than the exception', said: 'It is hard to overstate just how difficult it can be – for the person, for the court, and for other parties – when someone self-represents.'[6]

Judges soon reported that hearings involving unrepresented litigants were taking around 50% longer, on average, than proceedings involving two sets of lawyers. The National Audit Office reckoned that the cost of increased numbers of lawyerless court users could be £3 million in the family courts, based on an increase of 11,144 cases in which neither party was represented in 2013–14 and the £547 average cost of a family court case.

Such has been the chaos in the family courts that leading members of the judiciary have spoken out in the most stark terms. For example, in 2015 Mr Justice Mostyn complained that they had been 'flooded' with unrepresented litigants as a result of the 'savagery' of the 2013 legal aid cuts. 'Even allowing for the need to make cuts in order to reduce the fiscal deficit I do not accept that in the critically important area of private family law it has been necessary to sacrifice individual justice on the altar of the public debt, at least not to the extent that has happened,' he said. 'It is not clear to me why this particular pillar of the welfare state has had to fall.'[7]

Two years later, Mr Justice Bodey, a judge who had spent close to two decades in the family division before his retirement, spoke of how he felt 'first hand' about the frustration of unrepresented litigants, as he sometimes had to act as their counsel and ask questions on their behalf. 'I find it shaming that in this country, with its fine record of justice and fairness, that I should be presiding over such cases,' he said.[8]

Going it alone in Cardiff

For many people forced to go through our courts without a lawyer for whatever reason, the PSU offers some help in what can be a traumatic experience.[9] Cardiff PSU is on the ground floor of Cardiff's Civil Justice Centre.

After one passes through court security, the PSU is set off towards the back of the building, hidden away beyond the main courts. It would be easy to miss if you were not directed there. We spent a week shadowing its volunteers in June 2018. There are PSUs in 23 courts in 17 different cities across England and Wales. Cardiff PSU draws on a pool of 20 volunteers plus 20 law students. When we were there, there were two or three volunteers in court every day. Volunteers do not offer legal advice, but they can explain to people how to navigate the justice system without lawyers and how the courts work, help to fill out court forms and accompany people to their hearings.

When Mabel Thompson joined Cardiff PSU, four years prior to our visit, her volunteers were seeing on average 180 people a month; now they are seeing 450. By far the biggest category of work in Cardiff and throughout the PSU network is private family law – in other words, a dispute between two individuals (as opposed to 'public' family law, where the state intervenes to, for example, protect a child from harm).

Such cases, according to the PSU's submission to the Commission on Justice in Wales, 'can be particularly stressful and overwhelming for litigants in person at such an emotional time'.[10] "[The people we see] haven't got legal backgrounds," Thompson tells us. "They've never been in a situation like this [in court] before. They're totally on their own."

As we arrive at Cardiff PSU, one of the volunteers is assisting an evidently distressed man in his mid-20s whose partner has stopped contact with their child. "He's a boxer, a tough bloke; but he was crying his eyes out. He wanted to see his daughter so badly but just couldn't understand the forms," she tells us afterwards.

The volunteer – a law student – was helping the man complete a C100 form used to apply for court orders under the Children Act 1989. She then explained that he now needed to leave the court building and find Cardiff central library to use their photocopier. "Go and tell them you need a C100 copied, they'll help you," she says. "They do them all the time." The man isn't from Cardiff and the volunteer is keen to impress upon him the need to do it today rather than make a return journey, which he seems intent on doing.

It becomes evident that the young man is nervous about making a mistake on the form. "I'll call my aunt, see if she can help me. I don't understand computers," the man says at one point. The volunteer assures him that if he gets the forms copied now, she will double-check them and accompany him to the counter to ensure they go off correctly.

In their submission to the Commission on Justice in Wales, the Cardiff PSU estimate that around 90% of their clients need help with IT. "Seeing young people on their phones [is one thing] and expecting them to complete this complicated form on a computer [is another]," Mabel Thompson tells us.

Court users are directed to the PSU room by court staff before a hearing, or else they phone in advance. We saw a significant number of returning customers in our week. For example, one man rang up seven times regarding a dispute with a shop over a sofa purchase and then came in for an hour-long meeting.

Around half of the PSU's volunteers that we saw were law students honing their CVs and picking up first-hand court experience; the other half were older volunteers. "I don't care what anybody says, every bastard here does it for selfish reasons," said one retired volunteer who told us he was there to "keep my mind active".

Volunteers have two main roles: first, sitting round a table discussing the issue, filling out forms or drafting witness statements; and, second, going up to court to sit with a client and make notes for them. "We fill in more forms than we go upstairs [to court] to help people in hearings," explains Mabel Thompson.

"Forms are [written] to be completed by lawyers," one volunteer tells us. "Most people don't have lawyers so they can't understand them without help." As Thompson points out, court forms are "full of legal jargon. People have no idea what they mean." She argues that the courts "need to get real and make forms that are easy to complete". "Most people don't know what 'probate' is. Why say 'particulars of a case'? Just say 'details' and people will know what you mean."

'Only too often the litigant-in-person is regarded as a problem for judges and for the court system rather than the person for whom the system of justice exists,' reflected the former Lord Chief Justice Lord Woolf in 1995. 'The true problem is the court system and its procedures which are still too often inaccessible and incomprehensible to ordinary people.'[11]

Little has been done to assist unrepresented litigants. Court forms were described by an information expert in 2011 as 'the worst set of public documents I have even seen'.[12]

Lord Woolf was not a fan of the legal profession's fondness for words, often Latin, that the general public didn't readily understand, such as 'pro bono' (short for *pro bono publico*). "'I think one reason why pro bono is not playing its part in the provision of legal services as it should, is because of the very words pro bono,'" he said.[13]

The fact that non-lawyers don't understand what a litigant-in-person is hasn't stopped the phrase being widely used, despite moves to replace it with the self-explanatory 'self-represented litigants' or, as used elsewhere in this chapter, unrepresented litigants.

When we were with Cardiff PSU their volunteers were regularly advising unrepresented litigants from North Wales and, if they couldn't assist, referring them to their Chester service for help. 'The combination of an urban south coast and distant north coast, with rural communities in between, means that sources of help are patchy, and are largely focussed in the urban south, leaving the majority of the population with very little help,' they observed in their response to the Commission on Justice in Wales.[14]

They also pointed out that Blackwood Civil and Family Court served the population around Merthyr Tydfil, 'but with no trainline and poor bus routes'. The PSU coordinator in Liverpool, Dave Troughton, tells us his team similarly were approached by people from North Wales. "I regularly get people from Wrexham, Ruthin, Llandudno, Bangor, Holyhead, to name a few places we've had in the last two or three weeks," he tells us. They offer some support. "Unfortunately my advice to them is I can't come with you to your local court," he says. "All I can offer these people is either a chat over the phone, support over e-mail, or they can come in, and people do come in."

Litigants-in-person are 'a nightmare'

In the tiny waiting room outside the family court at Ipswich Magistrates' Court we wait for court business to start (7 November 2018). Audrey Ludwig, manager of Suffolk Law Centre, is there to introduce us to one of their volunteers who runs the court duty scheme. We talk with one of the two other people in the room waiting for the courts to open. She happens to be a legal aid lawyer who specialised in children's law before moving into academia and is there to observe the courts post LASPO.

An animated conversation between the three of us about the state of legal aid ensues. The only other person in the room, a smartly dressed woman, approaches us. She wants to ask us a few questions. We assume she is involved in proceedings, but no, she is a reporter from the *Guardian* writing an article about the impact of 2013 cuts.

During the course of our year of research there has been little, if any, serious mainstream media interest in the unfolding crisis in our courts. The chances of bumping into a journalist on our travels seem vanishingly slight.

In her article about her day in the family court in Ipswich the journalist, Amelia Hill, describes the judge, District Judge Hallett, gently 'trying to tease evidence' in a child contact case from 'the tearful, unrepresented mother'.[15] The woman has to sit opposite her former husband, who is represented by a barrister. The man hasn't seen his children for five years and accuses her of manipulating them into refusing to see him. The mother denies this.

'When the time comes for the main witnesses, the parents, to be cross-questioned, she has to do it herself,' Hill relates. 'His barrister will cross-question her afterwards. "Do you want to ask [your former husband] any questions?" Hallett asks her gently. "If you like, you can tell me what you'd like to know and I'll ask him for you."'

It is clearly an uncomfortable process; but, according to Hill, the judgment is 'an equitable one' and the mother 'quietly agrees to it'. Outside the court, she speaks of her frustration and the unfairness of the experience. 'I was totally executed by his barrister,' she is reported to have said as she wept.

'With no legal representative to explain what has happened in court, she misremembers and misinterprets,' Hill asserts. 'The judge didn't listen to me at all,' the woman goes on to say. 'Perhaps he'll listen when my daughter kills herself. She's threatened to. Maybe this time she will. Then they'll have to listen to me.'

According to the *Guardian*, representation in the family courts has 'dwindled to such an extent' that by 2017 only one in five family cases involved parties who both had representation; in more than one in three, neither party had a lawyer. Lord Woolf's 1995 view that the courts existed for unrepresented litigants (and that they shouldn't be treated as a problem) hadn't yet percolated to the judiciary. 'Litigants-in-person are a nightmare,' a family judge told the newspaper. '99.9% do not understand what is going on in court or outside court; they don't know a good point from a bad one; they don't understand the law; they don't understand what they have to prove and they don't know how to ask a question. It is my firmly held view that the courts are full of people who would not be there if they had been able to approach a solicitor.'[16]

★ ★ ★

Retired barrister Carole Parry-Jones was running the duty scheme organised by Suffolk Law Centre when we visited. How are judges equipped to deal with a new post-LASPO generation of unrepresented litigants? "They hate it," she answers. "I've been in a courtroom as a barrister with a litigant-in-person on the other side and I've seen judges being testy, rude, and dismissive. I have also seen them bending so far backwards that you sit there and think: 'Hang on, this isn't fair'."

Parry-Jones reckons that the Ipswich magistrates are "very professional". "They try to deal with everybody in the same way; but they'll say that the best thing is when the usher comes in and tells them that the next case on the list is represented. They think: 'Hooray, we can crack on'."

When she began in practice how often would she see an unrepresented litigant? "Never. Change started in a very small way about five or six years before LASPO and you would get the odd one or two," the lawyer recalls. "They tended to usually be the man who felt he knew better than anybody else and wasn't going to pay money for something that he could do."

Parry-Jones reckons that in seven out of ten cases there will be at least one party who is unrepresented. "It is not often the case where you get both clients unrepresented, but in the last three or four months I'm noticing it more and more," she says. What impact have the LASPO cuts had on the courts? "Waiting times for hearings have at least doubled and the time needed to deal with the case where one or both sides are unrepresented has doubled," she tells us. "I don't think it is an exaggeration to say that the system is grinding to a halt."

The government's big idea was to cut tax-funded litigation through LASPO, but to also promote mediation. It didn't work. The number of couples entering mediation, and thus diverted away for the courts, has gone into free-fall. The number of publicly funded mediation, information and assessment meetings to explore non-court options fell by two-thirds between 2012–13 and 2017–18 (66%) and actual mediations dropped by over half (54%). Couples aren't being signposted to less confrontational resolutions.[17]

As a practitioner in the post-LASPO environment, Carole Parry-Jones increasingly ended up acting against litigants-in-person (LiPs), which had its own problems. "A whole range of very obvious difficulties presented themselves," she recalls. "It started off with LiPs being very reluctant to speak with me. The court expects you to do a lot of work outside the courtroom with a view to helping the parties resolve the difficulties. There was a high level of tension and suspicion."

She found herself giving "an inordinate amount" of professional support to the other side. "I'd think to myself this is wrong," she recalls. "I am not here to act for this person." She might end up explaining to a father that, as the applicant, he would normally be expected to lead the case, although the court might expect her, as a lawyer to provide a neutral outline of the case for the court. "I realised my own client was looking at me askance. It was painfully obvious to me that it was getting harder and harder for everybody in the process, not just LiPs, but everybody."

As mentioned earlier, emotions often run high in the family courts. In Ipswich the risk of confrontation is heightened by the inadequacy of the facilities and, in particular, the stuffy waiting room where, as Parry-Jones puts it, "everyone is forced to sit cheek-by-jowl". Parties using the family courts are forced to "run the gauntlet" past the four criminal courts with their much larger waiting area. "Some of the women and the younger girls find it difficult," Parry-Jones says; adding that the security staff on reception are "fantastic". "If they have the feeling that somebody is scared or that it might kick off, they tend to separate out the men and make them wait in the corridor where they can keep an eye on them," she adds.

No safety net

As noted above, the 2013 LASPO cuts removed legal aid from private family law cases with one exception: domestic violence. At least, that is what was claimed. Under the LASPO regulations, to qualify for legal aid a victim of domestic violence would have to submit evidence in a prescribed form (for example, evidence of a former partner's unspent conviction or a letter from a doctor detailing injuries consistent with domestic violence) and from a period of just two years before the legal aid application.

In 2017 the legal charity Rights of Women reported that four out of ten female survivors of domestic violence had been unable to meet such stringent conditions and most were having to represent themselves in court. In December that year the Ministry of Justice was forced to scrap the time limit and widened the types of evidence required to prove abuse.[18] This came after a successful judicial review in 2016 by Rights of Women together with another small legal charity called the Public Law Project, which went to the Court of Appeal.

LASPO has its own 'safety net' – or, again, that is what was claimed. Under what is known as the 'exceptional case funding' regime, legal aid was supposed to be available for those whose cases were not covered by the regulations but did require public funding on human rights grounds. If it was a safety net at all, it was almost completely impossible to access. In its first year, 1,315 applications were made and only 16 people were granted funding – a success rate of just over 1%.[19]

Again campaigners had to take to the courts. The Public Law Project, alongside other campaign groups, have scored a run of notable successes in the courts to lessen the full impact of the LASPO cuts. For example, in 2013 the Lord Chancellor attempted to introduce a 'residence test' for legal aid, which would have meant that, subject to some exceptions, only people who were lawfully resident in the UK could get legal aid. That obstacle was fought all the way to the Supreme Court, where it was defeated in 2016.[20] The Public Law Project assisted a quarter of all applicants who were granted exceptional case funding in the first two years post LASPO.

A judicial review challenging the refusal to grant legal aid in immigration cases recorded that the success rate for exceptional case funding applications had risen to 13%. The case went to the Court of Appeal, which ruled the guidance was not compatible with the European Convention on Human Rights. Applications to the scheme doubled from 1,516 in 2013–14 to 2,975 in 2018–19, but they remain significantly lower than the Ministry of Justice's own predictions of between 5,000 and 7,000 applications each year.

A survey of legal aid providers by Public Law Project revealed that, unsurprisingly, there was little faith in the exceptional case funding system. Only 5% of respondents strongly believed that the scheme operated effectively to ensure clients can access legal aid. Nearly half had not even applied for exceptional case funding in the past year. Reasons included the risk of not being paid, previous applications being refused and the time-consuming application process.[21]

★ ★ ★

In June 2020 a victim of domestic violence known as 'Claire' who was on Universal Credit challenged the legal aid regime that had effectively forced her to cross-examine her former partner in court. 'The Legal Aid Agency is saying that I have to sell my house in order to fight to be in my house, or to get my fair share of it,' she said. 'It's obvious that I can't do that. The alternative is to represent myself. The idea of seeing my abuser again in court is utterly terrifying.'[22]

Claire recalled the experience of confronting her ex-partner. 'His barrister was pushing for a "zonal order", which would have allowed my ex-partner back into the house, but I had no idea what it meant at first. They were using legal jargon I didn't understand,' she said. It was the first time she had seen him or heard his voice in four weeks. 'He was really angry. It was awful. I was petrified,' she said. 'I had nobody to help me. When I heard his voice I was physically sick in the courtroom. There was such an inequality of power. He had his barrister and I didn't have anybody. I was fighting on my own.'

She had then to return to court another three times over child arrangement orders. She managed to find a solicitor to act for her pro bono, but still had to pay for the barrister for the court hearings. The solicitor persuaded the barrister to agree to represent Claire on legal aid rates. 'But even at legal aid rates my Mum ended up taking out a loan and selling some of her furniture and her rings to pay for me to have a lawyer to represent me in court,' Claire said. 'She can't afford to do that again, and I'm on Universal Credit.'

Once again Public Law Project together with Rights of Women were involved in the challenge. Claire had been denied legal aid because the Legal Aid Agency's interpretation of its means test took into account 'trapped capital' in the home she jointly owned with her ex when assessing her eligibility, despite the fact that she was not in a position to access that equity.

Olive Craig, senior legal officer at Rights of Women, said they frequently advised women who could not afford to pay for representation but who were considered to be financially ineligible. 'We hear from victims of abuse who are having to resort to foodbanks to feed their children but are assessed as financially ineligible for legal aid,' she said. The Public Law Project solicitor Katy Watts pointed out that Claire was on Universal Credit and cared for two small children. 'There is no way she could pay for legal representation on her own,' she explained. 'The Legal Aid Agency's decision means that our client is expected to sell her house in order to pay for lawyers to represent her in proceedings which relate to the sale of her house. This is an absurd catch-22 that denies legal aid to highly vulnerable individuals.'

9

Death by a Thousand Cuts

When the attorney general Sir Hartley Shawcross introduced the Legal Aid and Advice Bill in Parliament in 1948, he called it 'a charter of the little man to the British courts of justice'.[1] The new legislation, the barrister promised a war-weary nation, would do its bit in building a new, fairer and more egalitarian Britain. 'It is a Bill which will open the doors of the courts freely to all persons who may wish to avail themselves of British justice without regard to the question of their wealth or ability to pay,' he declared.

Sir Hartley, who served as the lead British prosecutor at the Nuremberg war crimes tribunal, repeated 'the familiar taunt' (his words) about the courts being open to all 'just as the grill room at the Ritz Hotel is open to all'. In other words, theoretically available but only accessible to the rare few who could afford to pay their way. In fact, he quipped that the Ritz had become a more democratic institution than our courts 'at any rate in the grill room', where he reported that costs were 'largely controlled' compared to the costs of court users which were 'not subject to any legal limit at all'.

Sadly, Sir Hartley's point is as valid today as it was then. His taunt is reminiscent of the Lord Chancellor's 2015 damning assessment of 'a two-nation justice system'.[2]

★ ★ ★

This book has so far been focused on the impact of 'austerity' and the 2013 legal aid cuts on the justice system. It would be wrong to leave readers with the impression that the problems faced by the legal advice sector somehow began in 2010. The demise of the advice sectors in Manchester (as outlined in the Chapter 6) and elsewhere long predate the arrivals of New Labour and of the Coalition government. This chapter provides an overview of the legal aid scheme and a history of access to justice.

As we will explain below, the legal aid scheme never delivered 'access to justice' in any comprehensive sense. Nor was legal aid one of 'the pillars' of the welfare state. That was a claim often made by advocates of publicly funded law in the debate over LASPO; but it is based on misunderstanding of its origins.

New Jerusalem (1945 to 1970)

In the year of the D-Day landings (1944), a former Conservative MP and barrister, Lord Rushcliffe, was tasked with setting up a legal aid system. His report was to be 'a very small and unobtrusive part of the plans for a New Jerusalem,' noted the legal academic Tamara Goriely. 'It was a time of social solidarity. Disaster was no longer individual but something whole communities had shared.'[3]

The Beveridge Report, the founding document of the welfare state, was published in the midst of the Second World War.[4] It had been drafted by the Liberal economist William Beveridge with the promise of reform to the system of social welfare to address the 'five giants on the road of reconstruction': want, disease, ignorance, squalor and idleness. It promised reward for a beleaguered people's wartime sacrifice.

The welfare state was to be based upon four pillars:

- a national health service
- universal housing
- state security (welfare benefits)
- universal education

But not legal aid. As far as a system of publicly funded law was concerned, Rushcliffe recommended:

- legal aid should be available in those types of case in which lawyers normally represented private individual clients;
- legal aid should not be limited to those people 'normally classed as poor' but should include those of 'small or moderate means';

- there should be an increasing scale of contributions payable by those with income or capital above minimum levels, below which legal aid would be free;
- in addition to the means test, cases should be subject to a merit test, designed to be judged by legal practitioners independent of government, on a similar basis to those applied to private clients;
- legal aid should be funded by the state but administered by the Law Society. The Lord Chancellor should be the minister responsible, assisted by an advisory committee;
- 'adequate' remuneration should be paid to barristers and solicitors working under the scheme.

As idealistic as that sounds, legal aid's origin story was not free from professional self-interest. The Law Society needed an extension of legal aid 'not least because it was concerned that its members would find it difficult to re-establish their practices after the war'.[5] The solicitors' group was particularly keen to wind up the salaried divorce department it had been forced to run during the war and which it saw as unhelpful competition.

From the start there was some support for a state-funded national network of legal advice agencies. In a submission to the Rushcliffe Committee, the Haldane Society of Socialist Lawyers argued that for the poor to depend on charity for legal advice was 'wrong in principle' and did not work in practice. Instead, they wanted to build a brand new service on the structure of the newly created network of Citizens Advice Bureaux, as described in Chapter 3.

In the end, the Rushcliffe Committee recommended that legal advice should be provided by salaried solicitors employed directly by the Law Society. Help should be available to a wider income group than 'those who are normally classed as poor'. 'The term "poor person" should be discarded and the term "assisted person" adopted,' the Committee said. An assisted person would 'be a man or woman whose net income (after deduction of income tax and certain other items) does not exceed £420 a year'. An assisted person would have to contribute 'what (if anything) he could afford', it continued.

Aneurin Bevan, the minister of health and housing and chief architect of the National Health Service, felt that Rushcliffe was handing too much power to solicitors. He was opposed to any scheme whereby a committee of lawyers decided whether a category of cases should 'result in the payment of fees to the legal profession'. Bevan considered that, compared with his own tough negotiations with the leaders of the medical profession, the Lord Chancellor's department had 'given in' to the Law Society. 'Bevan was right,' wrote Tamara Goriely. According to 1948 costings, it was anticipated that the salaried divorce department together with an initial advice scheme would comprise 44% of the entire aid budget.

Rushcliffe's final report was published in 1945 in the same month that Germany unconditionally surrendered to Allied forces. In the end, the Tory peer largely accepted what the Law Society proposed: a legal aid scheme provided by solicitors in private practice and, where appropriate, barristers.

The Legal Aid and Advice Act 1949 never lived up to Sir Hartley's billing. When the legal aid scheme started in 1950 it covered almost 80% of the population but 'access to justice' was skewed to a very particular demographic. In the first 17 years of the scheme some 860,000 people received support, but 80% of the cases funded related to matrimonial proceedings.[6]

The Society of Labour Lawyers put this into useful context when, drawing on the experience of three poor man's lawyer services in London, they reported that between 15% and 25% of cases involved family law problems. In its influential 1968 *Justice for All* pamphlet, the society called for 'a new approach': 'A new institution is required capable of bringing high quality legal services to those parts of our cities were the need for them is greatest, and attracting men of ability to the service of the community.'[7]

The report was written by a committee including human rights lawyers such as Geoffrey Bindman and Benedict Birnberg, who went on to set up the leading human rights firms Bindmans and Birnberg Peirce, respectively. They were taking their inspiration from the neighbourhood law firm movement in the US.

Michael Zander, then a *Guardian* journalist and now professor emeritus in law at the London School of Economics and Political Science, reported on Lyndon B. Johnson's 'War on Poverty' and the creation of neighborhood law firms. In fact, Johnson's landmark Economic Opportunity Act 1964 did not mention lawyers at all, but section 205 provided for 'community action programs'.

In the two years that followed, some $59 million was spent on neighborhood law firms under that provision, staffed by salaried lawyers and based in deprived urban communities. Programmes were funded in 37 of the 50 largest cities in the US, with plans for nine more, comprising 551 offices manned by 1,157 lawyers. The vision was to take specialist legal advice to those communities that needed it, recognising that people who needed help were unlikely to go to commercial legal practices.

The *Harvard Law Review* noted in 1967 the 'psychological barriers' that prevented 'many indigents from visiting a downtown legal services centre' in the following disparaging terms:

> For many urban slum-dwellers a trip outside the ghetto is a sharp break from their usual habits, and the middle class aura of a downtown office is strange and hostile. Whatever the causes, the reluctance to leave the ghetto is real, and if all the poor are to receive legal service, the lawyers must be located in the slum neighbourhood.[8]

There were four offices in the run-down Lower East Side in New York, and the Bowery office had a van stationed on a block for a week at a time before moving on to the next block.

The mainstreaming of legal aid (1970 to 2010)

In 1970 the first law centre opened in North Kensington in a former butcher's shop, as recounted in Chapter 2; and by the mid-1980s there were over 60.[9] But, as the law centre movement grew, legal aid was swiftly absorbed into the mainstream of the legal profession.

By 1986 publicly funded legal advice represented a substantial income stream at 11% of solicitors' income, which was an increase of 5% in just ten years. This growth had been fuelled by the establishment of the Green Form scheme, which provided funding for advice and assistance on any matter of English law on the basis of a simplified test of income and expenditure which was carried out by the solicitor, as well as by the implementation of the PACE (Police and Criminal Evidence Act) reforms, which established the right to a lawyer for suspects in police stations.

The case for the Green Form scheme had been made by the Law Society on the basis that it would fund social welfare law work as pioneered by law centres; but over half of the Green Form cases in 1986 related to personal injury, crime and family matters. There was also exponential growth in the number of Green Forms in social welfare law, from 27,000 in 1975 to 172,000 in 1985; but as a percentage of the total number of cases the increase in social welfare law advice increased from just 11% to 17%.

Increasingly, the perceived excessive costs fuelled criticism of the legal aid scheme. When the Conservatives returned to power under Margaret Thatcher in 1979, ministers' attention turned to reform. Lord Mackay, who was Lord Chancellor between 1987 and 1997, slashed eligibility from 77% to 47%, leaving what the Legal Action Group called 'largely a sink-service for people on means-tested benefits'.

In 1986 control over legal aid was finally wrestled out of the profession's hands. The scheme was to be run by a government quango (the Legal Aid Board), but concerns about costs only increased. In 1985–86 the total cost was £319 million. This rose to £1.4 billion by 1995–96, comprising £675 million for civil (including family); £530 million for criminal; and £272 million for advice and assistance. In the ten years up to 1996, the average annual increase in expenditure was 16%, and for three consecutive years (1990 to 1993) the annual rise was 20%. In one year it was closer to a third.

The number of Green Form cases increased by 50% in the ten years to 1997. There was shocking abuse from some solicitors milking the system. For example, Timothy Robinson was convicted in 2001 of conspiring to systematically defraud the legal aid system of millions of pounds over a period of almost six years. The police investigation began eight years earlier and was reported to have cost several million pounds. This was fraud on an industrial scale. The Serious Fraud Office and three police forces took more than 3,000 witness statements and seized 21 tonnes of documents from the offices of his firm, Robinsons, as they investigated the scam. Some 21 former employees were reported to have pleaded guilty or were found guilty of the conspiracy in a total of five trials.[10]

One of the solicitor's former employees reckoned that up to 90% of the Green Forms submitted by one of the firm's offices were fraudulent. 'The jury heard time spent with clients was exaggerated, prison visits were claimed twice, clerks billed for cases which had never existed and crimes that clients may have mentioned in passing, but never wanted advice on, were put down in claims form,' one newspaper reported.[11]

New Labour's Access to Justice Act 1999 represented the biggest shake-up of legal aid since 1948. It replaced the Legal Aid Board with the Legal Services Commission (LSC), scrapped legal aid for personal injury cases, introduced the hard cap on overall expenditure and set out a vision for a Community Legal Service.

The Conservatives had previously created a system of legal aid franchises, and a firm's performance was measured against quality standards. Now firms had to hold a specialist quality mark in order to apply for a block contract to undertake legal aid work. The Green Form was replaced by the 'Legal Help' scheme to cover initial advice. When the new system came into force, about 5,500 contracts were awarded to firms and organisations which possessed franchises, including 50 of the then 52 law centres. The contracts allowed a fixed number of cases or 'matter starts', which could not be exceeded without the explicit approval of the LSC. This began the period of 'top down' management of the legal aid scheme, described in Chapter 6, with costs controlled through the system of contracts and fixed fees.

Divide and conquer (2000 to 2010)

One of the principal reasons why the LASPO cuts have had such a catastrophic impact is that they were inflicted on a sector already destabilised by years of 'reform' and unwelcome reorganisation. In 2016 we interviewed barrister John Nicholson as he and other veteran campaigners were planning to set up the Greater Manchester Law Centre.

The chaos inflicted upon Manchester's legal advice sector over the past two decades illustrates the point. Nicholson explained the extent of the devastation of the city's advice sector. "There are ten districts in Manchester. There used to be nine law centres," he recounted. "There are only two now left, Bury and Rochdale, and they are struggling against the odds to keep going. The whole of the inner area – so Manchester city, Salford and Trafford – is a law centre-free zone."

Greater Manchester Law Centre rose from the ashes of South Manchester Law Centre, which had been forced to close its doors in 2014 as a result of the coming into being of what was known as the Manchester Community Legal Advice Service (CLAS).

The Manchester CLAS, as it was known, was part of New Labour's aborted reorganisation of the legal advice sector known by two more unlovely acronyms: CLACs and CLANs. The idea behind a CLAC, or community legal advice centre, was for 'jointly funded, face-to-face legal and advice services', specialising in social welfare law and bringing together disparate services in a one-stop shop – or 'a souped up' law centre, as Roger Smith of the law reform group JUSTICE once called it. CLANs, community legal advice networks, were to operate in disparate rural communities.

The big idea at the heart of the initiative was acknowledgement that vulnerable people often have more than one problem going on in their lives at any one time. They lose their job, they can't afford to pay the rent or the mortgage, they have problems claiming welfare benefits, and so on. The reality of this spiral might seem blindingly obvious, and came as no surprise to anyone who had worked in the advice sector and was familiar with clients arriving with a bulging Tesco bag full of unopened correspondence.

Offering people holistic advice, housed under one roof (a community legal advice centre), would stop vulnerable people being shunted from pillar to post around various advice agencies and law firms and, more likely, disappearing between the cracks.

The policy was informed by an influential research paper, *Causes of Action*, published in 2006, which highlighted the phenomenon of 'problem clusters', where problems are experienced 'simultaneously or in sequence by the same person'. That research became the evidential base for the proposed national network of community legal advice centres.[12]

It highlighted a failing which is as valid and relevant now as it was then. A 1999 consultation paper described the sector as 'ad hoc, unplanned and uncoordinated', and the project was meant to reshape that into a proper safety net of advice.[13] The LSC, which succeeded the Legal Aid Board only to be replaced by the Legal Aid Agency in 2013, reckoned that only six firms in England and

Wales provided specialist advice in all five areas of social welfare law (community care, debt, employment, housing and welfare benefits), and not a single law centre.

The emergence of the community legal advice centre also marked a fundamental shift in legal aid policy with the LSC taking a more central role in the commissioning of local advice. The New Labour government created a market-based legal aid system. To tackle spiralling legal aid costs, control mechanisms were introduced: fixed fees and a system of competitive tendering whereby providers would bid for contracts.

The initiative combined the best and worst of policy thinking on legal aid. The central case for the community legal advice centre (better local planning of services) was unarguable; but the means of delivery through a crude tendering process showed no regard for existing providers or the wishes of the people who depended on their help. Beleaguered providers were deeply cynical from the start, and suspected that the policy was driven by a desire to drive agencies out of the sector. As it happened, their cynicism was well founded.

In 2006 the LSC reckoned that England and Wales could be covered by up to 75 new-style community legal advice centres and 36 networks. In the end only a small handful ever were set up. The first community legal advice centre was established in Gateshead in 2007, followed by others at Leicester, Derby, Portsmouth and Hull. The Hull CLAC was typically controversial, forcing the city's Citizens Advice Bureau, one of the oldest and largest in the network, to close following a successful out-of-town tender by an employment training company known as A4e.

A coalition of groups including Age Concern, the Child Poverty Action Group, the Legal Action Group, Liberty and Shelter called the closure of Hull's bureau a 'wake-up call'. 'If the government pushes ahead with its plan to impose a network of community legal advice centres without regard to existing providers, like they have done in Hull, it's going to fundamentally change the way in which the poor and the not-so-poor access advice about their legal and consumer rights,' warned Steve Hynes, who chaired the alliance. 'It could well end up devastating that network.'[14]

That A4e had no track record in legal services was no obstacle to its success. In fact, the Sheffield-based Action for Employment (as it was originally known) began life equipping unemployed steel workers with new skills. The LSC and Hull City Council put £3.5 million into the Hull CLAC and so Hull Citizens Advice lost its two main sources of funding (£649,000 from the authority and £47,000 from the LSC).

A4e quickly became mired in various scandals, with MPs Fiona Mactaggart and Margaret Hodge calling on the UK government to suspend contracts with the company in 2012. Six former employees received jail sentences for forging files in a scam that was said to have cost taxpayers almost £300,000 in 2015.[15]

The first community legal advice network was established in the East Riding of Yorkshire in 2010, and shortly after the last CLAC was announced at Barking and Dagenham. The initiative swiftly ran out of steam. A revealing study was published drawing on interviews with 831 CLAC clients in 2010. Almost one third claimed to have a long-standing illness; more than four out of ten suffered from stress, depression or a mental health problem; almost a third had no academic qualifications; and most had household incomes less than £15,000. Half of the respondents said they spent 'all of their time' worrying about the problems they were seeking help for.[16]

So what went wrong? 'The trouble was that the LSC lacked the political clout to force local government to share its vision or funding for local advice by pooling resources with the LSC for holistic advice and assistance provision,' wrote the former Court of Appeal judge Sir Henry Brooke in his history of legal aid. 'In addition, the problems of replacing 5,000 traditional firms with up to 50 large-scale providers proved insurmountable.'[17]

★ ★ ★

Curiously, in Manchester the council, together with the LSC, pushed on. In 2010 a decision was made to reconfigure the cash they currently spent on legal advice services into a competitive tender for what became Manchester Community Legal Advice Service. That tender was won by Citizens Advice in a partnership with private law firms together with an independent advice centre. For the local advice sector, if you weren't in partnership with Citizens Advice, you were history.

"The whole CLAC thing divided the city," recalls Denise McDowell, director of Greater Manchester Immigration Unit and a trustee of Greater Manchester Law Centre. When she first started work in the immigration advice sector in the city in 2008 there was Wythenshawe Law Centre, South Manchester Law Centre and North Manchester Law Centre. "That was just in the city of Manchester itself," she says. There were also law centres in Bury, Trafford and Oldham.

By the time South Manchester Law Centre closed in August 2014, the city of Manchester didn't have a single law centre. McDowell, like many others, was never convinced by the CLACs/CLANs experiment. "I always questioned what it was about. What was the agenda? It was about bringing in the private sector and competition and streamlining services. But streamlining services in the climate of cutting costs."

Nonetheless, the policy chimed with the politics of Manchester town hall. A 2010 review found that local provision was 'fragmented and did not consistently provide access to advice to residents across the city'. That review included a memorandum of understanding signed with the LSC following a meeting with Lord Willy Bach, then parliamentary under secretary of state for the Ministry of Justice.

Bach was later to head Labour's 2015 Bach Commission on Access to Justice (see Chapter 10). The memorandum covered three legal aid contracts to be awarded in Manchester with a combined value of £9 million over three years. 'This will make the Manchester Community Legal Advice Service the largest service of its kind in the UK and will enable Manchester to develop a new model of services which will vastly improve the legal advice landscape for residents at a time when demand for advice has increased exponentially as a result of the recession,' it said.

The tendering process pitched the city's advice agencies against each other. "When Citizens Advice got the citywide advice service contract, in one fell swoop South Manchester Law Centre and Wythenshaw lost the city council funding which had been a significant element of their financial viability for the past 20 to 30 years," McDowell explains.

The competition for contracts poisoned relationships. "Some of that still exists today. Trust has gone," says McDowell. The city-wide advice service contract in Manchester that used to include face-to-face advice was to be delivered through three hubs:

Wythenshawe, Moston in North Manchester and Moss Side to the south. According to McDowell: "A lot of money was invested into buildings and then, very shortly after, a decision was made to 'go digital' rather than face-to-face and almost overnight the buildings were vacated."

Greater Manchester Law Centre presently occupies the building that was supposed to be the home of the Manchester Community Legal Advice Service. That explains why the room where we met the Greater Manchester Law Centre team in Chapter 6 is painted Citizens Advice colours (blue and yellow). "The irony isn't lost on us," says McDowell.

★ ★ ★

South Manchester Law Centre went down fighting, challenging the LSC in court. According to Denise McDowell, it was that legal action that "bound" the small group of campaigners together who then went on to set up Greater Manchester Law Centre. As she puts it, "It's part of our history."

South Manchester Law Centre took the LSC to court over its assessment process in deciding its award of immigration and asylum legal aid contracts for the 2010 to 2013 period. Nine organisations in Greater Manchester had bid for the contracts. Eight, including South Manchester Law Centre, tied, scoring 53 points each; the ninth scored 54 points on the basis of having a case-worker who had made an application to be considered for accreditation at 'level 3' of the Law Society accreditation system (but at the time of the bid was not actually accredited).

As a result the winning bidder, the Immigration Advisory Service, was awarded 80% of the cases allocated to the entire Greater Manchester region, with the other eight organisations having to share the remaining cases between them. That result threatened the law centre's viability.

In 2011, within a year of the Immigration Advisory Service winning the contract, the charity which had offices throughout the country went bust, leaving stranded tens of thousands of migrants who were pursuing asylum and immigration cases. The service was reported to be advising 36,000 clients and opening 7,000 appeal files a year when it went into administration over a weekend. More than 200 staff discovered it had closed its doors when they turned up for work and found notices warning clients that the service had ended.

The LSC issued a statement saying: 'During recent stewardship activities the LSC raised concerns around financial management and claims irregularities, which prompted IAS [Immigration Advisory Service] trustees to conclude that the organisation was no longer financially viable.' Staff blamed the government and the move from being paid by hourly rates to a single fixed fee in 2007 – then £495 for an asylum case and £260 for immigration.

Sheona York, the charity's principal legal officer, warned trustees that the impact would be "cataclysmic". York had joined the charity in January 2009 after 29 years at the Hammersmith and Fulham Law Centre. "Imagine meeting someone, learning their entire life history, obtaining legal documents, researching the political situation of their country – you can't obtain that amount of information and write proper legal arguments in that time," she says.

That sorry saga was a case of history repeating itself. A year earlier the charity Refugee and Migrant Justice had been forced to close its doors on some 10,000 asylum seekers. "These files are people's lives and they are sitting there on desks and shelves," an Immigration Advisory Service case-worker in Manchester told us.[18] She reported that staff wanted to work on urgent cases on a pro bono basis after the charity went bust, explaining: "We do asylum work. Sometimes this is life and death." She claimed that she was told to stop working immediately by the administrators and was not allowed to refer clients elsewhere. "I just told them to fuck off."

★ ★ ★

The chaos inflicted on the Manchester legal advice sector was not unique. Cardiff, together with the Vale of Glamorgan, was identified as a possible venue for a community legal advice network. "The council was very keen on it," recalls Warren Palmer, director at the Speakeasy Advice Centre in Cardiff (see Chapter 4). He describes the tender as "set for somebody like A4e to apply". "Only a commercial outfit with a tendering department could compete," he says.

The community legal advice network idea was kicked into touch at the last minute following a report by consultants DG

Legal commissioned by the Welsh Government; however, the LSC launched a tender in 2010 which was to prove to be a disaster for the city's advice sector. In 2009 the LSC redesigned its civil legal aid contracts and prepared a tender requiring the winning bidders for the new social welfare law contracts to provide services in housing, benefits and debt work. The number of family law contracts was reduced by almost half (46%), with some established firms losing out and new entrant firms winning everything.

Palmer recalls the 2010 social welfare law tender. "If you were the dominant player, you could bid for everything," he says. One of the main players was Morgans Solicitors, a local firm run by a well-respected sole practitioner, Roy Morgan. A successful bid by Morgans threatened to leave Cardiff Citizens Advice Bureau, Cardiff Law Centre, Shelter Cymru and the Speakeasy without legal aid income. However Morgans Solicitors collapsed shortly after its bid and the LSC's offer was retracted. The firm later went into administration.

The tendering process had a predictably calamitous impact on the local sector. "Within three years from 2010, our income from legal aid went from £160,000 a year on average to zero," Palmer recalls.

"One of the real difficulties of working under the last Labour government was that it was so controlling," Warren Palmer says. "A huge amount of time and money was wasted as they tried to completely overhaul the system and micromanage everything in a completely top-down, imposed style and at a time when organisations had such fine margins and operated so close to insolvency anyway." Between 2006 and 2010 it was reckoned that the LSC issued no less than 30 consultation papers on its plans for reforming legal aid.

In October 2011 Cardiff Citizens Advice became insolvent and Wales's capital city was left without even a CAB. Bureaux in the Vale of Glamorgan, Rhondda Cynon Taff, Caerphilly and Newport stepped in to provide an interim service. Cardiff Law Centre, one of the oldest in the network, closed in 2016, leaving Wales without a law centre.

Katie White, senior solicitor with the housing charity Shelter Cymru, recalls the impact of its closure. "Law centres are part of the community in a way that Shelter Cymru and private firms aren't," she says. "It's very much in the community and people come for all different kinds of reasons. It's more than just legal advice. It's such a huge thing to lose." Alison Jones, a solicitor also now with Shelter Cymru, worked at the law centre and remembers the LASPO cuts as "the final nail in the coffin".

Jones remembers its end days. "The funding had gone and there was very little case-work going on, hardly any." There was huge demand but "no one to refer people to". The newly saved Citizens Advice "would help with form filling" but "you couldn't get appointments", she adds.

In May 2019 the Speakeasy became the Speakeasy Law Centre, the newest addition to the network. Again, Wales has a law centre.

Magna Carta (1215 to 1945)

The purpose of this chapter is to provide a historical context for our research. The notion of 'access to justice' in the UK long predates our modern system of legal aid as briefly set out above. The principle was most famously enshrined in the charter that King John signed at Runnymede on 15 June 1215. Chapter 40 of Magna Carta is as clear and as concise a statement of that principle as it is possible to frame: 'To none will we sell, to none will we deny, or delay, the right of justice.'

There is a long tradition of pro bono or unpaid legal work. In 1495, Henry VII introduced a law requiring judges to assign counsel to the poor under the *in forma pauperis* procedure; and in 1648 the radical lawyer John Cooke advocated in his book *The Poor Man's Case* that barristers should be required to donate 10% of their time to work unpaid (Paul Im Thurn had a similar idea to support Greater Manchester Law Centre; see Chapter 6).

John Cooke led the prosecution of King Charles I, which the human rights lawyer Geoffrey Robertson QC has said was the first-ever war crimes trial of a head of state.[19] Cooke's vision of an organised legal aid system in which lawyers provided pro bono services as part of their professional duty was not taken up by Parliament at the time.

The Poor Man's Lawyer service, developed in the late 19th century, established a system of organised pro bono legal services that grew out of the settlement movement inspired by the work of Samuel Barnett, a clergyman working in the impoverished East End of London, as discussed in Chapter 2. In 1926 the founder of the Poor Man's Lawyer movement, F.C.G. Gurney–Champion, said that without access to justice the rule of law was a 'make-believe'. At the time, a prisoner in court who could not afford a lawyer could rely upon 'dock briefs' or volunteer barristers. In 1944 one journalist reported the 'general scuttle' of counsel leaving court when a prisoner asked for representation.[20] On being asked if he had anything to say before sentence was passed, one defendant was reported to have replied: 'Nothing my Lord, except to plead the youth and inexperience of my counsel.'[21]

The rank stench of moral hypocrisy

In 2015, on its 800th anniversary, the Lord Chancellor paid tribute to the great charter which has become a symbol of liberty, right and justice recognised around the world. At the time the occupant of that ancient office was Chris Grayling, who was reckoned to be the first non-lawyer to hold the post for at least 440 years.[22]

Beginning a year of celebrations, Chris Grayling paid tribute to 'quite a remarkable document: the Magna Carta'. 'That document, signed on the fields by the Thames at Runnymede in 1215, as part of a truce between King John and his feuding barons, has become a foundation stone not just for our legal system, but for many other countries too,' Grayling hymned in his opening speech at the Global Law Summit, which took place at the Queen Elizabeth II (QE2) Conference Centre, opposite the Houses of Parliament, to mark the occasion.

The conference was ostensibly a celebration of the legacy of the charter; however, it was a thinly veiled opportunity to bang the drum for the successful business that is commercial legal practice in the UK, which, as Grayling went on to point out, contributed 'over £20 billion to our GDP'. The event was dubbed the 'Davros of the law' and was attended by representatives from 110 countries, more than 100 ministers, attorneys general and chief justices, plus, the minister teased, 'a very talented British actress'. Tickets were priced at £1,750 for the opportunity rub shoulders with the likes of US attorney general Eric Holder as well as the Oscar-nominated actress (Carey Mulligan).

At the time when Chris Grayling was presiding over a global celebration of Magna Carta, he was also continuing an unprecedented assault on 'access to justice' that began with the 2013 legal aid cuts.

Grayling's tenure as Lord Chancellor proved controversial and deeply divisive and included his attempts to impose a book ban on prisoners and to privatise the probation service, which was reversed six years later. As for legal aid, Grayling attempted to impose the 'residence test', which would have deprived of legal aid those who had lived in the UK for less than 12 months.

Grayling also attempted to cut legal aid for prisoners. When challenged in the House of Commons, he told MPs that his opposition to prisoners have access to taxpayer-funded legal advice was "ideological". In other words, the politician believed prisoners had forfeited their rights to justice. He also pushed for a fee cut of unprecedented magnitude (17.5%) on criminal defence lawyers, who claimed not to have a pay rise for 20 years.

As Grayling was planning the Global Law Summit conference, he was trying to find ways to curb the use of judicial review, which he had variously derided as 'a must use tool for pressure group lobbyists' and 'a promotional tool for countless left wing campaigners'.[23]

The irony of that particular Lord Chancellor presiding over the Magna Carta celebrations was not lost on commentators. The 'rank stench of moral hypocrisy' hung over the QE2 Conference Centre, wrote Peter Oborne in the *Daily Telegraph*.[24] While the big corporate law firms were out in force, the journalist advised delegates not to bother looking for small solicitors' firms which 'for pitiful fees have made a precarious living out of advising legal aid customers'. 'This is an occasion where only legal oligarchs, along with their wealthy clients, are welcome,' he continued.

Meanwhile, the newly formed campaign group the Justice Alliance walked the 42 miles from Runnymede to the QE2 Conference Centre accompanied by a giant papier mâché effigy of Chris Grayling in the stocks and dressed as King John. The campaigners delivered a letter to the conference quoting the famous words of the charter, given that it was 'not quoted anywhere in the brochure for the event'.

Speakers at the demo outside the conference included members of families who could provide first-hand accounts of what 'access to justice' meant and highlight what the LASPO cuts imperilled. They included Marcia Rigg, whose brother Sean Rigg had died in police custody and who spoke about the intrusive legal aid means-tested forms that her family was required to complete in order to be represented at the inquest; and Michelle Bates, sister of Barry George who wrongly spent eight years in prison for the murder of Jill Dando.

In the House of Lords, peers debated the government's latest assault on access to justice. Lord Pannick QC highlighted the seeming hypocrisy of the Lord Chancellor. 'My message to him is that if you wrap yourself in the Magna Carta, as he does, you are inevitably going to look ridiculous if you then throw cold water on an important part of its legacy, that is, judicial review.'[25]

'The Global Law Summit demonstrates that global capital has hijacked human rights,' Professor Costas Douzinas, law professor and founder of the Birkbeck School of Law, told campaigners outside the conference centre. 'It demonstrates that global law is for capital, not for humans.... Law without justice is like a body without a soul. It is a dead letter.'[26]

10

A Way Forward

> I genuinely believe 'access to justice' is the hallmark of
> a civilised society. (Kenneth Clarke, Lord Chancellor,
> 2011)[1]

We too believe access to justice is the hallmark of a civilised society.
But what – if anything – does 'access to justice' mean? This book
is our attempt to answer that question.

The phrase has been devalued by politicians of all colours who
have invoked it to sell policies to the public that (at best) pay lip-
service to the notion and, on occasion, actively undermine it.

This is not a party political point. As illustrated in the last chapter,
it was New Labour's Access to Justice Act 1999 that laid the
groundwork for the reforms discussed that had such a calamitous
impact on the advice sectors in Manchester, Cardiff and elsewhere.

It is hard to argue with the main intention of that legislation
(to impose coherence on a disparate and patchy coverage offered
by the civil legal aid sector), putting to one side the reality of its
execution (forcing the closure of advice agencies through a crude
tendering process).

The legislation also capped the legal aid budget, linking the civil
and criminal schemes, creating an artificial crisis in the system.
Social welfare law became smothered by a spiralling criminal
budget that was fuelled in part by New Labour's law and order
obsession, as evidenced by the 3,600-plus new offences created
during their tenure.[2]

When politicians and commentators in the press talk about 'legal
aid', invariably it is in the context either of alarm over its cost or

else abuse of the system by lawyers and their unworthy clients 'riding the gravy train'.

That narrative has now unfairly dominated the public discourse about 'access to justice' for over three decades. Legal aid has become a casualty of the political populism that has infected the discussion of all 'justice' issues since Tony Blair coined the mantra 'tough on crime and tough on the causes of crime'.[3]

The one politician in recent years who has been an advocate of legal aid has been Jeremy Corbyn, a doughty supporter of unfashionable causes. His own party dismally failed to oppose the LASPO cuts. Sadiq Khan, then justice minister and now London mayor, told MPs in 2011 that the legal aid budget was "not sustainable, especially in the current economic context".[4] It was a surprising response.

In another life, Khan had been a legal aid lawyer. In fact, he had been co-partner of a leading human rights practice (Christian Khan) with the veteran campaigning lawyer Louise Christian. She later wrote a coruscating open letter to her former colleague saying that it was 'simply unsustainable that Labour could let LASPO remain on the statute book with people forced to rely on foodbanks unable to get legal advice'. Addressing her former colleague directly, Christian wrote: 'Although you have spoken at demonstrations against legal aid cuts, you have just repeated a mantra about not reversing the cuts. There has been no passion, no commitment to principle, and no inclusion of access to justice among Labour's core values.'[5]

A recent example of how the media reports legal aid was the furore over a Court of Appeal ruling in July 2020 that Shamima Begum, who as a 15-year-old schoolgirl from Bethnal Green went to Syria to join Islamic State, must be allowed to return to the UK. Prime minister Boris Johnson immediately promised to review the 'odd and perverse' rules that governed eligibility for legal aid.[6] 'JIHADI BRIDE IS HANDED LEGAL AID,' was the *Daily Mail*'s front-page headline.

Confected outrage about recipients of legal aid has become standard tabloid fare, from drink–driving football players to suspected Islamic terrorists who are judged to be unmeritorious recipients of publicly funded legal advice. There is little sympathy for or understanding of the important principle that everybody –

no matter what they have done or are alleged to have done – is entitled to equal treatment before the law.

The phrase 'access to justice' has also been undermined by its lawyer-allies who have conflated it with 'legal aid' and, more often than not, with legally aided advice and representation as provided by lawyers working in private practice.

Only a minority of the people whom we interviewed going through the justice system between October 2018 and October 2019 actually had a lawyer; fewer still received legal aid; most wouldn't have been eligible anyway under the means test, even if their case had fallen within the hugely restricted scope of the scheme.

★ ★ ★

'What the ★&^! does "access to justice" mean anyway?' was the question posed in the very first article of the Justice Gap website just after the passing of LASPO in 2011.[7] 'Frankly,' replied Roger Smith, the former director of the law reform group JUSTICE, 'the phrase is just best avoided by everybody.' Smith, whose career began at Camden Law Centre in 1973, argued that in its original conception 'access to justice' had a precise definition; however, taken away from its roots it had become completely meaningless.

Its derivation comes from the Italian jurist Mauro Cappelletti. In the 1970s the law professor directed a research project funded by the Ford Foundation on 'access to justice in modern societies' and which led to a four-volume series called, unsurprisingly, 'Access to Justice'. Cappelletti said:

> The right of effective 'access to justice' has emerged with the new social rights. Indeed, it is of paramount importance ... Effective 'access to justice' can be seen as the most basic requirement, the most basic human right, of a system which purports to guarantee legal rights.[8]

The campaigning human rights lawyer Michael Mansfield QC argued that 'access to justice' was a much broader concept than simply having a lawyer. 'It encompasses a recognition that everyone is entitled to the protection of the law and that rights are meaningless unless they can be enforced,' he said. 'It is about protecting ordinary and vulnerable people and solving their problems.'[9]

Shami Chakrabarti, then director of Liberty, now a peer and shadow attorney general, acknowledged the constitutional value of access to justice. 'Fundamental rights and freedoms and the rule of law are vital checks and balances in any civilised society – but meaningless without "access to justice" or the practical means of understanding and enforcing the law of the land,' she said.[10]

Chakrabarti rightly identified that, as a cause, access to justice had never enjoyed popular support. While 'we all love schools and hospitals,' she noted, legal advice and representation 'doesn't seem important until you're really in trouble'.

The law ('like joy and grief') can be a great leveller, Chakrabarti argued. 'There is no longer a level playing field. Unlike many countries in the world, no one checks your wallet in the emergency room. But when it comes to legal advice, the rich can pay, the not-so rich will struggle to find the means and under new reforms, even the poorest may be shut out from a legal aid system that we were once proud of.'

Our courts remain like the Ritz – theoretically open to all but, in reality, closed off to all but the wealthy.

* * *

We argue that, over the last eight years, 'access to justice', a conceptually elusive idea at the best of times, has been so debased as to be rendered meaningless. What we have documented in this book during our 12 months of research starting in October 2018 are the human consequences of a society in which the state has abandoned its commitment to ensuring proper 'access to justice'.

So what should it mean? For us, the phrase encapsulates three ideas:

1. a fully funded system of publicly funded legal advice and support which has at its heart 'social welfare law';
2. the ability to access that advice through a national network of providers; and
3. an ability to enforce rights through the courts if necessary.

Recommendations

There has been no shortage of reviews of legal aid over the years since the LASPO reforms were introduced. The government published its own five-year LASPO review in 2019, which proposed some small-scale tinkering with the regime, including changes to the means test, the exceptional case funding and early legal advice. The government's review failed to address fundamental structural problems exacerbated by the LASPO reforms and was (rightly) dismissed by the Conservative MP Bob Neill, chair of the House of Commons justice select committee, as 'kicking the can down the road'.[11]

The Commission on Justice in Wales, launched by the Welsh Government, published its review of the impact of legal aid cuts in 2019, which prompted a call by a former head of the judiciary for Wales to have its own fully devolved justice system.[12]

The 2017 Bach Commission on Access to Justice was chaired by the Labour peer Lord Willy Bach and supported by the former Court of Appeal judge Sir Henry Brooke. We believe that the Bach Commission makes an important contribution to the debate and its headline recommendation of a Right to Justice Act offers a way forward. The Bach Commission came shortly after other powerful reports into the devastating impact of the LASPO cuts, for example, by Amnesty, which concluded that the 2013 reforms were made with 'insufficient regard for the potential negative and profound impacts on the protection of human rights in the UK';[13] and by the Trades Union Congress, which included a survey of justice sector workers in which almost nine out of ten staff (87%) agreed that the increase in unrepresented litigants had had a detrimental effect on the ability of family and civil courts to deliver justice.[14]

The first major post-LASPO report came from the Legal Action Group's Low Commission, chaired by the Liberal Democrat peer Lord Colin Low, specifically considering the future of social welfare law in 2014.[15]

We finish with our recommendations as to how best we might revive the idea of 'access to justice' and make it meaningful; and how to address what we believe to be the worst excesses of the post-2013 regime.

Access to justice must be a right

There is an urgent need for a wholesale reappraisal of what a properly funded system of legal support looks like. That must involve a restoration of the post-war political consensus around 'access to justice' that ended with LASPO – in other words, the cross-party agreement that legal redress should not be restricted to those with enough money to pay for legal advice.

As we explained in Chapter 9, the pre-LASPO regime was far from perfect and we are not suggesting a reversal of the 'cuts'; nor are we harking back to some legal aid 'golden age' that never existed. We make clear that the scheme was always narrow in focus and never delivered on the idealism expressed in the immediate aftermath of the Second World War. That said, the 2013 cuts represent a nadir in the debate about our system of publicly funded law and its relationship to the welfare state.

To this extent, we back the Bach Commission's big idea, a Right to Justice Act. This would place a right to 'access to justice' (that is, for people to have legal assistance without incurring costs that they cannot afford) on the statute book.

It could also give flesh to what we believe 'access to justice' actually means. A legally enforceable right would be underpinned by principles that could cover, for example, the scope of the legal aid scheme; the importance of an accessible and comprehensible system of eligibility; plus the role of early legal help and public legal education.

The Bach Commission called for a Justice Commission to replace the Legal Aid Agency to take a proactive role in enforcing and defining the right to justice. Too often the Legal Aid Agency has become a barrier to justice rather than an enabler. A Justice Commission would have a watchdog function and the new statutory right could be proactively enforced in the courts.

Public funding of legal cases frequently strays into the political: for example, the legal challenge by a single mother of the council's decision that she was 'intentionally homeless' after she had fallen into arrears as a result of a £34 shortfall between housing benefit and rent. As we note in Chapter 3, there were more court applications fighting for legal aid than there were devoted to the important issues of what was rightly described to be a test case.

The legal aid scheme must be run by an independent body operating at arm's length from the government. In its short life, the Legal Aid Agency has proved itself to be a bureaucratic and inefficient organisation that has fostered an unhealthily adversarial relationship with practitioners. In the course of our research, the Legal Aid Agency has been variously described as exhibiting a 'culture of disbelief', being 'hostile', 'punitive' and 'having lost all pragmatism' in its dealings with practitioners (Chapter 8).

A statutory 'right to justice' provides a new way of looking at 'access to justice'. It reconnects the idea to a common understanding of people's basic rights as citizens which date back to Magna Carta (see Chapter 9). It is an opportunity to set out what 'access to justice' means in principle and practice and places the notion at the heart of the relationship between citizen and state. Specifically, it locates legal aid where we think it ought to be: as a valuable and valued part of the welfare state.

Legal aid must make sense

Time and again, we spoke to people who were suffering because they did not qualify for legal aid. More than that, interviewees did not understand 'legal aid': they had little idea of what the scheme might cover, whether or not they would be eligible or where to go to for help.

That is no surprise. Legal aid has been cut back to the bone. Social welfare law has been removed from the scheme, except where the government is obliged to offer minimal cover under international human rights commitments. What remains makes little sense. Lawyers working in private practice have largely abandoned publicly funded law, as the introduction of fixed fees made legally aided work non-viable in the context of the more remunerative rates for private work; and the not-for-profit legal advice sector has suffered for years as a result of legal aid, local authority and other funding cuts.

'Legal aid' is withering on the vine. People who might be eligible for what remains of the scheme are unlikely to access it, as they don't understand that they could be helped; they incorrectly assume that it won't be available; or else they can't find someone who can help them. Public understanding needs to be restored.

A right to justice requires a funding system that offers broad and accessible coverage and that makes sense. We agree with assertions by the Trades Union Congress that legal aid 'enables people to enforce their human right to justice', and by Amnesty that legal aid is 'a prerequisite for effective human rights'.[16]

The present system fails to achieve that.

The system should be informed by statements of principle. Access to legal aid should be based on need. Instead, it has been reduced to a residual and arbitrary benefit dependent on what can be afforded.

'Access to justice' is a luxury that few can afford. We have a two-tier legal system: open to those who can afford it; but increasingly closed to the poor and the vulnerable and the not-so-poor.

Addressing this requires a straightforward and generous formula. The means test should be based on an easily understandable calculation, a simple assessment of gross household income, according to family size. This would increase the number of households eligible for legal aid and people who should qualify for legal aid, including those who can pay part of their legal costs.

We talk about the inadequacies of the overly restrictive means test in the Chapter 5. Even if someone is on welfare benefits they may have to make a contribution, exposing a justice gap above the poverty line in which many will need to choose whether to go without advice or else somehow raise funds at the risk of pushing themselves further into poverty.

It is reckoned that the proportion of people currently eligible could be as low as 20% of the population, as compared to 80% in 1980. The Bach Commission recommended that everyone who receives a means-tested benefit should be automatically eligible for legal aid without further assessment. We agree. The separate capital assessments for legal aid should be scrapped.

There need to be effective mechanisms allowing for funding for those people who arbitrarily fall outside the scheme and are denied access to justice. LASPO's 'safety net' provisions (for example, the exceptional case funding, and for domestic violence cases; see Chapter 8) have been a disaster and serve to demonstrate the recklessness of the cuts.

Legal aid must protect the vulnerable

LASPO has had a disproportionate impact on the disadvantaged and marginalised. According to the Amnesty report, these groups included vulnerable young people, migrants and refugees, and people with 'additional vulnerabilities' (for example, mental health conditions, learning disabilities, low numeracy and literacy levels, language problems, medical conditions such as terminal illness, and alcohol and drug dependency).[17]

Following the structure of our book, we highlight the following broad areas.

- *Housing/homelessness* (Chapters 1 to 3): LASPO removed legal aid for housing cases except where there is risk of homelessness; in cases of housing disrepair, it is available only where there is 'serious risk of harm'; and beyond that legal aid is available for only a small number of narrowly defined cases (for example, accommodation in relation to asylum support). Legal aid is crucial to prevent and resolve housing issues, which quickly escalate into crisis and homelessness. Before LASPO, housing lawyers could provide initial advice in a disrepair case and send an early letter of claim to a landlord. According to the housing charity Shelter, that would usually persuade the landlord to carry out the necessary repairs and so resolve the issue at little public cost. Cutting publicly funded legal advice (together with cuts to welfare benefits, see below) has left the vulnerably housed exposed in the midst of a housing crisis. The problems of LASPO are compounded by the shortage of specialist housing lawyers.
- *Debt and welfare benefits* (Chapters 4 and 5): LASPO scrapped legal aid for advice and representation on matters to do with welfare benefits, except for appeals. Our research took place during a period of great upheaval in the benefits system, not least the troubled implementation of Universal Credit. Debt cases were almost entirely removed from the scope of the legal aid scheme in 2013, except where there was an immediate risk to the home. Up until May 2020, the only way to obtain publicly funded advice for a debt problem (also for discrimination and special educational needs cases) was through a telephone

helpline known as the mandatory gateway, which had proved to a barrier.[18] It is well documented that as people fall into crisis, their problems 'cluster' – in other words, they experience different issues simultaneously, and frequently problems relating to debt and their entitlement to benefits.

- *Immigration and asylum* (Chapters 6 and 7): Post LASPO, legal aid is available only for asylum cases; immigration detention; immigration-only cases (that is, non-asylum) where there has been domestic violence, human trafficking or slavery; as well as for appeals. Vulnerable people have been left to represent themselves in a notoriously complex and ever-changing area of the law in the context of Theresa May's 'hostile environment' policies. We report that the problems of LASPO have been exacerbated by concerns over the quality of advice and exploitative fees. Separately, we noted concerns about separated migrant children who no longer qualify for legal aid for advice or representation in their non-asylum immigration claims. We echo the Bach Commission's calls for the reinstatement of legal aid for all cases with children.

- *Family* (Chapter 8): LASPO scrapped legal aid for all private law family cases. Public family cases involving the protection of children remain within scope; however, divorce or separation cases do not have public funding unless there is evidence of domestic violence or child abuse (even then the Legal Aid Agency has taken an alarmingly narrow view of what it is prepared to accept as evidence). As a result of LASPO, parents have been left to struggle alone to navigate the courts, causing chaos in the justice system and increasing acrimony and misery in the breakdown of relationships.

Legal aid coverage must be comprehensive

Geography plays a critical role in how people experience 'access to justice'. The present system too often presents a postcode lottery, and so people suffer not just because of the gaps in a much reduced scheme as described above but also due to the failure of the government to provide even coverage.

We spent time in the so-called 'legal aid deserts', parts of the country where help is not available through legal aid or where there is only one provider locally (for example, Suffolk in Chapters 3 and 8, and North Wales in Chapter 5).

A recurring theme of our book is the failure of legal aid planning, which delivers a chaotic and threadbare patchwork quilt of coverage, if it provides coverage at all. This leads not only to geographical gaps in provision (the 'deserts') but also to 'droughts', where firms and advice agencies are not using cases allocations, despite demand for services, because they are losing money on fixed-fee cases (see Chapter 7).

Local failures in 'access to justice' have been exacerbated by the severity of the government's court closure programme (Chapter 6). Court users and witnesses are forced to travel large distances, or else not attend at all.

Early advice is crucial

We heard repeatedly how people's problems had snowballed for want of early advice. Someone loses their job, then they have a problem with their welfare benefits (notably, Universal Credit with its infamous five-week wait for the first payment), fall behind with their rent payments and end up faced with losing their home.

It is a downward spiral that causes untold misery for individuals, their families and loved ones. It leads to depression and adverse physical health outcomes, which, in turn, puts strain on a range of public bodies and services, including the NHS, causing unnecessary expense.

LASPO means that legal aid is no longer available for early advice in social welfare (that is, support prior to representation in courts and tribunals). The 2013 cuts were predicated on the cost savings of £350 million a year at a time of fiscal pressure. Yet, such savings did not reflect the inevitable downstream costs as a result of scrapping timely publicly funded legal advice.[19]

An academic study prepared for the Low Commission, drawing on existing research, reckoned that for every pound invested in advice the state could save between £2 and over £9 in other expenditure.[20] It cited research carried out by the think-tank the New Economics Foundation on behalf of AdviceUK that estimated a social return on investment of over 1:9 in housing and debt cases.

The authors of the study noted that some of this research drew on some 'rather heroic assumptions'; but the chaos inflicted on the family courts by the post-LASPO generation of unrepresented litigants is a vivid illustration of the point. According to the National Audit Office, this could cost the courts as much as £3 million a year.[21]

In the government's post-implementation LASPO review, ministers agreed to test forms of early intervention and evaluate whether they were cost-effective. We back calls for the restoration of legal aid for early legal help for social welfare law. Potential cost savings from preventing the escalation of problems justify additional funding being put into legal aid for advice.

Advice must be (hyper)local

Provision of publicly funded legal advice needs to go directly to the people and the communities who need it, where they need it. Local expertise is critical in ensuring that access to justice works in practice.

Time and again we saw the effectiveness of legal advice surgeries provided by local agencies in innovative settings: foodbanks (such as Hammersmith and Fulham in Chapter 4), homeless shelters (for example, in Birmingham with SIFA Fireside in Chapter 3) and MPs' surgeries (with Dan Carden in Walton, Liverpool and with Ian Lucas in Wrexham, North Wales in Chapter 6). We also support social welfare legal advice clinics in healthcare settings such as GPs' surgeries.[22]

The Low Commission proposed that local authorities should work with or commission local advice and legal support plans with local not-for-profit and advice agencies, embedding advice in settings where people regularly go. Local advice providers know best the need that is on their doorstep, where problems arise from and how to most effectively target help. Responsibility and resources need to be devolved to the local level, and the benefits of seeing access to justice as part of the broader web of local welfare provision must be encouraged.

We looked at New Labour's legal aid reforms in Chapter 9. They provide a cautionary tale, illustrating the perils of the commissioning of legal services without local support. New

Labour's reform of legal services foundered because the LSC (as it then was) was largely unable to persuade local authorities to work collaboratively on the commissioning of advice services. However, when the LSC and councils were prepared to work together, the competitive tendering regime proved hugely divisive as it pitched advice agencies, law firms and charities against each other.

There is an important role for the likes of Citizens Advice; but there also has to be access to specialist advice to complement the generalist support largely provided by volunteers. As we record throughout the book, the legal not-for-profit sector has been hit hard by the double whammy of the 2013 legal aid cuts and local authority cuts. Many agencies have been forced to close, and those that remain open offer a diminished service at a time of significantly increased need. Every Citizens Advice Bureau, law centre and advice agency we spoke to was overwhelmed, and all reported major funding problems.

The value of law centres as providers of specialist legal advice needs to be properly recognised and a properly funded and comprehensive national network of law centres and advice agencies needs to be established.

We were heartened to see a new post-LASPO generation of law centres that have been established in the most impossible of circumstances – Suffolk (Chapter 3), Cardiff (Chapter 4) and Manchester (Chapter 6). Their emergence has been in spite of, not because of, our system of publicly funded legal advice.

Courts are a public service – and must act like one

There must be a duty on the court service, the judiciary and the legal profession to ensure that court users are not prejudiced simply because they don't have a lawyer.

Our experience shadowing duty schemes in the courts (for example, Stratford Housing Centre in Chapter 1, and Manchester Civil Justice Centre and PSU Cardiff in Chapter 8) is that the 'lucky' ones managed to receive help from a duty adviser. Typically, this was less than five minutes before a hearing and, with all due respect to the lawyers who run these important schemes, was no substitute for proper advice and representation.

The duty scheme is illustrative of the chaos of publicly funded legal advice. Some courts have duty schemes, some don't; some are funded by the Ministry of Justice, and some aren't. For the court user, even if there is an adviser on duty there is no guarantee that they will be able see him or her and it is entirely possible that the court user might not even be aware that such a service exists.

It is difficult to overstate the hurdles faced by unrepresented litigants. Interviewees would frequently describe their experience of the courts in the same emotional language: 'overwhelming' and 'harrowing'.

Little concession was made to the court user. Signposting in courts to duty schemes was poor and there was little, if any, written advice or guidance available at court. Interviewees had little understanding of the legal process that they were involved in and would struggle to understand court forms that they were required to complete.

The courts are an important public service and must work for the people who use them (not just for the legal professionals who work in them). Making courts usable means providing legal advice at the point of access: legal advice that is guaranteed by the state and funded through legal aid.

Clear advice about legal rights must be readily available – and jargon banned

The reality for most people is that the law and legal system are confusing and overwhelming. 'Access to justice' doesn't simply mean having a lawyer. People find 'the law' incomprehensible because, frankly, it is, to all but those who practise it.

We agree with the Low Commission, which recommended that public legal education should be given higher priority; and with the Bach Commission, which recommended that public legal capability (the public's capacity to understand and confront legal problems) should be improved. Both called for public legal education to be brought into the school system, ensuring that people learn from an early age what their rights are and how they can enforce them.

We would stress that people need access to information about legal rights, and guidance about legal process and legal costs in plain English. There is a dearth of high-quality, freely available, independent information about the justice system. There are some notable exceptions; but they are tiny dots is the vast information desert out there. There needs to be a centrally branded and easily navigable portal for online information and advice.

There should be a ban on legalese in court forms and guidance, including the removal of unnecessary technical language (for example, litigant-in-person) and Latin terms (such as pro bono).

Wales must have its own fully devolved legal system

Decisions on justice made from London feel remote and out of touch; and (as we explain in Chapter 4) the Welsh Government has repeatedly had to step in to fill funding gaps created in the local advice sector by the UK government's austerity programme.

We have seen at first hand the advice deserts that blight the country's rural and post-industrial areas in the South Wales Valleys (Chapter 4) and in North Wales (Chapter 5). We agree with the recommendation of the Commission on Justice in Wales that 'only full legislative devolution, combined with executive powers, will overcome the obstacles of the current devolution scheme'.[23]

The Commission on Justice in Wales persuasively argued that devolution would enable the proper alignment of justice policy and spending with social, health, housing, education and economic development. It also flagged integrating legal aid and third sector advice, bringing health and justice resources together.

Revisiting access to justice

At the time of writing, we are in the grips of COVID-19. There was no need for a devastating pandemic to expose the frailties of our justice system, suffering already from the best part of a decade of austerity: they were all too visible as we toured England and Wales in the year of our research.

The majority of people we spoke to were in precarious situations before coronavirus: vulnerably housed; dependent on minimum wage or zero-hours contract jobs, and on welfare benefits or foodbanks to feed themselves and their families; or else victims of the 'hostile environment'.

The same people who bear the brunt of the pandemic suffer disproportionately from austerity and a broken justice system. The idea that the virus is a 'great leveller' is a cliché and a myth. The consequences of the pandemic are not the same for everyone. It is those on low incomes who struggle the most. A survey of 285 low-income families shortly after the March 2020 lockdown revealed that eight out of ten families living close to the poverty line reported a significant deterioration in their living standards, pushing them further into debt.[24]

It is tempting to treat the pandemic as an opportunity to reset the justice debate. Politicians, lawyers and the judiciary push solutions to the challenges of a new age, and the crisis becomes an opportunity; hence the calls for bigger (Nightingale) courts, increased use of technology and remote justice, or else limiting trial by jury.

Little thought is given to dealing with the intractable structural problems that so beset the justice system. We argue that the 2013 legal aid cuts represent the death of an idea: the end of the post-war political consensus around 'access to justice' and, in particular, the notion that legal redress should not be the preserve of the wealthy. We call for a return to the notion that our right to justice and equal treatment before the law should not be contingent upon wealth or the vagaries of a failing justice system.

We are not calling for a reversal of the LASPO cuts. It would be wrong to suggest that the legal aid system established in the wake of the Second World War was some kind of idyll. In Chapter 2 we recalled the poor patiently waiting in line in East London for legal advice at Toynbee Hall, harking back to Victorian-era philanthropy. When there are more than 2,000 foodbanks in England and Wales, there is no room for complacency. While legal aid's original architects had in mind an ambitious and transformative idea, it was never delivered.

We urgently need to revive that idea.

Notes and References

Introduction

1 Robins, J. (2011) 'Access to justice is a fine concept. What does it mean in view of cuts to legal aid?', *Guardian*, 6 October (an edited version of Robins, J. (2011) '"Access to justice": what the @%!? does that mean?', *The Justice Gap*, 4 October).

2 It should be noted that there were concerns about clients receiving little or no help under the fixed fee scheme as they tried to 'game' the system, particularly in the area of immigration law (see Chapter 7).

3 Gove, M. (2015) 'What does a one nation justice policy look like?', Ministry of Justice, 23 June, https://www.gov.uk/government/speeches/what-does-a-one-nation-justice-policy-look-like

4 Bach Commission (2017) *The Right to Justice: The Final Report of the Bach Commission*, http://www.fabians.org.uk/wp-content/uploads/2017/09/Bach-Commission_Right-to-Justice-Report-WEB.pdf

5 Hirsch, D. (2018) *Priced Out of Justice? Means Testing Legal Aid and Making Ends Meet*, University of Loughborough, University of Loughborough, Centre for Research in Social Policy, www.lawsociety.org.uk/en/topics/research/legal-aid-means-test-report

6 United Nations (2019) *Visit to the United Kingdom of Great Britain and Northern Ireland: Report of the Special Rapporteur on Extreme Poverty and Human Rights*, https://www.ohchr.org/EN/Issues/Poverty/Pages/CallforinputUK.aspx

7 Freedland, J. (2006) 'The most friendless wing of the welfare state', *Guardian*, 11 October.

Chapter 1

1 Office for National Statistics (2018) *Housing Affordability in England and Wales: 2018*, London: Office for National Statistics.

2   Cribb, J., Hood, A. and Hoyle, J. (2018) *The Decline of Homeownership among Young Adults*, London: Institute for Fiscal Studies.

3   Law Society (2019) *Parliamentary Briefing: Housing Legal Aid Deserts.*

4   Singh, M. (2018) 'Is the rentquake analysis a spurious correlation?', *Numbercruncher Politics*, 18 March, https://www.google.com/url?q=https://www.ncpolitics.uk/2018/03/is-the-rentquake-analysis-a-spurious-correlation/&sa=D&source=editors&ust=1613390771376000&usg=AOvVaw0vxaUkbikBCjW12v6PB642

5   May, T. (2018) 'PM speech to the National Housing Federation summit', National Housing Summit, London, 19 September.

6   Walters, M. (2018) 'Government defeated over housing legal aid', *Law Society Gazette*, 22 June.

7   *R (Law Centres Federation Ltd t/a Law Centres Network) v Lord Chancellor* [2018] EWHC 1588 (Admin), 22 June 2018.

8   House of Commons Justice Committee (2019) *Court and Tribunal Reforms*, HC 190, London: HMSO.

9   Bowcott, O. (2018) 'Court closures: sale of 126 premises raised just £34m', *Guardian*, 8 March.

10 McKinney, C.J. (2015) 'Legal aid lawyers aren't on £200 an hour', *Full Fact*, 6 July, https://fullfact.org/law/legal-aid-lawyers-arent-200-hour/

11 Law Society (2019) 'Left-behind communities out in the cold without publicly funded housing legal advice', 25 April, https://www.lawsociety.org.uk/en/contact-or-visit-us/press-office/press-releases/left-behind-communities-out-in-cold-without-publicly-funded-housing-legal-advice&sa=D&source=editors&ust=1613390771392000&usg=AOvVaw018lxdlwNU32bm87eVi-OQ

12 Chakrabortty, A. (2018) 'It took a UN envoy to hear how austerity is destroying lives', *Guardian*, 14 November.

13 Shelter (2018) *Homelessness in Great Britain: The Numbers Behind the Story*, London: Shelter.

14 Combined Homelessness and Information Network (2019) *Annual Bulletin Greater London 2018/19*, London: Combined Homelessness and Information Network.

15 United Nations (2019) *Visit to the United Kingdom of Great Britain and Northern Ireland: Report of the Special Rapporteur on Extreme Poverty and Human Rights*, https://www.google.com/url?q=https://www.ohchr.org/EN/Issues/Poverty/Pages/CallforinputUK.aspx&sa=D&source=editors&ust=1613390771408000&usg=AOvVaw1oubw8gVR7KAWQLB8sTQvI

Chapter 2

1   Hynes, S. and Robins, J. (2009) *The Justice Gap: Whatever Happened to Legal Aid?*, London: Legal Action Group.
2   Hynes and Robins (2009).
3   ITV, *World in Action* (1970) 'Law Shop', 7 December.
4   As quoted in Robins, J. (2007) 'The uncertain future of law centres', *Independent Lawyer*, 19 April.
5   Ibid.
6   F.C.G. Gurney-Champion, *Justice and the Poor in England*, London: Routledge 1926, as quoted in Hynes and Robins (2009).
7   Toynbee Hall (2019) *Impact Review 2018/2019*, London: Toynbee Hall.
8   Fabian Society (2017) *The Right to Justice: The Final Report of the Bach Commission*, London: Fabian Society.
9   Robins (2007).
10 Robins, J. (2017) 'Underfunded and overstretched: the lawyers seeking justice for Grenfell', *Guardian*, 24 July.
11 Shelter (2018) *One Year On from Grenfell*, London: Shelter.
12 Lambeth Council (2017) *Housing Strategy*, London: Lambeth Council, https://moderngov.lambeth.gov.uk/documents/s93071/Appendix%2520A%2520-%2520HfL%2520Business%2520Plan.pdf&sa=D&source=editors&ust=1613394107212000&usg=AOvVaw0umXaNPG8p47tqnRMBZ8Ym
13 Heath, L. (2020) 'Housing legal aid cases given funding fall by almost 40% in a decade', *Inside Housing*, 7 February.
14 Shelter (2018) *Shelter Evidence to the Statutory Review of LASPO: The Impact of Changes to Civil Legal Aid under the Legal Aid, Sentencing and Punishment of Offenders Act 2012*, London: Shelter.
15 Heath (2020).
16 BBC Newsnight (2017) Grenfell Tower report, BBC2, 14 June, 22:45hrs.
17 BBC Law in Action (2017) Interview with the Lord Chancellor, BBC Radio 4, 29 June, 20:00hrs.
18 Robins (2017).

Chapter 3

1   Shelter (2019) *This Is England: A Picture of Homelessness*, London: Shelter.
2   Barker, N. (2019) 'Homelessness Reduction Act increasing temporary accommodation numbers', *Inside Housing*, 26 March.
3   House of Commons Debates, 6 March 2012, cols 258–62WH.

4   Citizens Advice (2019) *Annual Report*, https://www. citizensadvice.org.uk/about-us/our-work/annual-reports/&sa= D&source=editors&ust=1613399821254000&usg=AOvVaw0G 76daUS_cFdAJKNJO2yOL

5   Citizens Advice (2010) 'Towards a business case for legal aid', Paper presented to the Legal Services Research Centre's Eighth International Research Conference.

6   Citizens Advice (2014) Written evidence to the Justice Select Committee inquiry into the impact of the Legal Aid, Sentencing and Punishment of Offenders Act 2012, https://www. citizensadvice.org.uk/global/migrated_documents/corporate/ citizens-advice-submission-to-jsc-on-impact-of-laspo-april-2014. pdf

7   Citizens Advice (2014) 'Nowhere to turn: Citizens Advice speaks out on impact of legal aid cuts', 8 July, https://www. citizensadvice.org.uk/about-us/about-us1/media/press-releases/ nowhere-to-turn-citizens-advice-speaks-out-on-impact-of-legal- aid-cuts/

8   Cameron, D. (2010) 'Big Society' speech, 19 July, https://www. gov.uk/government/speeches/big-society-speech

9   Adisa, O. (2018) *Access to Justice: Assessing the Impact of the Magistrates' Court Closures in Suffolk*, Suffolk University, https:// www.uos.ac.uk/sites/default/files/Research%20Report%20 Access%20to%20Justice%20FINAL.pdf

10   Platt, L., Sunkin, M. and Calvo, K. (2009) *Judicial Review Litigation as an Incentive to Change in Local Authority Public Services in England and Wales*, Colchester: Institute for Social and Economic Research.

11   https://www.independent.co.uk/news/uk/home-news/single- mother-supreme-court-housing-benefit-homeless-children- unlawful-cpag-shelter-a8954936.html

12   BBC News (2019) 'Court backs woman in rent row with Birmingham council', 13 June, https://www.bbc.co.uk/news/ uk-england-birmingham-48625914.

13   Bowcott, O. (2019) 'Homelessness lawyers complain of legal aid "culture of refusal"', *Guardian*, 26 June.

14   Law Society (2019) 'Left-behind communities out in the cold without publicly funded housing legal advice', 25 April.

15   Bach Commission (2017) *The Right to Justice: The Final Report of the Bach Commission*. London: The Fabian Society.

Chapter 4

1 Citizens Advice (2019) 'One in two people Citizens Advice helps with Universal Credit struggle to pay for housing as they wait for payment', 6 February, https://www.citizensadvice.org.uk/about-us/about-us1/media/press-releases/one-in-two-people-citizens-advice-helps-with-universal-credit-struggle-to-pay-for-housing-as-they-wait-for-payment/

2 Commission on Justice in Wales (2019) *Justice in Wales for the People in Wales*, Cardiff: Welsh Government, p 8.

3 Commission on Justice in Wales (2019), p 10.

4 Legal Action Group (2019) 'LASPO cuts bite as social welfare law practice to close', April, https://www.lag.org.uk/article/206262/laspo-cuts-bite-as-social-welfare-law-practice-to-close

5 DC Pritchard has since retired.

6 Various authors (2019) 'Food banks are no solution to poverty', *Guardian*, 24 March.

Chapter 5

1 Smith, R. (2019) 'Pound notes, canned soup and common goals', *New York Times* (online), 30 January.

2 United Nations (2019) *Visit to the United Kingdom of Great Britain and Northern Ireland: Report of the Special Rapporteur on Extreme Poverty and Human Rights*, https://www.ohchr.org/EN/Issues/Poverty/Pages/CallforinputUK.aspx

3 Fouzder, M. (2019) 'Legal Aid Agency seeks to reduce dependency on troubled billing system', *Law Society Gazette*, 5 July, https://www.lawgazette.co.uk/practice/legal-aid-agency-seeks-to-reduce-dependency-on-troubled-billing-system/5070884.article

4 Hirsch, D. (2018) *Priced Out of Justice? Means Testing Legal Aid and Making Ends Meet*, University of Loughborough, Centre for Research in Social Policy, www.lawsociety.org.uk/en/topics/research/legal-aid-means-test-report

5 *R (Unison) v. Lord Chancellor* [2017] UKSC 51. The introduction of employment tribunal fees in 2013 coincided with a massive drop in applications: a comparison of the first quarters of 2013 and 2015 shows a 72% fall in claims accepted. LASPO removed almost all employment cases from scope, except for cases concerning discrimination. 'The imposition of these fees has compounded the impact of LASPO on people's ability to resolve employment law issues,' the Equality and Human Rights Commission said in its 2017 report, *The Impact of LASPO on Routes to Justice* (Research report 118).

6   Loughborough University (2018) 'Struggling families disqualified from justice despite Supreme Court verdict', 20 March, www.lboro.ac.uk/news-events/news/2018/march/struggling-families-supreme-court-verdict/

7   House of Commons Debates, 11 September 2018, vol 646, col 251WH.

8   Glaze, B. (2019) 'Tories warned over Universal Credit that I, Daniel Blake film "is becoming reality"', *Daily Mirror*, 7 January.

9   Barrie, J. (2017) '"Real I, Daniel Blake" man who can't work after being stabbed faces Christmas eviction after Universal Credit blunder', *Daily Mirror*, 17 December.

10   BBC Panorama (2018) 'The Universal Credit Crisis', BBC2, 17 November.

11   Chartered Institute of Public Finance and Accountancy (2019) 'Decade of austerity sees 30% drop in library spending', 6 December, https://www.cipfa.org/about-cipfa/press-office/latest-press-releases/decade-of-austerity-sees-30-drop-in-library-spending

12   Wrexham.com (2018) 'Local MP backs campaign to save Wrexham's Citizens Advice office', 23 May.

13   Robins, J. (2015) 'A brave new dawn', *New Law Journal*, 1 October.

14   Hogan Lovells LLP and All-Party Parliamentary Group on Pro Bono (2017) *Mind the Gap: An Assessment of Unmet Legal Need in London: A Survey of MPs' Surgeries.*

15   Ministry of Justice (2019) *Post-Implementation Review of Part 1 of LASPO*, 7 February, https://www.gov.uk/government/publications/post-implementation-review-of-part-1-of-laspo

16   Tyrell, N. (2019) 'Universal Credit puts strain on council's already stretched budget', *Liverpool Echo*, 6 December.

17   House of Commons Debates, 11 September 2018, vol 646, col 251WH.

Chapter 6

1   Kirkup, J. and Winnet, R. (2012) 'We're going to give illegal migrants a really hostile reception', *Daily Telegraph*, 25 May.

2   Joiner, S., Lombardi, A. and O'Neill, S. (2019) 'Hostile environment: Home Office makes £500m from immigration fees', https://www.thetimes.co.uk/article/hostile-environments-home-office-makes-500m-from-immigration-fees-vgpbm2h6j

3   House of Commons Debates, 24 March 2014, col 94W, https://
    publications.parliament.uk/pa/cm201314/cmhansrd/cm140324/
    text/140324w0003.htm#14032517000020

4   BBC News (2018) 'Barry lawyer says Windrush families are living
    in fear', 7 May, https://www.bbc.co.uk/news/uk-wales-43913263

5   Jasper, L. (2013) 'Ms Brown comes to London town', Operation
    Black Vote, 7 May, https://www.obv.org.uk/news-blogs/ms-
    brown-comes-london-town

6   House of Commons Debates, 16 April 2018, vol 639, col 28,
    https://hansard.parliament.uk/Commons/2018-04-16/
    debates/7234878F-ACEE-48DD-A94C-9013B38FA465/
    WindrushChildren(ImmigrationStatus)

7   *Pokhriyal v. The Secretary of State for The Home Department*, CA,
    5 December 2013.

8   *Patel and Others v. Secretary of State for the Home Department* [2019]
    UKSC 59.

9   Baxi, C. (2017) *Legal Hackett's Brief*, 'Immigration judge bemoans
    "worse than useless" Home Office officials', 8 November.

10 Simmons, R. (2019) 'Average BPTC fee passes £16,000 as all but
    three law schools raise prices for 2019/20', *The Lawyer*, 9 May.

11 Robins, J. (2016) 'We will have a law centre owned and run by
    the people for the people', *The Justice Gap*, 24 June, https://www.
    thejusticegap.com/will-law-centre-owned-run-people-people/

12 Ryan, F. (2017) 'Remember when legal aid was slashed? The
    awful effects are taking hold', *Guardian*, 9 February.

13 Robins, J. (2016) 'We will have a law centre owned and run by
    the people for the people', *The Justice Gap*, 24 June, https://www.
    thejusticegap.com/will-law-centre-owned-run-people-people/

14 Ibid.

15 Barlow, N. (2016) 'A levy on Manchester's Corporate sector
    should help fund legal fees for the vulnerable', *About Manchester*,
    6 July, https://aboutmanchester.co.uk/a-levy-on-manchesters-
    corporate-sector-should-help-fund-legal-fees-for-the-vulnerable-
    say-law-centre/

16 Hurst, P. (2018) 'Nigel Farage slams EU "gangsters" at Brexit rally
    in Bolton', *Manchester Evening News*, 22 September.

17 Robins, J. (2011) 'Removing chunks of social welfare law from
    Citizens' Advice Bureaux bodes ill', *Guardian*, 15 February.

18 Holland, D. (2017) '"Staggering" disparity in number of refugees
    settled in Bolton compared to rest of UK', *Bolton News*, 6 April.

19 BBC News (2018) 'Andy Burnham's threat to stop housing
    asylum seekers in Greater Manchester', BBC, 2 November.

20 Pad, H. (2018) 'Attack on refugee family highlights rising hate crime in Bolton', *Guardian*, 16 December.
21 Scheerhout, J. (2018) 'City star Vincent Kompany pledges testimonial cash to Manchester's homeless', *Manchester Evening News*, 29 September.

Chapter 7

1   Sanctuary on Sea (2015) 'What makes Brighton and Hove a City of Sanctuary?', 10 June, https://brighton-and-hove.cityofsanctuary.org/2015/06/10/what-makes-brighton-hove-a-city-of-sanctuary
2   Condon, R., Hill, A. and Bryson, L. (2018) *International Migrants in Brighton and Hove*, Brighton and Hove City Council.
3   Open Doors (2018) *World Watch List*, https://opendoors international.exposure.co/2018-world-watch-list-top-10
4   Butler, P. (2017) 'Number of rough sleepers in England rises for sixth successive year', *Guardian*, 25 January.
5   Wilding, J. (2019) *Droughts and Deserts: A Study of Legal Aid Market Failure*, University of Brighton, https://www.researchgate.net/publication/333718995_Droughts_and_Deserts_A_report_on_the_immigration_legal_aid_market
6   Legal Action Group (2018) 'Advice deserts set to grow as LAA tenders fail to attract bids', 13 April.
7   Yeo, C. (2020) *Welcome to Britain: Fixing Our Broken Justice System*, London: Biteback.
8   Some details have been changed to ensure the woman's anonymity.
9   May, T. (2016) 'Defeating modern slavery', Home Office, 31 July, https://www.gov.uk/government/speeches/defeating-modern-slavery-theresa-may-article
10 National Crime Agency (2019) *National Referral Mechanism Statistics: End of Year Summary 2018*, https://nationalcrimeagency.gov.uk/who-we-are/publications/282-national-referral-mechanism-statistics-end-of-year-summary-2018/file
11 BBC News (2019) 'Birmingham homeless charity helps 50 slavery victims in two years', 12 April, https://www.bbc.co.uk/news/uk-england-birmingham-47908790
12 Crown Prosecution Service (2019) 'CPS secures convictions in largest ever modern slavery prosecution', 5 July, https://www.cps.gov.uk/south-east/news/successfully-prosecutes-second-major-modern-slavery-case-month

13   West Midlands Police (2018) 'Freedom of information: modern slavery (676_18)', https://foi.west-midlands.police.uk/modern-slavery-676_18-2/

14   Anti-Trafficking and Labour Exploitation Unit (2018) 'Legal aid and immigration advice for victims of modern slavery', 30 April, https://atleu.org.uk/news/legalaidimmigrationadvice

15   *BF (Eritrea) v. Secretary of State for the Home Department* [2019] EWCA Civ 872.

16   Ibid.

17   Refugee Council (2019) 'Court of Appeal rules the Home Office age assessment policy as unlawful', 24 May, https://www.refugeecouncil.org.uk/latest/news/court-of-appeal-rules-the-home-office-age-assessment-policy-as-unlawful/

18   Morris, J. and Clayton, J. (2019) 'Asylum seekers: "They didn't believe I was a child"', BBC *Newsnight*, 25 June, https://www.bbc.co.uk/news/uk-48750708

19   Gibbons, L. (2019) 'The "culture of disbelief" that fails child asylum seekers', *The Justice Gap*, 19 July, https://www.thejusticegap.com/the-culture-of-disbelief-that-fails-child-asylum-seekers/

20   Independent Chief Inspector of Borders and Immigration (2014) *An Investigation into the Home Office's Handling of Asylum Claims Made on the Grounds of Sexual Orientation*, https://assets.publishing.service.gov.uk/government/uploads/system/uploads/attachment_data/file/547330/Investigation-into-the-Handling-of-Asylum-Claims_Oct_2014.pdf

21   Slack, J. and Grove, J. (2015) 'Woman with the guts to tell the truth over migrants', *Daily Mail*, 6 October. https://www.dailymail.co.uk/news/article-3262645/Woman-guts-tell-truth-migrants-Theresa-faces-backlash-big-business-Left-following-conference-speech.html

22   Yeo (2020).

23   Barendrecht, M. et al (2014) *Legal Aid in Europe: Nine Different Ways to Guarantee Access to Justice?*, The Hague: Hague Institute for the Internationalisation of the Law.

24   Ford, R., Ames, J. and Swinford, S. (2020) 'Lawyers scupper Priti Patel's bid to send Channel migrants to Spain', *The Times*, 28 August.

25   Hyde, J. (2020) '"Activist' tweet deleted – as Number 10 targets 'loudmouthed lawyers"', *The Law Society Gazette*, 28 August.

26   Osborne, S. (2016) 'Theresa May speech: Tory conference erupts in applause as PM attacks "activist left wing lawyers"', *Independent*, 5 October.

27   No Accommodation Network and Refugee Action (2018) *Tipping the Scales: Access to Justice in the Immigration System*, https://naccom.org.uk/wp-content/uploads/2018/07/Access-to-Justice-final-version.pdf

Chapter 8

1   Personal Support Unit (2018) *Response to Call for Evidence from Commission on Justice in Wales*, https://llyw.cymru/sites/default/files/publications/2018-06/Submission%20to%20the%20Justice%20Commission%20from%20the%20Personal%20Support%20Unit.pdf

2   Citizens Advice (2016) *Standing Alone: Going to the Family Court without a Lawyer*, https://www.citizensadvice.org.uk/about-us/our-work/policy/policy-research-topics/justice-policy-research/access-to-justice-policy-research-and-consultation-responses/access-to-justice-consultation-responses/standing-alone-going-to-the-family-court-without-a-lawyer/

3   National Audit Office (2014) *Implementing Reforms to Civil Legal Aid*, 20 November, https://www.nao.org.uk/report/implementing-reforms-to-civil-legal-aid/; House of Commons Debates, 784, 2014–15.

4   Trinder, L., Hunter, R., Hitchings, E., Miles, J., Moorhead, R., Smith, M., Sefton, M., Hinchly, V., Bader, K. and Pearce, J. (2014) *Litigants in Person in Private Family Law Cases*, Ministry of Justice, https://assets.publishing.service.gov.uk/government/uploads/system/uploads/attachment_data/file/380479/litigants-in-person-in-private-family-law-cases.pdf

5   Ibid.

6   Civil Justice Council (2011) *Access to Justice for Litigants in Person (or self-represented litigants)*, https://www.judiciary.uk/wp-content/uploads/2014/05/report-on-access-to-justice-for-litigants-in-person-nov2011.pdf

7   Hilborne, N. (2015) 'Mr Justice Mostyn: Nobody anticipated "savagery" of legal aid cuts', *Legal Futures*, 1 July, https://www.legalfutures.co.uk/latest-news/mr-justice-mostyn-nobody-anticipated-savagery-of-legal-aid-cuts

8   Bowcott, O. (2017) 'Senior judge warns over "shaming" impact of legal aid cuts', *Guardian*, 13 October.

9   In October 2019 the Personal Support Unit rebranded as Support Through Court.

10   Personal Support Unit (2018).

11   Lord Woolf (1995) *Access to Justice, Interim Report*, June, Lord Chancellor's Department.

12   Robins, J. (2011) 'Changes mean outlook is bleak for unrepresented litigants', *Guardian*, 14 November.

13   Berlins, M. (2002) 'The battle for pro bono', *Guardian*, 8 October.

14   Personal Support Unit (2018).

15   Hill, A. (2018) 'How legal aid cuts filled family courts with bewildered litigants', *Guardian*, 26 December.

16   Ibid.

17   Taddia, M. (2020) 'We can work it out', *Law Society Gazette*, 27 January.

18   *Rights of Women, R (on the application of) v. The Lord Chancellor and Secretary of State for Justice* [2016] EWCA Civ 91.

19   Ministry of Justice (2014) *Legal Aid Statistics in England and Wales Legal Aid Agency 2013–2014*, 24 June.

20   *R (Public Law Project) v. Lord Chancellor* [2016] UKSC 39; see also *R (oao Law Centres Federation Ltd) v. The Lord Chancellor* [2018] EWHC 1588 in the successful challenge to the tender for the Housing Possession Court Duty Scheme (see Chapter 3).

21   Public Law Project (2020) 'PLP survey shows lack of faith in legal aid scheme', 20 January, https://publiclawproject.org.uk/uncategorized/improving-exceptional-case-funding-providers-perspectives/

22   Public Law Project (2020) 'Domestic violence: Challenge to legal aid means regulations', 10 June.

Chapter 9

1   House of Commons Debates, 15 December 1948, vol 459, col 1221.

2   Gove, M. (2015) 'What does a one nation justice policy look like?', Ministry of Justice, 23 June (as quoted in the Introduction).

3   Goriely, T. (1994) 'Rushcliffe fifty years on: the changing role of civil legal aid within the welfare state', *Journal of Law and Society*, vol 21, no 4, 545.

4   William Beveridge (1942) *Social Insurance and Allied Services*, Cmd 6404.

5   Smith, R. (1997) *Justice Redressing the Balance*, London: Legal Action Group.

6   Society of Labour Lawyers (1968) *Justice for All*, Fabian Research Series 273, London: Fabian Society.

7   Ibid.

8   Lowenstein, D. and Waggoner, M. (1967) 'The new wave in legal services for the poor source', *Harvard Law Review*, vol 80, no 4.

9   This section draws on Hynes, S. and Robins, J. (2009) *The Justice Gap: Whatever Happened to Legal Aid?*, London: Legal Action Group; and Brooke, H. (2016) *History of Legal Aid: 1945 to 1997*, London: Fabian Society.

10   Press Association (2004) 'Legal aid fraudster had criminal history', *Guardian*, 26 October.

11   Ibid.

12   Pascoe, P. (2006) *Causes of Action: Civil Law and Social Justice*, Legal Services Research Centre, https://www.researchgate.net/publication/271209992_Causes_of_Action_Civil_Law_and_Social_Justic

13   Hynes and Robins (2009).

14   Robins, J. (2008) 'A threat to legal help in the town that needs it most', *Guardian*, 20 July.

15   Wiggins, K. (2012) 'Margaret Hodge urges DWP to suspend A4e Work Programme contracts', *Third Sector*, 22 February.

16   Robins, J. (2010) 'Legal advice centres need to help clients, not contractors', *Guardian*, 23 July.

17   Brooke (2017).

18   Robins, J. (2011) 'Legal aid cuts to immigration could mean "injustice, hardship and even loss of life"', *Guardian*, 15 July.

19   Robertson, G. (2007) *The Tyrannicide Brief*, London: Vintage Books.

20   *News Chronicle*, 14 April 1944, as quoted in Hynes and Robins (2009).

21   Hynes, S. and Robins, J. (2009).

22   Gimson, A. (2015) 'Grayling – As Lord Chancellor, "it's an advantage not being a lawyer"', *Conservative Home*, 21 January, https://www.conservativehome.com/thetorydiary/2015/01/interview-grayling-as-lord-chancellor-its-an-advantage-not-being-a-lawyer.html

23   Criado-Perez, C. (2014) 'How Chris Grayling is killing off judicial review – and why it matters', *New Statesman*, 9 December.

24   Oborne, P. (2015) 'The hypocrites have jumped aboard the Magna Carta bandwagon', *Daily Telegraph*, 8 January.

25   As quoted in Robins, J. (2016) 'Summit wrong?', *New Law Journal*, 6 March.

26 McCabe, M. (2016) 'Law without justice is like a body without a soul', *The Justice Gap*, 23 February.

Chapter 10

1 As quoted in Robins, J. (2011) 'Access to justice is a fine concept. What does it mean in view of cuts to legal aid?', *Guardian*, 6 October.

2 Hare, D. (2010) 'Labour's criminal record – 3,600 new offences, and 86,637 inmates', *Guardian*, 4 April.

3 New Statesman (2015) 'From the archive: Tony Blair is tough on crime, tough on the causes of crime', *New Statesman*, 28 December, www.newstatesman.com/2015/12/archive-tony-blair-tough-crime-tough-causes-crime

4 As quoted in Robins, J. (2011) '"Immoral and crazy": legal aid bill hits the Lords', *The Justice Gap*, 24 November.

5 Christian, L. (2015) 'Dear Sadiq Khan', *Legal Action*, May.

6 Brown, A. (2020) 'Boris Johnson to review "odd and perverse" legal aid rules after Shamima Begum judgement', *Sun*, 21 July.

7 Robins, J. (2011) '"Access to justice": what the @%!? does that mean?', *The Justice Gap*, https://www.thejusticegap.com/access-to-justice-what-the-f-does-that-mean/

8 Ibid.

9 Ibid.

10 Ibid.

11 Ministry of Justice (2019) *Post-Implementation Review of Part 1 of LASPO*, London: Ministry of Justice.

12 Commission on Justice in Wales (2019) *Justice in Wales for the People in Wales*, Cardiff: Welsh Government.

13 Amnesty (2016) *The Cuts that Hurt: The Impact of Legal Aid Cuts in England on Access to Justice*, October.

14 Trades Union Congress (2016) *Justice Denied: Impacts of the Government's Reforms to Legal Aid and Court Services on Access to Justice*, https://www.tuc.org.uk/research-analysis/reports/justice-denied-impacts-governments-reforms-legal-aid-and-court-services

15 Low Commission (2014) *Tackling the Advice Deficit: A Strategy for Access to Advice and Legal Support on Social Welfare Law in England and Wales*, London: Legal Action Group.

16 Amnesty (2016); Trades Union Congress (2016).

17 Amnesty (2016).

18   Brendon, P. (2018) *The Civil Legal Advice Telephone Gateway*, London: Public Law Project (PLP). PLP reported that the number of cases started through the gateway was substantially lower than anticipated: debt, 90% lower; discrimination, 60%; and special educational needs (SEN), 45%. The number of Legal Help matters in debt had fallen by 50% and discrimination by 58%. Referrals for face-to-face advice in discrimination and SEN had been significantly lower than estimated: 0.2% rather than 10% in discrimination; and 0% rather than 10% in SEN.

19   As confirmed in House of Lords Debates, 21 November 2011, vol 732, col 931. Lord Phillips of Sudbury quoted a Ministry of Justice statement confirming the 'lack of a robust evidence base', which meant that the department was 'unable to draw conclusions as to whether wider economic and social costs are likely to result'. "What are we doing?" asked Phillips. "We know the suffering, the disenchantment and the cynicism that will follow. We have made no attempt to calculate the financial costs in social or other terms."

20   Legal Action Group (2014) *Economic Benefits of Advice*, July.

21   National Audit Office (2014) *Implementing Reforms to Civil Legal Aid*, 20 November.

22   Beardon, S. and Genn, H. (2018) *The Health Justice Landscape in England and Wales: Social Welfare Legal Services in Health Settings*, London: UCL Centre for Access to Justice. The research identified more than 380 health justice partnerships across the UK, often run by Citizens Advice and Macmillan Cancer Support. Funding tended to come from charities.

23   Commission on Justice in Wales (2019) *Justice in Wales for the People in Wales*, Cardiff: Welsh Government.

24   Howes, S., Monk-Winstanley, R., Sefton, T. and Woudhuysen, A. (2020) *Poverty in the Pandemic: The Impact of Coronavirus on Low-income Families and Children*, London: Child Poverty Action Group and Church of England.

Index